Place and Ideology in Contemporary Hebrew Literature

Judaic Traditions in Literature, Music, and Art
Harold Bloom and Ken Frieden, *Series Editors*

Other titles from Judaic Traditions in Literature, Music, and Art

American Hebrew Literature: Writing Jewish National Identity in the United States
Michael Weingrad

Classic Yiddish Stories of S. Y. Abramovitsh, Sholem Aleichem, and I. L. Peretz
Ken Frieden, *ed.*

Finding the Jewish Shakespeare: The Life and Legacy of Jacob Gordin
Beth Kaplan

Here and Now: History, Nationalism, and Realism in Modern Hebrew Fiction
Todd Hasak-Lowy

The Image of the Shtetl and Other Studies of Modern Jewish Literary Imagination
Dan Miron

Intimations of Difference: Dvora Baron in the Modern Hebrew Renaissance
Sheila E. Jelen

Missing a Beat: The Rants and Regrets of Seymour Krim
Mark Cohen

The New Country: Stories from the Yiddish about Life in America
Henry Goodman, *trans. & ed.*

The Passing Game: Queering Jewish American Culture
Warren Hoffman

Translating Israel: Contemporary Hebrew Literature and Its Reception in America
Alan L. Mintz

Place and Ideology in Contemporary Hebrew Literature

Karen Grumberg

SYRACUSE UNIVERSITY PRESS

First Edition 2011

11 12 13 14 15 16   6 5 4 3 2 1

This book was published with the support of a University Cooperative Society Subvention
Grant awarded by the College of Liberal Arts at the University of Texas at Austin.

∞ The paper used in this publication meets the minimum requirements
of the American National Standard for Information Sciences—Permanence
of Paper for Printed Library Materials, ANSI Z39.48-1992.

For a listing of books published and distributed by Syracuse University Press,
visit our website at SyracuseUniversityPress.syr.edu.

ISBN: 978-0-8156-3259-7

Library of Congress Cataloging-in-Publication Data

Grumberg, Karen.
    Place and ideology in contemporary Hebrew literature / Karen Grumberg. — 1st ed.
        p. cm. — (Judaic traditions in literature, music, and art)
    Includes bibliographical references and index.
    ISBN 978-0-8156-3259-7 (cloth : alk. paper) 1. Hebrew literature—History and criticism.
2. Place (Philosophy) in literature.   I. Title.
    PJ5012.P53G78 2011
    892.409'006—dc23   2011036267

Manufactured in the United States of America

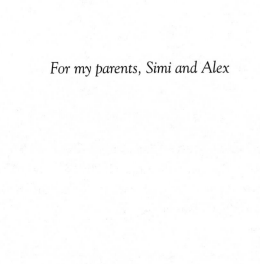

For my parents, Simi and Alex

Karen Grumberg is associate professor of Hebrew studies in the Department of Middle Eastern Studies and the Program in Comparative Literature at the University of Texas at Austin.

Contents

Preface

As I complete this manuscript a week after a cease-fire ends the Gaza War, Gazans attempt to clear streets filled with debris, to reopen shops, to rebuild homes, schools, hospitals, prisons, police stations, factories, and mosques, bombed because they allegedly harbored arms caches or were situated on top of tunnels used by Hamas for smuggling weapons and ammunition. In Sderot, the southern Israeli town whose eight-year pummeling by Hamas rockets instigated the Gaza invasion, eerily empty streets reflect the dubious nature of the Israeli "victory" that has left residents hesitant to venture outdoors. The Israel-Palestine conflict has always been about territory. Yet it is becoming increasingly apparent that "territory," that is, swaths of land subject to national sovereignty and delineated by maps and borders, is not the only type of place that determines the political and ideological configurations of the conflict. Ordinary, everyday places resonate as much in the minds of Israelis and Palestinians as does the more abstract concept of "territory" that has dominated debates on the conflict since the early twentieth century. Photographs of Gaza show houses turned literally inside out, their interiors now exteriors, intimate artifacts of private life pornographically on display to the outside world. A lone man on a Sderot sidewalk says he is happy to be able to smoke a cigarette outside again, without fear of rockets. These, more than the ceding or gaining of territory, are the spatial consequences of this war. This book examines the Hebrew literary representation of "vernacular" places such as these to illumine the intricate processes by which ideology invades—in the case of the recent war, quite literally—everyday lived experience, and shapes Israeli identity.

The question of what it means to be Israeli is not an easy one to answer, and I do not purport to resolve it here. I do, however, seek to expose the often overlooked spatial factors that contribute to Israelis' understanding of themselves as Israeli. With a few exceptions, Israeli authors do not represent explicitly the conflict that periodically bursts into the foreground of everyday life. Israeli literature rarely takes place in settings of war and political violence, but is replete with evocative descriptions of quotidian places. The resultant displacement of ideological elements from clearly political topoi such as contested borders to these ordinary, seemingly apolitical places, and its effect on the individual Israeli's self-conception, are the main concerns of this book. The imaginative spatiality of literature proffers alternative mappings of Israeli identity: bound less by the walls, fences, barriers, and borders that characterize the current political-spatial discourse in Israel, Israeliness and the ideological elements that determine it are increasingly defined according to diverse Israelis' experiences of everyday sites. The significance of vernacular places and of their sometimes discrete ideological components, this book demonstrates, alerts us to the dynamic complexity of Israeli identity. Acknowledging the relationship between places, ideology, and identity not only brings us a step closer to understanding ourselves, but also enables us to better understand the one we consider *other*.

Acknowledgments

Although in its current form this book hardly resembles the dissertation from which it was born in 2004, I would like to begin by thanking my adviser at UCLA, Arnold Band, for all that he taught me. He has accompanied this project since its inception almost a decade ago. The idea for the dissertation emerged from discussions I had with Yigal Schwartz at the Hebrew University of Jerusalem over the course of 1999–2000.

At UCLA, the Department of Comparative Literature, the Department of English, and the Center for Jewish Studies provided countless opportunities to enrich my knowledge and develop my ideas. Michael North, David Myers, and Gil Hochberg imparted insightful feedback in the earliest stages of this project. I owe a special thanks to my dearest friend Rebecca Hopkins, who has read through most of the various phases of this book's slow metamorphosis over the years. Her sharp eye, critical acuity, and seemingly inexhaustible patience have been invaluable.

UT Austin welcomed me into its vibrant community in 2004. It would be impossible to overstate how encouraging and supportive my colleagues and friends have been over the past seven years. I am particularly grateful to Esther Raizen, who has devoted many long hours to discussing this project's development. Kristen Brustad and the Department of Middle Eastern Studies, Kamran Aghaie and the Center for Middle Eastern Studies, and Elizabeth Richmond-Garza and the Program in Comparative Literature have created an institutional atmosphere conducive to vigorous academic inquiry. A semester's leave from teaching and a summer research grant awarded by UT's College of Liberal Arts provided opportunities for ongoing research and writing.

Special thanks to several cherished friends and colleagues who have made Austin and our department a true home: Samer Ali, Yoav Di-Capua, Tarek El-Ariss, Stephennie Mulder, and Na'ama Pat-El. Na'ama and Esther Raizen also helped with tricky translations and transliterations. Outside Austin, Lital Levy read, reread, discussed, suggested, and argued almost every point of this book over the course of several years. The intellectual rigor and commitment of this remarkable group of scholars and friends continues to challenge, inspire, and nurture me.

Many others have contributed in some way to shaping and refining the ideas in this book. I thank those who have offered helpful insights and encouraging words as I presented my ideas at conferences, colloquia, and seminars. In bringing this book to press, I must also thank my editors at Syracuse, who have made this process smoother than I imagined it could be.

I would like to extend my thanks to my students at UT, whose critical and theoretical sophistication never fails to impress and delight me, and from whom I continue to learn every day.

Finally, I cannot adequately express my gratitude to my parents and sister, who have encouraged and supported me through a decade of thinking and writing about place. Whether I'm in Lyons or Los Angeles, Jerusalem or Tel Aviv, Oslo or Austin, I have a home in them.

✳

I gratefully acknowledge permission to use the following copyrighted material:

Excerpts from *shetah hefker: shirim* by Anton Shammas © 1979 by Hakibbutz Hameuchad—Sifriyat Poalim.

Excerpts from *im ha-layla ha-ze* by Leah Goldberg © 1964 by Hakibbutz Hameuchad—Sifriyat Poalim.

Excerpts from *kro u-khtov* by Ronit Matalon © 2001 by Hakibbutz Hameuchad.

Excerpts from *Dolly City* by Orly Castel-Bloom © 2010 by Dalkey Archive Press (previously © 1997 by Loki Books); and from Orly Castel-Bloom via The Institute for the Translation of Hebrew Literature.

Excerpts from *heykhan ani nimtset* by Orly Castel-Bloom © 1990 by The New Library (previously held by Zmora-Bitan).

Excerpts from *The Sabra: The Creation of the New Jew* by Oz Almog © 2000 by University of California Press.

Excerpts from *va-yehi boker* by Sayed Kashua by Keter Books Ltd.

Excerpts from *sefer yosef* by Yoel Hoffmann by Keter Books Ltd.

Excerpts from *kristus shel dagim* by Keter Books Ltd.

Foucault, Michel and Jay Miskowiec. "Of Other Spaces." *Diacritics* 16:1 (1986), 22–27. © 1986 The Johns Hopkins University Press. Reprinted with permission of The Johns Hopkins University Press.

Quotes from THE ONE FACING US by Ronit Matalon. English language translation copyright © 1998 by Metropolitan Books. Reprinted by permission of Henry Holt and Company, LLC.

Quotes from BLISS by Ronit Matalon. English language translation copyright © 2003 by Metropolitan Books. Reprinted by permission of Henry Holt and Company, LLC.

Ben-Gurion Archives, Speeches and Articles Division (Sde Boker, Israel, acquired in 2010).

Excerpts from DON'T CALL IT NIGHT copyright © 1994 by Amos Oz and Keter Publishing House Limited, translation copyright © 1995 by Nicholas de Lange, reproduced by permission of Houghton Mifflin Harcourt Publishing Company.

Excerpts from A PERFECT PEACE copyright © 1982 by Amos Oz and Am Oved Publishers Ltd. Tel Aviv, English translation copyright © 1985 by Amos Oz, reproduced by permission of publisher Houghton Mifflin Harcourt Publishing Company.

Excerpts from TO KNOW A WOMAN copyright © 1989 by Amos Oz and Keter Publishing House, Jerusalem Ltd., English translation copyright © 1991 by Nicholas de Lange, reproduced by permission of Houghton Mifflin Harcourt Publishing Company.

Various excerpts by Yoel Hoffmann, Translated by Eddie Levenston, David Kriss, and Alan Treister, from KATSCHEN & THE BOOK OF JOSEPH, copyright © 1987, 1998 by Yoel Hoffmann. Reprinted by permission of New Directions Publishing Corp. (British Commonwealth rights granted by The Deborah Harris Agency.)

Various excerpts by Yoel Hoffmann, Translated by Eddie Levenston, from THE CHRIST OF FISH, copyright © 1991, 1999 by Yoel Hoffmann. Reprinted by permission of New Directions Publishing Corp. (British Commonwealth rights granted by The Deborah Harris Agency.)

Excerpts from *Human Parts* by Orly Castel-Bloom are reprinted with permission of Key Porter Books. Copyright © 2003 by Orly Castel-Bloom; also acquired permission from Orly Castel-Bloom via The Institute for the Translation of Hebrew Literature.

Excerpts from *Let It Be Morning* © 2004 by Sayed Kashua, translation copyright © 2006 by Miriam Shlesinger. Used by permission of Grove/Atlantic, Inc. (UK English-language rights granted by Grove/Atlantic UK.)

Excerpts from *Dancing Arabs* copyright © 2002 by Sayed Kashua, translation copyright © 2004 by Miriam Shlesinger. Used by permission of Grove/Atlantic, Inc.

Parts of chapter 5 originally appeared in *Scritture Migranti/Migrant Writings* as "Migration as Place: Airplane and Airport in Ronit Matalon's *The One Facing Us and Bliss*" (2010).

Parts of chapter 1 originally appeared in *Das Gelobte Land* as "Schwellengangst."

Place and Ideology in
Contemporary Hebrew Literature

Introduction

Places of Ideology and Ideologies of Place

> The discourse of space is one which we enter as we enter ideology.
> —BILL ASHCROFT, *Post-colonial Transformation*

In her novel *Ha-sefer he-hadash shel orli kastel-bloom* (Taking the trend; literally, The new book by Orly Castel-Bloom) (1998), the Israeli author Orly Castel-Bloom introduces us to a heroine who breathlessly follows trend after trend in search of even the most superficial sense of belonging. Set in a Tel Aviv whose culture and language change continuously, the narrative follows the adventures of this nameless heroine. In one chapter of the novel, entitled "The Ugliest Place in Israel," she relates the trend of naming places that have or make "the best": the best hummus, the most beautiful furniture, the best place to hike. These superlatives notwithstanding, she reveals that her friend has outdone this trend by discovering the ugliest place in Israel:

> But everyone who lives in Israel knows that there are a lot of places that can make you vomit. Places so ugly that it just makes you want to stop the car and vomit.
>
> The ugliest place in Israel was located a few days ago by a friend of mine who passes there all the time and didn't notice until she was stuck behind a line of cars that stood quietly waiting for the ugly train to pass from here to there. It was around eleven in the morning . . . and she realized that she was situated exactly in the fifty square meters that are *definitely* the ugliest in Israel. The reference is of course to the right-hand turn from Shitrit Street south to Mivtsa Kadesh Street in Bnei Brak, on

1

the way to the Ayalon Mall, which is tumultuous in all directions: to the right the green Yarkon Park, in the middle the heavy and repulsive traffic and up and to the left enormous trucks that transport what to where, and to the left more huge concrete barrels that release smoke, and between them designer shopping malls that sell plastic furniture from China. And between all these, signs that say which show to watch on what channel, and what phone the president of the United States uses, and what a character who doesn't exist did in the never-ending program called Everything for Everything. (Castel-Bloom 1998, 60–61)[1]

The narrator's friend is so repulsed by this place that she contacts the newspapers, asking them to send a photographer to document its hideousness. The photographers, however, refuse to come: "They all know the place—it's stuck hard in their visual memory—but they don't want to eternalize it in any way" (1998, 61). The narrator, her friend, and all the people who are familiar with this ugliest of places attribute its unsightliness to its mundanity. Even the friend who has made this "discovery" passes through it regularly. Far from noticing anything extraordinary, she cites only the most ordinary details as contributing to the place's overall ugliness. Signifiers of production, transport, consumption, and advertising, the banal underpinnings of any industrialized society, are represented here as comprising an exceptionally blighted landscape. Then again, as our heroine asks her friend rhetorically, "What does it matter?" (1998, 62).

Castel-Bloom is not the only Israeli author to devote her attention to ugly places. Ronit Matalon, in her short story "*Yalda be-kafeh*" (Girl in a café), describes a young girl who works in a café "that was, in truth, a rather sorry place and that's that. What more can you say about the look of a place whose ugliness sticks out like a stupid curl from a stocking cap?" (1992, 54). Some authors choose to emphasize boredom rather than

---

1. For texts that have been translated into English, I cite from the translation. The exceptions, which are noted, are cases when I offer an alternate translation to elucidate a point not clear from the available English translation. All translations from Hebrew texts unavailable in English are my own.

ugliness. Thus Etgar Keret, in his novella *Ha-keytana shel kneler* (Kneller's happy campers) (1998), represents the afterlife of successful suicides as located in a place just like the Tel Aviv the protagonist, Mordy, knew when he was alive, only a little bit worse: "a dump" (2004, 93). Keret's fantastic world, with its convenience stores, gas stations, and dirty beaches, is notable for its distinct ordinariness.

Unnervingly and explicitly negative in these examples, the literary representation of common, often unsightly places is an innovation neither in Israeli nor in other literatures. Yet, despite the ubiquity of quotidian places in textual and the extratextual worlds, they are consistently passed over as a subject of academic study and intellectual discussion in favor of places considered more relevant to certain political, cultural, and social processes. Particularly in Israeli spatial discourse, which is dominated by religious- and political-territorial debate, everyday places are overlooked. As demonstrated by the above examples' disconcerting combination of indifference and barely concealed anger over their surroundings, however, ordinary places are far more complex and powerful than they may seem. Why do these places evoke such strong imaginative responses? What role do they play in the shaping of Israeli culture and identity? How do Israelis interact with them? What kind of relationship do these places have with those that are considered ideologically significant, such as the nation or the border? This book seeks to answer these questions by analyzing the depiction of ordinary "vernacular" places in Israeli literature.

The geographer credited with having coined the term "vernacular landscape," John Brinckerhoff Jackson, establishes a dualistic relationship between the vernacular and what he calls the "political landscape."[2] He

---

2. Jackson's discussion centers on the vernacular *landscape* and the various types of place that comprise it; to this end, he devotes a good deal of his study to an analysis of the concept of landscape and to historicizing the notion of vernacular landscape. The present study, which addresses landscape as such only minimally, adopts Jackson's political and vernacular as particular spatial categories applicable not only to landscape broadly speaking but to the topoi within a landscape. Jackson himself discusses "the American vernacular dwelling," for instance, as one such place that he locates within the American vernacular landscape (1984, 86).

identifies the features of the political landscape as "the visibility and sanctity of boundaries, the importance of monuments and centrifugal highways, the close relationship between status and enclosed space" (1984, 149). It includes "spaces or structures designed to impose or preserve a unity on the land, or in keeping with a long-range, large-scale plan" (149). A vernacular landscape, on the other hand, is "one where evidences of a political organization of space are largely or entirely absent" (149). It reflects vernacular culture, which implies "a way of life ruled by tradition and custom, entirely remote from the larger world of politics and law; a way of life where identity [derives] not from permanent possession of land but from membership in a group or super-family" (149). In the context of vernacular landscapes, Jackson examines places such as the garage, the strip mall, and the road to demonstrate the extent to which they have shaped cultural life in the United States. For Jackson, the vernacular and the political constitute "two very different but complementary elements in our landscape" (xii). They serve dissimilar people and ends, emerge from disparate cultural, social, and economic circumstances, and reflect the divergent priorities linked to these differences. The mutually exclusive nature of vernacular and political, for Jackson, constitutes a primary division of landscape.

In the case of Israel, it would be difficult to argue convincingly for any place that is vernacular in the apolitical sense that Jackson proposes. But this does not mean that the vernacular landscape and its attendant places are absent there. For the purposes of my study, Israeli vernacular places, concrete sites encountered regularly and used for ordinary purposes, are not constructed or understood *primarily* as political or ideological. Nonvernacular places are primarily political, often formal, institutional, abstract, or metaphorical in nature. Vernacular place in Israel, I argue, serves or reacts to ideology implicitly or explicitly. The sometimes jarring combination of the ideological elements of the Israeli vernacular on the one hand and its commonplace, ubiquitous, and unremarkable nature on the other hand speaks to the complexity of the Israeli identity it helps to shape. Whereas Jackson's definition of vernacular place is well founded in the European and American contexts he examines, the Israeli case presents an altogether different spatiality for which the concept of vernacular place must be reconfigured. My goal is not to challenge or reject Jackson's ideas, which are invaluable for their recognition, articulation, and typology of different types of place, but rather to modify them to accommodate the Israeli situation.

I propose, then, that the Israeli spatial vernacular as it is represented and produced in literature not only complements the Israeli political landscape but is actually inextricably entangled in it. Through close readings of Israeli literary texts, I examine quotidian places that are burdened with overtly political obligations and expectations, resulting in the despair of the characters who inhabit them. The bulk of this study, though, is devoted to what I find more revelatory and interesting: the literary portrayal of those vernacular places that seem, like Jackson's vernacular landscapes, "entirely remote from the larger world of politics and the law." To this end I focus on mostly apolitical vernacular places to demonstrate the pervasiveness of politics and ideology in the most mundane of Israeli spatial interactions. This pervasiveness, in turn, leaves an indelible mark on the Israeli self-conception, initially effecting disorientation and anxiety and ultimately leading to a subtle resistance of the nation-centered paradigm of Israeli identity. In short, vernacular place in Israel, while inseparable from the political landscape, offers alternatives to institutionalized ideological assumptions that simply do not account for the diverse possibilities of Israeli experience and identity. Since this diversity contradicts the notion of culturally homogeneous unification at the foundation of the nationalist endeavor, studying the nation itself as a constitutive space of identity formation can get us only so far. If Israeli identity is so intimately bound up with place (as well as absence of place), then an alternative spatial paradigm is in order. Many have made claims about the centrality of place from theological, nationalist, and other cultural perspectives, and the trope of nationalism has provoked discomfort even among patriotic Zionists. My study, then, modifies Jackson's conception of vernacular landscape to account for the unique characteristics of the Israeli engagement with place. By mobilizing Israeli vernacular places in my examination of literature, I demonstrate how embedded ideological concepts are resisted or confirmed in particular topoi, from the "vernacularized" political to the politicized vernacular.

In this work, I analyze places represented in contemporary Hebrew novels to argue for a particular narrative of the development of spatial relations in Israel. I begin by examining several specific types of place that accord with the conventional Israeli conception of space. The first chapter establishes how Zionist ideology has influenced representations of space in Israeli culture. I find the existence of certain "Zionist places," places that provide physical and geographical expression of mainstream Zionist ideology. These places are identified and defined against the perceived wildness and chaos of the "uncivilized" space beyond. Barriers, both literal and figurative, often separate these two types of spaces and discourage trespassing. This chapter argues that representations of the kibbutz, the garden, and the southern development town, critical as they may be, conform to the Zionist conventions associating spaces inside a border, fence, or wall with order and civilization, and the spaces outside them with chaos and primitive nature. Drawing on works by Amos Oz, a prominent author and a leading figure on the Zionist Left, this chapter presents mainstream Israeli thinking about place. The fact that Oz's representation of these "Zionist places" is itself tinged with apprehension demonstrates that subscribing to Zionist ideals does not preclude ambivalence regarding the implications of their spatial implementation.

In the next two chapters I examine reactions to this mainstream Israeli conception of place by two authors whose literary portrayals deviate from those established conventions. Each chapter focuses on a different crisis of subjectivity resulting from this deviation. In chapter 2 I deal with the fragmentation of national identity and the isolation of the individual Israeli. Through the prisms of cultural geography and mental illness, I examine the representation of spaces Foucault terms "heterotopias of deviation," such as mental asylums and cemeteries, in terms of the terrifying alienation of place brought about by the place formulation outlined in chapter 1. The settings of one of Israel's most provocative authors, Orly Castel-Bloom, exemplify the fragmentation of self that results from the inability to conform to the unifying ethos of the state. In chapter 3 I illustrate the added complexity of the notion of home for "native outsiders," people whose experience of place is characterized by paralysis, in this case Israeli Palestinians (Palestinian citizens of Israel, also known as Israeli Arabs). The Israeli-Palestinian village and the checkpoint, spaces suspended between two nations but participating fully in neither, are the focus of this chapter. Like chapter 2, this chapter demonstrates interactions with a place that is inadequately accounted for by the mainstream Israeli place narrative. Comparing this site as it emerges in the novels of an Israeli-Palestinian author writing in Hebrew, Sayed Kashua, I identify paralysis as a definitive characteristic of his perception of place. I argue in both chapters 2 and 3 that the inability to conform to the conventional understanding of place in Israel leads to a crisis of subjectivity, suggesting a crucial link between identity and the manner in which place is represented.

The final two chapters respond to these crises by suggesting an altogether different interpretation of place from the periphery of the Israeli context. Inherited memories of the forsaken pre-Israeli past are central in the texts I examine here, shaping the way characters interact with place in the Israeli present. The ordering paradigm of space introduced in the first chapter, whereby "inside" is rational and civilized and "outside" is wild and threatening, is not reversed so much as rejected in favor of an altogether different configuration of multiple, nonhierarchical spaces and places. In chapter 4 I consider how, though the elite status of European Jews in Israel is ironically predicated on their rejection of "diasporic" traits in favor of "native Israeli" ones, many Jews who immigrated to Israel from Europe maintained their diasporic sensibilities despite the derision this sometimes evoked. I examine the unapologetic diasporic orientation of Yoel Hoffmann's characters using Bakhtin's notion of time-place ("chronotope") to argue that bourgeois urban "salon spaces" in Israel constitute a "diaspora chronotope" that resists de-historicization. In the final chapter, I examine sites outside Israel such as an African shantytown and the postcolonial house, suggesting that the acts of seeing and moving within these and other places themselves constitute an alternative, subversive space. Analyzing the representation of place by Ronit Matalon, a Jewish Israeli author of Egyptian origin, I use postcolonial and migration theory to demonstrate that her emphasis on movement differs profoundly from the Western-based Zionist valorization of *arrival*, radically reconfiguring the notion of place. Both chapters suggest alternative spatial conceptions, departing from nationalistic modes of understanding place and creating in their stead new spatial narratives to account for the diversity of Israeli experiences.

Historically, this project is situated in modern times. I trace the representation of place and space over the course of a riveting period in Israeli literary history. Several events, notably the defeat of Labor and the rise to power of the right-wing Likud party in 1977, the public Israeli outcry against the 1982 invasion of Lebanon, and the publication of revisionist histories in the early 1980s by the Israeli "New Historians," reflected an increasingly favorable disposition toward collective Israeli self-criticism. This shift in mood encouraged the flowering of new and different literary voices in Israel, particularly in the 1980s and 1990s. These events, along with later ones such as the two Palestinian Intifadas and the emergence of the controversial notion of "post-Zionism," accompany and influence the literary phenomena I examine here.

To provide a sense of the tremendous changes wrought over the course of those two and a half decades, this book focuses on works published in that time period by a diverse array of authors. Far from representing a single, unitary notion of Israeliness, the authors in question include a former member of an elite kibbutz, a second-generation Israeli Palestinian, and the daughter of Francophone Egyptian Jews. Their works, by extension, offer a number of different lenses through which to examine and interpret place. This plurality demonstrates the need for an alternative to the predominantly European and Jewish conception of Israeli identity. Yet the authors examined in this study were chosen not because they are seen to represent Israel but because their portrayals of place parallel the development of a broader, continually evolving narrative of spatial relations within Israeli society. All of the authors included here, with the sole exception of Oz, began publishing in the 1980s or later; though Oz began publishing in the 1960s, his novels examined here were all published in the 1980s and 1990s. My focus on this particular moment in Israeli literary history is intended to demonstrate the range of reactions inspired by earlier conceptions of space and place. One can look to the beginning of the twentieth century, at Yosef Hayim Brenner's seminal 1911 essay *"Ha-janer ha-erets yisraeli va-avizareyhu"* ("The land of Israel genre and its accessories") (1978–85), as an early attempt to articulate the uneasy relationship between literature, place (specifically, the *Yishuv*), and ideology.[3] In the 1940s and 1950s, authors such as S. Yizhar, Moshe Shamir, Yigal Mossinsohn, and others produced works that were involved—sometimes ambivalently in their own right— in creating the concept of Zionist place. These earlier authors and their literary production warrant a study of their own. What concerns me in the present work is not so much the genesis of these conceptions of place but the way contemporary Israelis have interacted with them. The spatial sensibilities of Castel-Bloom, Kashua, Hoffmann, and Matalon all, to some extent, respond to, react against, or evade the ideological tropes embedded in the dominant spatial model that Oz represents and with which his characters struggle.

Given the complexity and diversity of Zionist thought and its continually evolving nature over the course of the past century or so,[4] a clarification of what I mean by Zionism and Zionist ideology is in order. In using these terms, I refer to the mainstream contemporary Israeli understanding of Zionism and its historical endeavor, specifically the social, cultural, and political efforts exerted to create a national Israeli identity. This understanding, rooted in Labor Zionism,[5] is based on several

3. For an analysis and contextualization of Brenner's complex essay, see Hasak-Lowy 2008, 41–49.

4. For a presentation and analysis of the wide range of some of the most influential Zionist thinkers, see Hertzberg 1972. For a more recent assessment of Zionism and its role in Israel, see Hertzberg 2003.

5. The contemporary Israeli understanding of Zionism is rooted in socialist Zionism, which, as the historian Anita Shapira notes, "was the most dynamic force in Zionism since the early 1920s and was to a large degree representative of the widest body of opinion in the Zionist camp" (1992, ix). She reminds us that, for five decades, Mapai (the left-wing workers' party that later merged into the Israeli Labor Party) predominated in the political

fundamental points: Zionism sought to restore the Jews to their ancestral homeland, *erets yisrael*, or the Land of Israel; to create a virile, physical, and engaged "New Jew," the antithesis of the cerebral Diaspora Jew; to revive the Hebrew language and establish a new secular Hebrew culture that would, to a great extent, supplant religious Judaic culture; and thereby to produce a new national identity based, like the European nation-state, on a shared territory and common language. Like all nationalist movements, Zionism aimed to forge a national identity through a unity of purpose, a sense of shared fate and history, and a common political vision leading to action. However, the cultural and linguistic homogeneity that provided the basis for the European nation-state that early Jewish nationalists like Moses Hess (1812–1875) hoped to emulate had to be induced in the Jewish state, since its Jewish inhabitants hailed from a wide range of places. Zionism was the brainchild of European thought and hence was adopted and realized by European (Ashkenazi) Jews, who came to monopolize the political and cultural apparatus that led the state. Accordingly, in the quest for a cohesive national character, all Israelis were encouraged to adopt a Western cultural orientation. As we shall see, this drive for unity was manifested spatially as well. My use of the terms "Zionism" and "Zionist ideology," then, takes as its reference point the Labor Zionism that reigned for over half a century and that, even after its political downfall in 1977 and its weakened sociocultural position, continued to inform collective Israeli consciousness and identity as well as the various political movements that crystallized in the decades after its defeat.

Despite the critical stance it establishes vis-à-vis the conventional Zionist conception of place, this study does not conceive of itself as "post-Zionist" in nature. Post-Zionism as a concept remains too amorphous, too malleable, and too vague to constitute a coherent alternative to Zionism.

---

and ideological life not only of the *Yishuv* (the Jewish community in Palestine) and, later, the State of Israel, but also of the Zionist movement itself: "More than any other factor, it molded the Israeli ethos, defining its basic tenets and shaping the minds of young people associated with it" (ix).

There is still no consensus as to how, exactly, to define post-Zionism, which continues to be understood to mean dramatically different things by various thinkers. For some, it means anti-Zionism, for others, a-Zionism, for still others, it connotes a continuation and transformation of Zionism, and so on.[6] Just as I acknowledge that Zionism is not a monolithic,

---

6. The sociologist Uri Ram, for example, defines it as "a trend of libertarianism and openness, which strives to lower the boundaries of Israeli identity, and to include in it all relevant 'others'" (1999, 334). He interprets it as a civic identity that accentuates the "normalizing and universalistic aspects" of "classical Zionism" (Ram 1999, 335). For the philosopher Adi Ophir, "[post-Zionists] are presumably those who, while not necessarily accepting old anti-Zionist positions, deny the ongoing viability of Zionism" (2000, 185). Ilan Pappé, a political scientist, goes further, writing that "the term *post-Zionism* is a hybrid of anti-Zionist notions and a postmodernist perception of reality" (1997, 30, his emphasis).

Scholars representing a wide range of ideological conviction acknowledge the difficulty of pinning down a workable definition of post-Zionism, and usually end by defining it, rather vaguely, as representing a stance critical of Zionism. Anita Shapira writes that "The concept has never been precisely defined and different writers emphasize different elements as 'post-Zionism.' . . . Indeed, the term 'post-Zionism' has varied connotations, ranging from a critique of Israeli research on the Palestinians and their treatment by the Zionist movement and Israel, to the demand for a completely new approach to the history of Zionism and the history and sociology of Israel. . . . Its proponents do not question the existence of Israel, but their attitude to it is, at best, indifferent and, in more extreme cases, a priori suspicious and critical" (1995, 10–11). Shapira notes that the debate is not only about historiography, as suggested by the prominent place of the "new historians" in post-Zionist discourse (whether or not they subscribe to post-Zionism), but also about collective memory.

Ephraim Nimni notes that "definitions of post-Zionism are hard to find, and when they appear they are often not consensual. Supporters and detractors attribute to it different and sometimes conflicting meanings" (2003, 3). He summarizes Chaim Waxman's identification of three contrasting definitions of post-Zionism, only to reject all three for their limited applications: "The first is the anti-colonial argument sustained by old radical 'anti-Zionist' groups in Israel. The second results from a generational change in Israeli universities, as the generation of the 'founding fathers' retires and a new more 'eclectic' generation takes over. The third contribution results from an 'a-Zionist' interrogation of fundamental questions of Jewish nationalism, Judaism and ethnicity—questions that, according to Waxman, accompanied the Zionist enterprise from its origins. From a different perspective and opposing point of view, detractors use 'post-Zionism' simply as a term

one-dimensional, absolute entity, so do I hope the reader resists the facile categorization of any and all scholarship critical of Zionist paradigms as post-Zionist. Moreover, despite the absence of a consensus regarding the definition of post-Zionism, one thing is clear: it is a concept that is always defined in relation to Zionism.[7] The point I wish to make in this study is that a variety of different critical stances, expressed by a wide range of authors from Oz to Kashua and springing from diverse motivations, confront conventional nationalist conceptions of space and offer alternatives that are sometimes in dialogue *with* or *against* Zionist spatiality, and sometimes bypass it altogether to articulate notions of space and place that are independent of Zionism. As I see it, then, the manuscript offers an alternative not only to Zionism, but also to various understandings of post-Zionism in its reading of place.

I wish to emphasize at the onset that, though theoretically informed by a wide disciplinary spectrum, this study focuses on literature. Moreover, the authors I examine write from a cultural context that is primarily secular. No few studies on Israeli conceptions of space take as their starting point the biblical text and the concepts of exile and home developed there (in Hebrew one of God's names is *ha-makom,* the place). The more radical studies question and reconfigure the values attached to exile and home, but they still work from within a Judaic framework. While it would be difficult to dismiss religion and theology from any serious consideration

---

of abuse that encompasses any critique of Zionism that is not to their liking. None of the above is, however, fully satisfactory, for none can account for the wider use of the term beyond the limited audiences identified in Waxman's categories. The widespread use of the term indicates that the phenomenon goes beyond these limited audiences" (3–4). He argues that "in the transitional period that results from the shift in values taking place in Israel, the term post-Zionism is an 'empty signifier,' a concept not characterized by density of meaning, but by an emptiness of content that allows supporters and detractors to articulate it easily into conflicting discourses" (11). For Nimni, this situation presents an opportunity to inscribe post-Zionism with "unambiguous meaning" (11). For the time being, however, such clarity remains elusive.

7. Amnon Raz-Krakotzkin elaborates on post-Zionism as replicating Zionism's separation of Israeli Jews and Israeli Arabs (1997).

of Israeli identity, one of the challenges this book confronts is how to approach Israeliness that is situated outside the assumed normative Israeli identity—for instance, that of the non-Jewish Israeli Palestinian. Another reason I chose to focus on secular interpretations of place and space stems from my determination to examine place and its production on the most concrete level. Religious-theological debates on the nature of exile, while they certainly play a significant role in the Israeli self-conception as well as in policy making, deal with abstract notions of place and space. This book considers the Judaic conception of place to be one of many factors that have shaped the Israeli cultural landscape inhabited by Jewish and non-Jewish Israelis alike.

The literary works I analyze here are all Israeli; however, my theoretical concerns are widely applicable beyond the Israeli context. The importance of place in shaping ideology, and, in turn, of ideology in transforming place, is evident in an array of situations around the globe. Postcolonialism in Africa and Asia, migration in Europe and the United States, displacement and the creation of refugee populations in Iraq and Afghanistan: these familiar events and processes affect profoundly the way people relate to their places and to the political and ideological forces with which these are engaged, enacting a continual shaping and reassessment of identity. The narratives affected by global spatial shifts are not only the official histories of textbooks and newspaper headlines. They are also—to a greater extent—the unofficial stories of individuals who conquer, defy, establish, or resist these broad spatial configurations on a concrete, microcosmic level, by drawing water from a forbidden source, leaving home after a curfew, climbing a fence, avoiding a hostile neighborhood, or crossing a river.

This introduction provides the conceptual framework for the book as a whole, which is primarily devoted to close readings of literary texts. After briefly noting the main preoccupations of Israeli thinking on place, I outline the broader concerns of theorists of place and space working in different cultural contexts and disciplinary traditions. I examine two factors in particular: the role that various interpretations of place and space attribute to politics and ideology, and the particular contribution that literature can make to deepen our understanding of the way spaces and places actively shape identity.

On Place in Israel

It is difficult to conceive of space and place in the Israeli context separately from ideology. In that relentlessly contentious territorial situation, the epigraph at the beginning of this introduction does not require extensive elaboration. Working against the grain of Jewish statelessness to articulate a modern collective Jewish identity at the turn of the nineteenth century, political Zionism was centered by the idea of a physical homeland. The implementation of this idea, begun in earnest with the first wave of immigration in 1881 and formalized in 1948 with the declaration of Israeli statehood, was complicated further in 1967 by another spatially defined phenomenon. Occupation is, after all, first and foremost territorial. These two events, Israeli statehood and the Israeli occupation of 1967, are the formative components of the Israeli spatial narrative. Israelis' acute awareness of the centrality of the spatial is reflected in the many recent studies on the subject from various disciplinary perspectives. At the same time, the veritable explosion of interdisciplinary scholarship on the subject of space and place more generally since the 1970s has demonstrated the diverse possibilities of spatial analysis.

I seek to complement the existing thought on space and place in Israel while challenging the nationalist territorialist perspective from which much of it originates by integrating modes of spatial analysis that, though less apparent in the Israeli experience, nevertheless play a crucial role in the constitution of collective and individual Israeli self-conceptions. In doing so, I aim not to downplay the relationship between place and ideology but, to the contrary, to demonstrate that this relationship is at work even in apolitical spatial situations. Shifting the focus from the nation to other seemingly less loaded places will illuminate the extent to which ideological and political elements imbue even the most apparently neutral and personal sites.

The preoccupation in Israel with the national paradigm stems from the historical circumstances preceding the relatively recent establishment of the state. Since the condition of exile had come to be identified with Jewishness itself, the advent of Jewish nationalism was interwoven for most of its proponents with the notion of Jewish normalization. For Theodor Herzl,

Max Nordau, David Ben-Gurion, and others, nationhood would end, once and for all, the "abnormality" that had tainted the Jews for the duration of their long exile and that had made their assimilation in Europe impossible. Not all Jews agreed. Outside Israel, some non-Zionists claimed and continue to claim that nationalism threatens the very essence of Jewishness, which they locate in the condition of exile. This contention, rooted in Jewish history or biblical hermeneutics (though sometimes invoked in decidedly secular cultural terms), establishes exile as the true home of the Jew. Daniel and Jonathan Boyarin, for example, argue for "Diaspora as a theoretical and historical model to replace national self-determination" (1993, 711). Looking to historical models of European Jewish history, they hold that Zionism constitutes "the subversion of Jewish culture and not its culmination. It represents the substitution of a European, Western cultural-political formation for a traditional Jewish one" (712). George Steiner asserts that, in Judaism, the centrality of text and the condition of exile are inextricably bound and mutually dependent. For the Jew, he posits, the "text is home; each commentary a return" (1985, 7). The Jew's "at-homeness in the word" constitutes an at-homeness in exile (24). Similarly, Edmond Jabès recalls his family's departure from Egypt and his subsequent realization that "the Jew's real place is the book" (1991, 248). In the first half of the twentieth century, a few Zionists opposed the territorial focus that increasingly characterized Zionist ideology, but today Zionism is associated first and foremost with territory and statism.[8] The provocative ideas espoused by Boyarin, Steiner, Jabès, and others have gained little credence within Israel.

Yet Israeli scholarship increasingly acknowledges that statehood has not resulted in the hoped-for normalization of the Jewish relationship to

---

8. Perhaps the best known such figure is Ahad Ha-am, often characterized as a "cultural Zionist" (rather than a statist "political Zionist"). Other Zionists who formulated nonterritorial conceptions of Jewish nationhood include Simon Rawidowicz, Mordecai Kaplan, and Hans Kohn. For more on Rawidowicz, see Myers 2008; for an analysis of the contributions of Rawidowicz, Kaplan, and Kohn to the notion of nonstatist Jewish nationalism, see Pianko 2010.

place. Anthropologists Zali Gurevitch and Gideon Aran spawned controversy and heated discussions in a range of disciplines including literature,
art, architecture, and anthropology with their essay, 'Al ha-makom: anthropologiya yisraelit (On place: Israeli anthropology), reprinted in Gurevitch's
collection, 'Al ha-makom (On Israeli and Jewish place). In the introduction
to this collection, Gurevitch begins with the provocative statement that
"in Israel place is not in place. . . . [There] is a discomfort and an inability
to come to terms with Jewish nativeness [mekomiyut] itself" (2007, 7). He
characterizes the Israeli relationship to place as two-pronged: "we aspire to
it, we come to it, we miss it, we bless it, it is the big promise, but at the same
time place and nativeness [mekomiyut] also evoke recoiling, reservation,
even revulsion" (8). Though he acknowledges the effect of the contemporary political situation, including wars, occupation, and internal Israeli
divisions on the Israeli spatial consciousness, he traces the roots of this
consciousness to the Bible's articulation of a Judaic conception of place
and interprets "the insolubility of place . . . as flowing from the contradictory ideas shaking up the 'unified' Zionist world of place from within" (15).
Aran and Gurevitch conclude their well-known essay by expressing the
hope for "the Israeli possibility to be released from the burden of making
place 'entirely ours' and making ourselves 'entirely the place's'" (1991, 44).

In a later essay, Gurevitch further develops the idea that, instead of
viewing Israeli nationhood as the end of previous Jewish existence out of
place, we should consider it favorably as a continuation of the anomalous
Jewish relationship to place. Attempting to reconcile the Judaic and the
Zionist views of place by reading the Bible as "the book of the place,"
Gurevitch identifies an "ambivalence toward the place, the unresolved
core of what it means to be Israeli," which he links directly to "the Judaic
sources of that identity" (1997, 207). He locates what he calls "the double
site of Jewish identity" in the land and in the text, the place and the story.
It is the "puzzling gap between story and place" that leads him to insist
upon "the irreducibility of the story to the place, and hence the unrest, the
schism, perhaps, between the Israelis and their native place, namely Israel"
(204). The "double site of identity" is paralleled by the "double structure
of the book of place" itself, Gurevitch points out, since the Bible "both
places and is itself unplaced" (205). He concludes the essay by pointing

out, tellingly, that "the ambivalence characteristic of this discourse is not necessarily a sign of weakness, or thing to get rid of. It comes from and in fact expresses the deep core of Judaic understanding of what the place is. It draws from the powerful source of the book that tells the story of the place as the home in the world, and at once disowns it for fear that the place would become the beginning and the end to identity" (214).

Aran and Gurevitch's work has left an indelible mark on Israeli scholarship. Perhaps the most striking example is the recent study by the influential literary scholar Yigal Schwartz, subtitled *Handasat ha-adam u-mahshavat ha-merhav ba-sifrut ha-'ivrit ha-hadasha* (The design of man and the conceptualization of landscape in Hebrew literature). Schwartz notes "the discomfort that we, the Israelis, feel regarding our identity and regarding the place we define as our national home" (2007, 9). Proceeding from Aran and Gurevitch's central claim in his own observation of "a general agreement . . . that there apparently exists an unbridgeable gap between the Place and our place," Schwartz's book examines the literary contribution to the imagining and establishment of an Israeli national home, with its attendant ambiguities and contradictions (11). The study, Schwartz emphasizes, is concerned with the conception and representation of a national home in Israel, and with the reconciliation of the Zionist dream of such a home with the reality. Thus, landscape, border and boundary are basic elements of Schwartz's analysis. One of his book's most innovative contributions is its inclusion of an appendix of literary maps, constituting "a systematic attempt to develop a special graphic language for describing literary texts" (22). As the Israeli place is so deeply marked by the text, suggests Schwartz, so the highly spatial text itself is subject to cartography. History and place continuously inscribe one another.

Where We Are: Theories of Place and Space

The problem that has vexed most recent theorists of space and place in a broader context has been not the preponderance of the political, but rather just the opposite: the resistance of so many thinkers to the idea that place is even capable of being political. The juncture from whence this question emerges is the one where the temporal and the spatial meet. The attempt to define the relationship between these two forces is an exercise in frustration, not least because at the very onset of such an attempt we have to contend with the meaning of place and space. As these terms' definitions are contested not only across disciplines but even within them, no universally accepted distinction separates them. In this study, I employ the definition posited by Yi-Fu Tuan in his influential work, *Space and Place*: "In experience, the meaning of space often merges with that of place. 'Space' is more abstract than 'place.' What begins as undifferentiated space becomes place as we get to know it better and endow it with value" (1977, 6). This conception of "place" is well suited to the concreteness and specificity of the vernacular spatiality I discuss. I use the term "space" to emphasize the abstraction of a place.

Edward Casey, the author of a philosophical trilogy on place, considers space and time to be abstractions poised against the concreteness of place. Lamenting that "[for] an entire epoch, place has been regarded as an impoverished second cousin of Time and Space," he resolves to "accord to place a position of renewed respect by specifying its power to direct and stabilize us, to memorialize and identify us, to tell us who and what we are in terms of *where we are* (and where we are *not*)" (1993, xiv, xv). Michel Foucault, in his oft-quoted contribution to this discussion, has written that "[the] anxiety of our era has to do fundamentally with space, no doubt a great deal more than with time" (1986, 23). The radical geographer Doreen Massey similarly positions herself against what she considers a persistent and prevalent understanding of space defined as "stasis, and as utterly opposed to time" (1993, 143). Though she articulates the opposition as one between space and time rather than place and time, she echoes Casey's resistance to the widespread conviction that time is more active, more political and more important than the spatial. The major difference between their interpretations is not in their starting points but in their conclusions: While Casey argues for a "renewed respect" for place based on its contributions to human identities, Massey seeks to reject the binary structure separating space and time altogether, arguing that "space and time are inextricably interwoven" and that the spatial and the social therefore enjoy a reciprocal relationship (152). The spatial is not important *despite* its separation from time, but because it is, in fact, *inseparable* from time. "[Space] is not absolute, it is relational," she argues (152).

For comparative purposes, those scholars who work on space and place can be roughly divided into two often overlapping groups: one that considers the spatial to be primarily experiential, intimate, and phenomenological; and one that considers it to be primarily social, political, and ideological. These two modes of thinking about place are neither mutually exclusive nor even oppositional by any means, and they are equally committed to the expansion of spatial discourse beyond the purely quantitative and geometric. Yet they emphasize different aspects of spatiality. Since these differences form the crux of the contemporary discourse on space and place that shapes my theoretical approach, it is useful to outline briefly their contours.

The first, phenomenological group includes figures such as the philosophers Gaston Bachelard and Michel de Certeau and the humanistic geographer Yi-Fu Tuan. Bachelard, who used the term "topophilia" to describe his investigations into "the human value of the sorts of space that may be grasped, that may be defended against adverse forces, the space we love," approaches spatiality from the perspective of what he terms a "philosophy of poetry" (1969, xxxi, i). His topophilic explorations are focused on dwelling places but more generally are concerned with the concept of "space that has been seized upon by the imagination," which, according to Bachelard, "cannot remain indifferent space" (xxxii). His insistence on the role of the human imagination in enlivening and even empowering the spatial contributes to the deconstruction of the loathed time/space binary that posits the spatial as mere passive setting. Certeau is concerned with the imagination as well, particularly its role in the *practice* of space. He considers stories to be active forces in the constitution of spatial practice. Since stories arrange, organize, and pass through places, and since they transform place into language, "they are spatial trajectories. In this respect, narrative structures have the status of spatial syntaxes. . . . Every story is a travel story—a spatial practice" (Certeau 1984, 115). The idea of *practice* lies at the heart of Certeau's conception of place, and it is activated by narrative. In a similar vein, Mark Turner argues in *The Literary Mind* that everyday human experience and interaction can be understood as practiced spatial narrative: "Partitioning the world into objects involves partitioning the world into small spatial stories because our recognition of objects depends on the characteristic stories in which they appear" (1996, 17). Tuan, the philosopher-geographer considered one of the founders of the discipline of human or humanistic geography, argues that experience transforms abstract space into place. Human experience encompasses a wide range of meanings for Tuan: "Experience can be direct and intimate, or it can be indirect and conceptual, mediated by symbols" (1977, 6). While he never discounts or undervalues the importance of conceptual experiences such as nationalism in shaping spatial relations, he is most concerned with these and other experiences from the perspective of human emotion. The common thread that binds these interpretations of place and space, then, is the notion that the spatial must be considered through the prism of intimate interaction with humans, whether this interaction is described as imagination, narrative description, or experience.

The second group of theories of place and space, as outlined above, focuses on the social and political dimensions of the spatial. Scholars working in this vein include postcolonial theorists such as Homi Bhabha and Bill Ashcroft and cultural geographers working at the intersection of social theory, philosophy, and geography like David Harvey, Doreen Massey, and Edward Soja. For Bhabha the condition of "unhomeliness" (to be distinguished from homelessness) results from "history's most intricate invasions" into the domestic sphere: "In that displacement, the borders between home and world become confused; and, uncannily, the private and the public become part of each other, forcing upon us a vision that is as undivided as it is disorienting" (1994, 13). It is in the banalities of everyday life, suggests Bhabha, that such unhomeliness is most keenly experienced. Ashcroft argues that place and displacement occur as a result of a convergence of factors in the lives of colonized peoples, and identifies the visual as one of the most consequential of these. He argues that "the prominence of the visual, and the equation of knowledge and sight, have had a profound impact on the conception, representation and experiencing of place in the colonized world" (Ashcroft 2001, 127). Identifying cartography, perspective, surveillance, and the discipline of geography itself as spatially relevant manifestations of the Western "passion for the ocular," he argues that the representation of space can differ substantially from the way it is experienced (127, 128). Ashcroft considers the colonial experience to be one in which the colonized person is forced to engage visually with space in a way that is disorienting. Reasserting one's place in place, he posits, depends on habitation more than anything. Ashcroft's point is relevant beyond the colonial context: the visual engagement with place lays bare the ambivalence or fear embedded within even the most familiar and intimate spatial relations.

Even in spatial situations that are not overtly political, and in which social relations seem normalized, the potential for deception exists. "We must be insistently aware of how space can be made to hide consequences from us, how relations of power and discipline are inscribed into the apparently innocent spatiality of social life, how human geographies become filled with politics and ideology," warns Edward Soja (1989, 6). In a similar vein, the literary scholar Roberto Dainotto cautions against the "jargon of authenticity" (the phrase is Adorno's) that is so often invoked to express a natural and organic relationship between a particular people and a particular place (Dainotto 2000, 33, 170–71). Nationalist and regionalist claims of authenticity suggest that place is closed, static, and a-historical. Massey, too, interprets place as not only the site of social relations but also as their active agent: "the spatial is integral to the production of history, and thus to the possibility of politics," she insists (1993, 159). She goes on to posit a direct comparison between the human and the spatial, arguing that "the identities of place are always unfixed, contested and multiple" (Massey 1994, 5). The dynamic nature of place, its resistance to closure and to boundedness, its ambiguous position as the locus of security and simultaneously the potential site of exclusion and domination—all these characteristics contribute to the understanding of place as the nexus of human social relations.

Little wonder, then, that some place theorists have turned (or returned, some might argue) to the prospect of the disappearance of place. Edward Relph, a humanistic geographer, like Tuan defines places as "phenomena of experience," but he limits the experiential to the concrete: "Places are not abstractions or concepts, but are directly experienced phenomena of the lived world and hence are full with meanings, with real objects, and with ongoing activities" (1976, 44, 141). The most crucial factors in our relations to place, he argues, are the inside/outside dualism and the related "authentic" experience of place. "To be inside a place is to belong to it and to identify with it, and the more profoundly inside you are the stronger is this identity with the place," he writes. "The inside-outside division thus . . . provides the essence of place" (49). Appreciation of place and awareness of its significance signifies an "authentic" spatial attitude (80–82). Conversely, to be outside a place is to be placeless and "inauthentic." "Placelessness describes both an environment without significant places and the underlying attitude which does not acknowledge significance in places" (143). Fearing that "it is less and less possible to have a deeply felt sense of place," Relph calls for an approach to make places "authentically" to counter the "psychological consequences and moral issues in uprooting and increasing geographical mobility and placelessness" (80, 147). For all its resistance to the spatial homogeneity effected by mass culture and global economic forces, this notion does not acknowledge the political factors that bring about a *literal* placelessness for so many. It is a slippery slope from the heartfelt love for place and for its role in human experience that Relph expresses to the distortion of the concepts of authenticity and "insideness" and their appropriation to the more sinister ends that Dainotto warns about.

An entirely different interpretation of the phenomenon of placelessness has been articulated by the anthropologist Marc Augé. As an alternative to postmodernity, which dismisses the idea of progress, Augé suggests that we live in an age of supermodernity, characterized by an "overabundance" or excess of time and place that complicates contemporary thinking about these concepts. Rather than oppose place to space, he opposes place to non-place. A non-place is the product of supermodernity, "a space which cannot be defined as relational, or historical, or concerned with identity" (1995, 77–78). Even if such spaces are unconcerned with identity, however, they contribute to its flux. Together with places, non-places "are like palimpsests on which the scrambled game of identity and relations is ceaselessly rewritten. But non-places are the real measure of our time" (79). Significantly, the concept of non-places—unlike Relph's placelessness— designates *specific* types of places, those that are constructed to serve certain purposes such as transit or leisure, as well as the relations between people and such places (94). The relations people have with these spaces of mass transit, commerce, and leisure are the mechanisms that produce the placeless malaise that Relph decries. Yet for Augé these relations are not to be lamented or overcome; they simply express the state of supermodernity, in which people "are always, and never, at home" (109).

"Spatial Stories": Literature and the Production of Place

How, then, are we to make sense of these various interpretations of place and space, and to reconcile the phenomenological with the social? And how can we articulate the relationship between space and ideology in a manner useful and productive for literary analysis? In his seminal study, *The Production of Space*, Henri Lefebvre strives for "a truly unitary theory" of space (1991, 12) that accounts for what he terms "ideal space," which is mental or intellectual, as well as "'real space,' which is the space of social practice"—including sensory phenomena and products of the imagination (14). The separation of the social from the phenomenological is inconceivable for Lefebvre, who considers real and ideal space to be related and interdependent. His primary concern, and the one that brings us to the question of literature, is with the *production* of space. Space springs not from a vacuum but from an intricate web of social relations. This process of the production of space constitutes the lifeblood of ideology. "What is an ideology without a space to which it refers, a space which it describes, whose vocabulary and links it makes use of, and whose code it embodies?" asks Lefebvre. "More generally speaking, what we call ideology only achieves consistency by intervening in social space and in its production, and by thus taking on body therein. Ideology *per se* might well be said to consist primarily in a discourse upon social space" (44). The production of space, which in itself can consist of intimate phenomenological components as well as abstract conceptual ones, not only invites but actually *forms* ideology. Without space and the process of its production, according to Lefebvre, there can be no ideology.

In terms of literary study, the notion that production is as crucial as the product—space itself—has obvious implications. Certeau's assertion that "every story . . . is a spatial practice" and that stories "carry out a labor that constantly transforms places into spaces or spaces into places" clarifies the role of narrative in actively producing space (1984, 115, 118). Narrative description transcends representation in that, like space itself, it has *agency*. Discussing the role of literature in the production of place, Leonard Lutwack writes that "places are neither good nor bad in themselves but in the values attached to them, and literature is one of the agencies involved in attaching values to places" (35). Wesley Kort takes this interpretation further, arguing that place is at least as significant as character in narrative discourse. Arguing against the prominence of the temporal in narrative theory, he seeks to demonstrate the centrality and even the dominance of the spatial, at the same time insisting that these two forces are not opposed but intricately intertwined (Kort 2004, 10). Pleading against the dehumanizing abstraction of social space and spatial language, Kort invokes both Lefebvre and Edward Said. The atopic spatial discourses resulting from the disregard of material, concrete elements of space lead to an unjustified and misleading erasure of differences and, finally, to a dangerous conflation of vastly different experiences and identities. It is not that textual space need not be abstract—it *must* not be abstract.

It is in an attempt to heed the warning issued by Lefebvre and Kort that I turn to Israeli literature. As Yigal Schwartz's study, including its literary maps, demonstrates, Israeli literary spatial discourse has been considered in highly specific terms. Schwartz's book, the most comprehensive literary study to grapple with the notion of a "gap" between Judaic and Zionist interpretations of place,[9] focuses on the concept of national home. Other approaches to the question of place in Israeli literature examine particular types of place such as the desert[10] and the sea,[11] and the fantastic

9. Vered Shemtov, currently writing a book entitled *Verse and Place: Poetic Form Between Home and Exile in Modern Hebrew Literature*, has addressed the tension between a Jewish and an Israeli-Jewish conception of space in Yehuda Amichai's poetry. See Shemtov 2005.

10. For instance, Omer-Sherman 2006a; and Zerubavel, forthcoming.

11. For instance, Hever, 2006.

and imaginary landscapes of recent postmodernist literature.[12] The city, and Tel Aviv and Jerusalem in particular, have been the subjects of a large body of critical production.[13] What has so far remained unexamined has been the seemingly insignificant space of everyday Israeli life. Though the importance of the spatial subjects above is undeniable, it seems to me that Israel's spatial story has another, unacknowledged dimension that has the capacity to tell us a great deal about the way Israelis relate to their place. That is, the way Israelis interact with the vernacular places of their day-to-day lives potentially reveals as much about their identity as does the relationship they have with the nation.

In tracing the role of place in mobilizing, confronting, or resisting ideology in Israel, I do not purport in the following chapters to offer a resolution to the very real geopolitical issues that have become so deeply embedded in the Israeli consciousness, nor do I suggest an escape from these issues into atopic abstraction. Rather, I acknowledge the power of place in its contribution to an ever-developing, highly complex conception of Israeliness. If, as Schwartz provocatively asserts, in Israel there is an "unbridgeable gap between the Place and our place," this book aims to shift the focus in an effort to reconcile a gap that is potentially bridgeable: the gap between our places and our place.

12. For instance, Mendelson-Maoz 1996.

13. Examples of studies on Tel Aviv include Azaryahu 2006 and Mann 2006. A few examples of studies on Jerusalem and Tel Aviv in literature are Ezrahi 2007; Omer-Sherman 2006b; Elad-Bouskila 2001; Mann 2001; Ben-Ezer 1989; Govrin 1989; Ben-Porat 1987; Sokoloff 1983.

1

Zionist Places Against the Desert Wilderness

Amos Oz

> Is it conceivable that the exercise of hegemony might leave space untouched? Could space be nothing more than the passive locus of social relations, the milieu in which their combination takes on body, or the aggregate of the procedures employed in their removal? The answer must be no.
> —HENRI LEFEBVRE, *The Production of Space*

Zionist places are, first and foremost, spaces that have been constructed or designed in the service of Zionist ideology. They establish particular spatial relations that affirm and represent Zionist values and self-conception. The kibbutz, a site created for the convergence of the collectivist and agricultural values at the heart of Labor Zionism, is perhaps the best example of such an overtly ideological place. As the home of thousands of Israeli Jews and the usually rural site of mundane activities like farming and milking, the kibbutz qualifies as a vernacular place, albeit one with a decidedly ideological orientation. Even after the economic and social decline of the kibbutz, it remains deeply rooted in the Israeli psyche as an example of a uniquely *Israeli* (and decidedly not *Jewish*) type of place that, at least until its peak in the early 1950s, encapsulated all the ideals that the new state hoped to instill in its citizens. Despite the fact that a minority of Israelis actually lived on kibbutzim, the kibbutz and the values it espoused, such as closeness to the land and to nature, physicality, and an anti-bourgeois manner, defined Israeli identity. Yet not all Zionist places wave the flag of Zionism as explicitly as the kibbutz. To define the contours of Zionist places, it is instructive to examine places like the kibbutz to determine what it is, exactly, that makes them so well suited for their ideological purpose. That is, what is it in the kibbutz and other obviously Zionist places that make them Zionist— *besides* the fact that their members subscribe to Zionist ideology? Only after a sustained examination of the mechanics of spatial representation of such an explicitly Zionist place can we begin to identify similar spatial patterns embedded within seemingly apolitical vernacular places.

The spatial relationships central to Zionist praxis become apparent through the literary analysis of the kibbutz. Two other vernacular places, the garden and the southern development town, are marked by similar spatial tropes and can be considered part of the rubric of Zionist places. Though neither of these two places was constructed primarily for ideological purposes like the kibbutz, both emerge as locales shaped by the same concerns and ideas. All three of these Zionist places, moreover, are situated against the actual or metaphorical desert wilderness,[1] *midbar*. Several works by Amos Oz, one of the most prolific, well known, and frequently translated Israeli authors, illustrate these phenomena.

My analysis of Oz's representation of places and spaces is intended to serve as the counterpoint to the subsequent chapters. I identify a spatial pattern that emerges in Oz's texts sometimes subtly and at other times explicitly. The broader discourse of partition[2] finds its microcosmic manifestation in my reading of Oz's spatiality, which defines itself not only according to borders, boundaries, and frontiers, those abstract and highly politicized edges of space, but also according to walls and fences, the most common units of vernacular construction. This microcosmic "partition" often (but not always) functions *within* a relatively neutral space, not at a tense and disputed border. The separation it enacts points to the

1. The compound noun "desert wilderness" reflects the two terms' interchangeability in Zionist spatial discourse (*midbar/shmama*). For more on this interchangeability and its implications, see Zerubavel 2008.

2. For more on Oz and partition, see Cleary 2002.

sharp divisions within Israeli society and to deeply ingrained exclusionary tendencies. Yet it also reveals the underlying tensions accompanying such divisions, which can perforate boundaries and riddle their attendant spaces with ambivalence. In other words, Oz constructs literary places according to an existing spatial-ideological paradigm, but he does not do so uncritically.

The kibbutz, an explicitly ideological place, is an important site in Oz's works as well as in his life. Because of its obvious significance, it may seem strange to analyze it alongside the less politically charged sites of the garden and the development town. Yet a critical commonality binds together these disparate places: each one represents an attempt to ward off an invasion by chaotic, unrestrained nature, to act as a bulwark of civilization, to assert its power by keeping nature—and more specifically the wilderness—out. Moreover, the effort expended in maintaining them as such speaks to the tenuousness of their borders, both metaphorical and geographical, and the oppositions they establish. Tracing an imaginary boundary *within* the troubled national boundary, these places construct an exclusivist dialectics of inside/outside space, whereby inside the imagined boundary is equated with safety and order and outside with danger and chaos. Always just beneath the surface of this neat sociocultural mapping, however, lies the possibility of permeability, an antithetical tension that drives its incessant guarding and maintenance.

Oz, who insists on the distinction between his literary work and his politics, is a highly visible figure in the public political discourse in Israel, as an outspoken representative of the Zionist Left. His position in the Israeli public consciousness as a political commentator and a respected author, along with his ability to express himself eloquently and elegantly in English, have made him an international spokesperson of Israel. Several critics have argued correctly that the fiction of *dor ha-medina*, the State Generation, including Oz, in no way represents the experience of the majority of Israelis but only a small group of elite Ashkenazi Jews.[3] While

---

3. Yitzhak Laor, one of Oz's most virulent critics, derides what he considers the unfounded presumptions of collectivity in Oz's writing. See his "Hayei ha-min shel kohot

Oz himself has never made any claims of blanket representations, several factors have led to the Israeli and the international public's perception of him as the representative Israeli author. First, the Israeli literary establishment considers him an heir to the foremost Hebrew writers of previous generations, such as Berdyczewski, Brenner, and Agnon. The influence of earlier Hebrew literature is apparent in his writing, and he has acknowledged it in several interviews.[4] In addition to this Hebrew inheritance, Oz has been shaped by the Western canon and by Russian literature. His Western orientation, ironically, is another factor that adds to his capacity as representative, as Zionism is essentially a Western ideology and because Israel conceives of its cultural identity as primarily Western. Besides frequently contributing to Israeli newspapers, Oz is regularly invited by the European and American media to express his thoughts on political developments in Israel. Oz's biography, which includes his self-imposed transformation from the bookish son of tragic, multilingual European parents named Klausner to the kibbutz's adopted son, reflects his early adherence to the ideology and institutions of Labor Zionism. Finally, as an author born in British Jerusalem in 1937, who has been publishing regularly since the 1960s, Oz in his life and literary output has paralleled the development of the state of Israel itself. These factors have imbued him with the authority of both an astute observer of and an active participant in Israeli culture. His characters' routine experiences of and interactions with certain types of place are useful for outlining the particulars of Zionist spatial practice.

Desert as Heterotopia

The Negev desert, a vast, arid, and rocky swath of land marked by wadis, mountains, and craters, makes up more than half of Israel's land area. Each of the three vernacular places discussed in this chapter, the kibbutz, the

---

ha-bitahon: al gufaniyuto shel ha-yisraeli ha-yafe ve-ha-bit'honi etsel 'amos 'oz" [The sex life of the security forces: on the physicality of the salt-of-the-earth militarized Israeli in Amos Oz], in Laor 1995, 76–104.

4. See, for instance, Cohen 1990, 182.

garden, and the southern development town, encompasses the Zionist attempt to resist the desert's power and assert dominance over it. They do so not only because the desert acts as a constant reminder of exile and because of its seemingly organic connection to other peoples, which threatens the Zionist claim on the land, but also to assert spatial (and, by extension, national-psychological) "normalcy."[5] Each of these places is fenced, enclosed, or otherwise bounded; each necessitates a re-creation of type of landscape, a reshaping of the place; each is constructed to serve an ethnic-national hierarchy. I will focus less on the relationship between the two purportedly distinct places on either side of the binary, and more on the side that is enclosed, the place that is set up as the metaphoric or actual desert's foil. The kibbutz, the garden, and the development town were all conceived of in opposition to the desert. Instead, however, they remain inextricably bound to the desert they were intended to displace. The utopian impulse behind the construction of these places itself gives way to a reflection of the desert "heterotopia," to use Michel Foucault's term, even where the desert itself is not physically present. This reflection dictates the characters' interactions with the places. The spatial nuances alluded to by the behavior of the characters and, in some cases, of the personified place itself, allow an exploration of the more shadowy corners of Oz's spatiality.

Foucault's notion of heterotopia, or "other place," captures both the contradictions of the desert and its interconnectedness to other places. Heterotopias possess "the curious property of being in relation with all the other sites, but in such a way as to suspect, neutralize, or invent the set of relations that they happen to designate, mirror, or reflect" (Foucault 1986, 24). Identifying the desert in Oz's work as a heterotopia, first of all,

---

5. The concepts of national "normalcy" and "abnormality" occupy the center of Zionist discourse. The desire to create a "New Jew" and the related goal of establishing a Jewish state were both based on the internalization of anti-Semitic accusations of the European Jew's "abnormality," both in terms of his physical appearance and his lack of a nation. Spatial "normalcy," then, refers to an independent state bounded by political borders but also to a space that is definable on its own terms and not always in relation to the desert heterotopia.

establishes the ambiguous relationship between Zionist space, the "closed utopia of Western civilization," to use Joe Cleary's terms (2002, 151), and the "outer" space that threatens yet strangely contains it. Yael Zerubavel writes of this oppositional relationship in the context of the emergent modern Hebrew culture of the *yishuv* (prestate Jewish settlement in Palestine): "The use of the term *yishuv* implies not only a place that is populated but also a civilized place marked by its social and cultural life. By contrast, the desert constituted a mythical territory that lay outside Jewish space and was marked by its inherent opposition to the settlement. 'Desert' therefore does not relate to a specific geographical region or a space defined as such by certain scientific criteria related to amount of rainfall. . . . Rather, desert emerged as a *symbolic landscape*" (2008, 203). Accordingly, the utopian "no place" and the heterotopian "other place" both identify with *ideas,* and only then (if at all) with physical spatial specificity. Thinking of the desert as heterotopia also lets us first move past Oz's apparently binary spatiality and acknowledge the mutual exchange between the desert and other sites. At the same time, it posits the desert as *active*—as the locus of the designation of spatial relations—and as the place *against which* other places are defined and understood. Foucault writes:

> There are also, probably in every culture, in every civilization, real places—places that do exist and that are formed in the very founding of society—which are something like counter-sites, a kind of effectively enacted utopia in which the real sites, all the other real sites that can be found within the culture, are simultaneously represented, contested, and inverted. Places of this kind are outside of all places, even though it may be possible to indicate their location in reality. Because these places are absolutely different from all the sites that they reflect and speak about, I shall call them, by way of contrast to utopias, heterotopias. (1986, 24)

Foucault emphasizes the concreteness of heterotopic spatiality; in contrast to utopian no-place, the heterotopia signifies a place that contains all other places in its interaction with them. What is most interesting about the construction of place in Oz's novels, to my mind, is not just the establishment and breakdown of binary spatial structures corresponding to the characters' psychological or national-political tendencies, but the role of the desert as the quintessential heterotopia. The birthplace of the nation, it turns out, itself became a *counter-place,* an antithesis to the Place, *erets yisrael,* which was of course imagined in utopian terms by some of its most articulate ideologues. The desert not just as a real place but also as a culturally constructed heterotopian *idea* helps feed the construction of Zionist sites dialectically, but at the same time it also undermines their function and threatens their very existence.

As I see it, the pitting of "civilized" space against the wilderness parallels the broader spatial project of Zionism, the history and mythology of which are both replete with pioneers clearing swamps and "making the desert bloom" through settlement projects that depended on systematic irrigation and planting. To make the desert bloom in the way that the Zionists envisaged is actually to make the desert *no longer a desert.* This eradication was accompanied by the need to contain the newly transformed space within a fence or other enclosure to resist the desert's encroachment and reassertion of its dominance. The desert is squeezed out of territory, the territory redefined as "civilized" and "humanized," and the remaining wilderness relegated to the outskirts of these newly created "Zionist places."

The Zionist urge to eradicate the desert, however, was accompanied in the early twentieth century by reverence for the desert landscape and a perception that, because of its centrality in the biblical narrative, it represented the most authentic Hebrew place. As Oz Almog has demonstrated, an Orientalist admiration of Bedouin and other Arab natives of the desert led prestate and early Israeli youths to emulate their dress and gestures in an effort to cultivate (or, in their eyes, to reclaim) a "natural" relationship with this most authentic of places (1997). With statehood in 1948 and the rapidly crystallizing Israeli identity, increasingly based on the need to unify in the face of a common enemy, the romantic conception of the Arab native at home in the desert collapsed. Even before this collapse, though, the European Jewish fascination with the desert in Palestine was mingled with fear and suspicion, first because it differed from Europe's landscape, and second because of the biblical association of the desert with punishment and exile. Though the desert is the place where the Israelites purified themselves of the corruption of slavery and exile, it is also a place associated

with God's assertion of authority: it is where he punished those who wor-
shipped the Golden Calf, where he condemned Moses to die, where he
prepared his people, formerly slaves and presently nomads, to be rooted.
Zali Gurevitch argues that the desert is significant in Judaism not only
because of its status as a biblical "no-place" between Egypt or other exilic
locations and Israel, but also because it is from the desert that God speaks
and the Israelites are born as a collective (1997). Similarly, Schwartz calls it
the "mythological national melting zone" (2007, 402). Ilana Pardes locates
the Israelite nation's maturation, "an in-between zone between infancy
and adulthood," in its desert wanderings (2000, 104). The desert, which
appears in the Bible as an anti-place that is neither Egypt nor the Promised
Land, represents the ultimate wilderness in the Jewish imagination.

Zionist thought and practice in the six decades preceding statehood
transformed Judaic conceptions of *ha-makom*, the Place, the Land of
Israel, from an ephemeral dream-site to a concrete national homeland. It
could not do so without also rearranging the Jewish relationship to the
anti-place, the desert. In Zionist thought, the desert's role as the site of
national crystallization was diminished by the threat it seemed to pose to
the Zionist project, at the core of which was the desire to "make the desert
bloom." David Ben-Gurion, one of the most impassioned believers in the
desert as a site of regeneration of Zionist ideals and the ultimate frontier,
campaigned throughout his life for the settling of the Negev desert and
set a personal example by moving to a kibbutz there. He begins his 1955
speech "The Significance of the Negev" with a statement that encapsulates the ambivalent Zionist relationship with the desert: "The Negev is
the cradle of our nation, *its most dangerous weakness and its greatest hope*"
(1955, emphasis mine). In a series of sweeping comparisons of biblical and
modern Israel, he notes the shared concerns of the biblical King of Judah,
Uziah (Azariah) and the state of Israel:

> But this heroic and clever king was not satisfied to conquer by the sword.
> He understood that he must develop the land, expand its settlement and
> make the desert wilderness bloom. . . . The state of Israel cannot toler-
> ate a desert in her midst. *If the state does not eliminate the desert then the
> desert will eliminate the state.* The narrow strip between Jaffa and Haifa

15 to 25 kilometers wide that contains the vast majority of the people in Israel will not last long without a massive and fortified settlement in the expanse of the South and the Negev. . . . The people and the state of Israel will be tested in the Negev—for only in the joint effort of a willing people and a state that plans and carries out can we take on the great goal of blooming and settling the desert wilderness. (1955, emphasis mine)

In a similar vein, Yolek from Oz's novel *Menuha nekhona* (A perfect peace) (1982) believes that deserts are "a badge of shame, a mark of inequity, a disgrace to the map of Israel, an evil presence, an ancient enemy that must be subdued by armies bringing tractors, irrigation pipes, and fertilizer sacks until the last of its surly acres had been compelled to bear" (1985, 265). A lingering reminder of statelessness, the desert became a powerful force to be subdued. To this end, Zionist pioneers transplanted trees and flowers to create a "native" flora that resembled either the European landscape of their memory or the biblical landscape of their imagination.

A few scholars have acknowledged the binary spatial structure of Oz's texts and his characters' impulse to defy this structure. His short story "*Navadim va-tsefa*" ("Nomad and viper") continues to inspire the deepest and most sustained critical attention in terms of space and place. Part of Oz's first published book, the short-story collection *Artsot ha-tan* (Where the jackals howl) (1965), "Nomad and Viper" is a seminal text in Hebrew literature. The tension between the kibbutz and the chaos beyond is depicted in this story primarily in terms of the relations between the kibbutz inhabitants and the famished Bedouin just past its outskirts. In analyzing this story, several critics comment on Oz's representation of place "as a constantly negotiated network of relationships," to use Bill Ashcroft's words, not only between the kibbutz residents and the Bedouin, but also among the kibbutz residents themselves (2001, 161).

Like several other scholars,[6] Nurit Gertz identifies a definitive tension between "civilization" and "threatening nature and its representatives—

6. For instance, Mazor 2002 and Naveh 2002.

the jackals, the Arabs, the mountains"—and emphasizes its broader implications: "This isn't a simple struggle between opposite forces, but a struggle
between two worlds, each of which includes the same contradictions: the
civilized person contains wild instincts (*yetsarim*), and the world of nature
isn't just a world of threatening instincts but also a world that is significant,
real and attractive" (1980, 93). Despite the stark line dividing civilization
from threatening nature, elements of each leak into the other and compli-
cate their relationship. In Gertz's reading, this conflict between civilization
and nature comes to a head when "they are exchanged or blended into
each other, in a fatal, malignant merging" (116).

Yigal Schwartz further develops the concepts of leaking and absorption
that Gertz observes between the two types of space in the story. Utilizing
Homi Bhabha's concept of "third space" to analyze the collision of the
seemingly distinct spaces of civilization and wilderness, he devises a useful
cartographic reading of "Nomad and Viper" and Oz's first novel *Makom
aher* (Elsewhere, perhaps) (1966), identifying an "'upper map,' presenting
the described world in terms of a hierarchical-binary principal, and a 'lower
map,' located beneath the first and peeking through its tears, presenting
the world through the destruction of the binary-hierarchical principal"
(Schwartz 2007, 383). The "upper map" sketches the spatial surface of the
narrative, which is based on the sharp division between the civilized place
and the wild space, while the "lower map" breaks down the division. The
Hebrew literary establishment's sustained interest in socio-spatial relations
in Oz's early work demonstrates their relevance not only to subsequent
Hebrew literature but also to the role of place in Israeli society.

One of the most compelling interpretations of place and space in Oz's
work comes from outside Israeli academe. Joe Cleary identifies in Oz's novels a "preoccupation with borders" (2002, 147) and writes that "the spatial
field delineated here recalls the imaginative geography of classical Zionism, which conceived of Israel as a closed utopia of Western civilization
within an otherwise chaotic and desert-like Asiatic landscape" (151). He,
too, argues that the sharp spatial divisions on the surface of Oz's texts cannot conceal completely the inter-spatial trespassing that constantly threatens the realm of "civilization" and "order." He writes that the "spatial field
delineated in the opening chapters [of *Elsewhere, Perhaps*] is divided into

zones of order and disorder, but the border between the two turns out to be worryingly obscure and elusive" (152). For Cleary, Oz's "cartographic anxieties" constitute the crux of his spatial representation (153). Ultimately, he concludes, though the two spaces on either side of the borders in Oz's works seem to leak into one another, Oz invariably affirms the need for a border and for its impermeability to ward off this seepage (176).

Elsewhere, Perhaps takes place in northern Israel in a green and hilly landscape, but the desert occupies a prominent place in several of Oz's other works. Discussing *A Perfect Peace* in his study of the desert in Jewish writing, Ranen Omer-Sherman suggests that "the claustrophobia of the modern Jewish state, as well as the epic geospatial scope of Jewish history, conspire to goad the lonely individual into a nomadic (and hence regressive[7]) embrace of desert space" (2006a, 77). The desert in this novel, he argues, presents itself to Yonatan, the protagonist, as a site of redemption that allows him to transcend the stifling ideology of his kibbutz home. The desert overwhelms, however, leaving Yonatan with "a Hebraic rebuke to any literal belief in natural transcendence, any permanent consolation in the world beyond human organization" (81). Alongside this interpretation of the desert as a site of potential redemption for the spiritually lost Jew, Omer-Sherman posits a provocative post-colonialist reading, arguing that "[Yonatan's] aimless quest into the mysterious eastern desert in search of a gratification he cannot fully articulate may be viewed instead as a displaced version of the Zionist relation to territory. Ironically, the narrative's trajectory of escape positions the desert, particularly the taboo lure of Petra, as a feminized space invaded by the masculine interloper. This is not too distant from the gendered binaries that the late Edward Said claimed are always in the service of the East/West dichotomy of Orientalism" (91).

Cleary's reading of the novel accords with this idea to an extent, but develops it further. Following John Noyes's ideas about the ambivalence

---

7. Omer-Sherman's intention in this parenthetical statement is not to suggest that nomadism as a way of life is regressive but rather to consider that within the linear Jewish narrative of exile, wandering, and homecoming, nomadism constitutes a temporal regression—a return to a prior (not necessarily inferior) state.

of colonialist desires for wide open spaces, Cleary argues that the border dividing the desert establishes two distinct sets of gendered and sexualized relations between the novel's self and its other. While still in Israel, Yonatan's yearning for wide open desert space signifies a colonialist desire to *master* this space; once he crosses the border into Jordanian territory, however, it denotes "a destructively narcissistic longing for oneness with the landscape" (2002, 172–73). Gazing over wide open spaces toward the border induces a longing for appropriation, while actually crossing the border is understood as merging with a territory so radically Other that it annihilates subjectivity, amounting to suicide. Yet Oz's call for the respect of national boundaries, Cleary argues, stems not from his consideration of the rights of the Other but from his certitude of the death that awaits the trespassing Israeli Jew (176).

Despite the acuity and significance of Cleary's postcolonial analysis, it neglects the biblical historical significance of the desert that is central in Omer-Sherman's reading and that adds complex layers of interpretation to the contemporary political one. The desert is more than merely wide-open-spaces subject to a gazing colonial eye. Zionism's ambivalent relationship to Judaism leads to what is arguably a de-sacrilization of the desert, and its reconfiguration as a space of ethnic, geographical, and political alterity. At the same time, the desert's role in the Jewish national narrative makes it impossible to disregard the Judaic dimension. A space of contradiction, the desert simultaneously evokes reverence and loathing; is at once natural and culturally constructed; is the birthplace of the Jewish self in its past and the home of the feared Other in its present. This all-inclusive space not only relates to but actually *shapes* other locales.

The Kibbutz and the Transgression of Boundaries

As the fertile breeding ground of Israel's mythical native sons, the Sabras, the kibbutz holds a special place in the Israeli national consciousness. Promoting idealism, brotherhood, collectivity, and social justice, the kibbutz founders and residents (called *haverim*, or comrades) oversaw the creation of settlements that were as self-reliant as possible. As there are kibbutzim in every region of Israel, there is some diversity in their landscape and planning. For the most part, they are usually verdant sites, with sprawling lawns, numerous trees, and modest white homes arranged in relation to a range of collective buildings like the dining hall and the clubhouse. Neat paths wind among the various structures. Farmland and agricultural spaces, such as chicken coops and stables, are arranged around or at the edge of the kibbutz. The morally upstanding image of the kibbutz has been tarnished somewhat by revelations of systematic gender and ethnic discrimination, by disillusioned ex-kibbutzniks who remember with horror such experiences as the collective children's house, and by the economic disintegration of the kibbutz institution itself. Still, the mythical value attached to the kibbutz remains forceful in Israel, and it continues, at least in mainstream society, to occupy the top of the socio-spatial hierarchy. Part of the reason for this is that the idea of the kibbutz precedes the creation of the state by almost half a century,[8] and is thus associated strongly with the rough-hewn ethos of the *halutzim*, pioneers, who established the first kibbutzim in harsh conditions. This pioneering ethic constituted the initial expression of the desire to be close to the land, and to exorcise the studious and religious "Old Jew" from the new type of Jew that Zionists hoped to create in Palestine. Associated ideas could be enacted in the kibbutz: the concept of 'avoda 'ivrit (Hebrew labor), the indifference to material wealth, and the revulsion at all behavior and objects deemed "bourgeois" or "capitalist." Thus the kibbutz became a greenhouse for the cultivation of the New Jew and indeed of Israeli identity, the exemplar of the Jewish State that was being shaped, which would be characterized by a self-sufficient, principled collective existence.

An irony of the kibbutz lies in the fact that, while it supposedly functions as a social equalizer and represents the face of Israel, it is actually exclusive, since members are accepted according to criteria established by the kibbutz itself. As Efraim Ben-Zadok points out, "the kibbutzim are socially closed societies, populated by Ashkenazim" (1993, 116). Even in its heyday in the 1950s, its members included only a tiny percentage of the overwhelmingly urban Jewish-Israeli population. Nevertheless, this

8. The first kibbutz, Degania Alef, was founded in 1909.

small elite, privileged ethnically, socially, and culturally, is understood in the popular sensibility as representing an essential Israeliness. The kibbutz, accordingly, has served as the setting for films such as *Adama meshuga'at* (Sweet mud) (Dror Shaul, 2006) and *No'a bat 17* (Noa at 17) (Yitzhak Yeshurun, 1982) as well as stories and novels by Israeli authors, including Yonat and Alexander Sened, Yitzhak Ben-Ner, Savyon Liebrecht, and others.

As a boy of fifteen, Amos Oz chose to leave the Jerusalem of his childhood for a kibbutz, where he remained for several decades.[9] Oz has always willingly admitted the shortcomings of kibbutz life. They have been the topic of many of his stories and novels of disillusion and disappointment, such as *Elsewhere, Perhaps*, "Nomad and Viper," and "Derekh ha-ruah" (The way of the wind), collected in *Where the Jackals Howl*. In his essay "The Kibbutz at the Present Time" he defends the kibbutz as having "a social system that, for all its disadvantages, is the least bad, the least unkind," that he has ever seen (1995, 128). He goes on to list the advantages of the kibbutz as having evolved from a social experiment to a place "developing an organic character . . . [and] striking deeper roots, producing leaves, flowers, and fruit in due season and occasionally shedding its leaves. . . . The kibbutz lives in its own inner legitimacy, far from the domination of human legislators with their committees and conflicts. As with all inner legitimacy, so this too is mysterious, semi-visible, spurning all generalizations and definitions" (131). Here Oz addresses the legitimacy of the kibbutz as a mystical philosophy of life that stresses the good of the collective over that of the individual, enables harmonious wholeness over alienation, and strives for justice for all over the promises that capitalism makes to the individual. What is lacking in this assessment is a consideration of the kibbutz as a constructed place that transforms the geographic space as well as the individuals who inhabited it. Oz does examine this perspective indirectly in some of his aforementioned works. In "Nomad and Viper,"

9. He discusses this choice in his autobiography *Sipur al ahava ve-hoshekh* (A tale of love and darkness) (2002). See particularly pp. 516–55 (chap. *nun-vav* to *nun-tet*) and 569–74 (*samekh-alef*).

for instance, the kibbutz is ostensibly antithetical to the space beyond the borders of the kibbutz, and in *A Perfect Peace*, the ruined Arab village at the outskirts of the kibbutz is a constant presence. Nevertheless, Oz's primary concern in dealing with the kibbutz is with its internal strife, with the dilemmas that it poses as a social system for its inhabitants—not with the problematics of its ideology on a larger scale.

Of course, external threats are present in his represented kibbutzim—angry Arab peasants who insist that the kibbutz members are plowing their land (*Elsewhere, Perhaps*), shady Bedouin who swarm toward the kibbutz like insects ("Nomad and Viper"), sleazy Diaspora Jews who sneak into the kibbutz and cause upheaval and chaos within its orderly confines (*Elsewhere, Perhaps* and *A Perfect Peace*). But the central problem is always present prior to these external threats (always posed by ethnic and cultural others), and sprouts from within the kibbutz itself. Secondary outside forces do not initiate the problem, but only catalyze it. This is logical in the context of Oz's claim that "the kibbutz lives in its own inner legitimacy." Although not subject to the "human legislators" of the outside world, neither is it immune from inner conflict. In the quotation above, Oz invokes images of roots, flowers, and leaves to defend the "organic" legitimacy of the kibbutz, thereby making a case not only for the kibbutz's desirability but also for its *natural* place in the Israeli sensibility and landscape. Oz's insistence on this legitimacy sounds defensive of the kibbutz as a social system as well as of the issue that he does not confront in his essay, the kibbutz's exclusive and closed-off nature. Kenneth Helphand notes this characteristic in the kibbutz's architectural design: "The kibbutz itself has an oasis-like quality. This is most dramatic in the desert, but even in other regions the physical separation and distinctiveness, even isolation, of the kibbutz landscape is an important part of its character" (2002, 155). This purposeful isolation finds its way into *A Perfect Peace* in Oz's representation of Kibbutz Granot as a place that seems to function as a microcosmic society yet lacks spatial *independence*, as it cannot be defined outside the context of the desert in this novel, first in the guise of the abandoned Palestinian Arab village on its outskirts, Sheikh Dahr, and later, briefly, in the desert itself.

For Yonatan, the young native Israeli protagonist of *A Perfect Peace*, the kibbutz signifies order, routine, familiarity, suffocation; the desert signifies chaos, adventure, exoticism, freedom. There is nothing original in the representation of this opposition, yet Oz complicates it through his range of secondary characters and their disparate positions in and inter-actions with place. Besides Yonatan's parents, Hava and Yolek, and his wife, Rimona, several secondary characters are particularly relevant to Oz's representation of the kibbutz. Bolognesi, the Libyan ex-convict, prays and knits; Benya Trotsky, Yonatan's mother's wealthy ex-lover, lives in the United States and never actually appears in the novel yet constitutes a constant threat; and Azariah Gitlin, the stranger who arrives at the kib-butz, sets the novel in motion. Each of these characters sheds light on the kibbutz's relationship with the "other place" and the threatening phenom-ena associated with it: ethnic difference and diasporic Jewishness.

Bolognesi, referred to in the novel as "the Italian," is a delicate, pious man who had served fifteen years in prison for decapitating his brother's fiancée. The description that Oz provides of him at the beginning of the novel is the longest passage on Bolognesi:

> Bolognesi was not really an Italian. He was a Tripolitanian hired hand with a dark, stubbly face, a mouth that smelled slightly of arak, and a torn ear that resembled a rotten-ripe pear. A lanky, stooped man in his middle fifties, he lived by himself in a shack. . . . He wore a permanently pinched look, as if he had just bitten into a piece of spoiled fish that he could neither swallow nor spit out. . . .
>
> Since settling on the kibbutz, he had taken up in his free time the art of knitting he had learned in prison and made marvelous sweaters for the kibbutz children, and sometimes, for the young ladies, stylish outfits copied from knitwear magazines bought with his own money and studied carefully. He spoke little in his feminine voice and always with extreme caution. (Oz 1985, 18)

Bolognesi lives on the grounds of the kibbutz, yet he is not really a part of it. He is a "hired hand," not a member. He lives in half a tin shack, refusing to move into a bachelor's room. He is dark, dirty, and mysteri-ous, swinging between the absurd behavioral extremes of a violent past and an utterly emasculated present. Yitzhak Laor asks, "Could there be a greater antithesis to our suntanned, scrubbed, shampooed kibbutz than the figure of Bolognesi?" (1995, 91). Being Tripolitanian places Bolognesi on a particularly low rung of the kibbutz ladder, at the top of which is the aristocracy of Russians and Poles. Moreover, the narrator's pointed obser-vation that Bolognesi is "not really Italian" produces a sense of Bolog-nesi's inauthenticity.

The repulsive picture of Bolognesi takes on another dimension through Oz's insistence on his marked femininity, signaled by his "feminine voice" and his proclivity for knitting. Clearly, it is not just his ethnic-national identity but also his gender that is put into question: Bolognesi is not a part of the kibbutz because he is dark and drinks arak,[10] and also because he is not really a man. Azariah, too, is initially suspect because of his feminin-ity; unlike Bolognesi, however, he works to eradicate his femininity and to become more "masculine." It is crucial to keep in mind that Bolognesi is emphatically *not* European like Azariah—hence the sarcastic nickname "The Italian"—and is therefore at a distinct disadvantage in his placement in the kibbutz hierarchy. Despite his *choice* to stay in his shack on the edge of the kibbutz rather than move into a regular room and thus to remain on the fringes metaphorically as well as geographically, the extent of his marginality, as evidenced by Oz's hideous description of him, would clearly prevent him from gaining full acceptance in the kibbutz like Azariah.

Perhaps most telling and relevant to the question of spatiality is Bolog-nesi's prayer. He mutters "a kind of shrill prayer or incantation in a lan-guage that [is] neither Hebrew nor anything else, its accents guttural like the desert's and as though risen from the depths of some evil slumber" (Oz 1985, 78–79). By comparing his accent to the desert's and thus spatializing Bolognesi, Oz confirms Laor's observation that he is antithetical to the kibbutz, a closed Zionist place aiming to eradicate the desert's barrenness through agriculture. His strange, sorcerer-like "incantations" remove him from the realm of familiar Judaic prayer, particularly since they are not rec-ognizably Hebrew or even "anything else," that is, *human.* Symbolizing the apex of his disconcerting difference and its implicit violence, Bolognesi's

10. Arak is an alcoholic beverage made of grapes and aniseed. It is associated in Israeli popular culture with negative stereotypes about Mizrahim.

accent is not only reminiscent of the desert but also supposed to have been born of an "evil slumber." In this association of the desert with evil, Bolognesi becomes inhuman, without recognizable faith, without language, without gender, without place.

Years before Bolognesi would sharpen the ax with which he would murder his brother's fiancée, Yonatan's mother, Hava, had a passionate love affair with a Russian fellow pioneer named Benya Trotsky. After a pathetic and failed attempt to shoot Hava, Yolek, the kibbutz bull, and himself, he left when Hava chose Yolek over him. He ends up a hotel tycoon in Miami Beach, periodically sending large donations to the kibbutz. When Yonatan disappears, Yolek, fearing that the millionaire might tempt his son with money to come to America, composes an oft-quoted vitriolic letter to Benya:

> It's not Hitler or Nasser but you and the likes of you who will be responsible, I repeat, *responsible*, for the destruction of the Third Temple. No power on earth can possibly forgive me for the moronic pity I showed you in not digging your grave thirty years ago, when you were still just a kinky little syphilitic, sniveling insect. You are the lowest of the low. It's people like you who've been the poisonous cancer of the Jewish people for generations. You're the age-old curse of the Exile. You're the reason the gentiles hated and still hate us with an eternal, nauseated loathing. You with your money-grubbing, you with your Golden Calf, you with your foaming lechery, you with your swank way of seducing women and innocent goyim with your sweet-talk, stopping at no betrayal, sleeping on your filthy ducats that spread like germs from country to country, from exile to exile, from racket to racket, homeless, conscienceless, rootless, making us a laughingstock and a pariah among the nations. (Oz 1985, 190–91)

Yolek's diatribe against Benya is striking in its use of classical anti-Semitic imagery and metaphor. He portrays Benya as inhuman, by turns an insect, a rat, and a vampire; and also as diseased and spreading disease, a "syphilitic" creature and a "poisonous cancer," spreading germs even through his "ducats," a word that invokes immediately Shakespeare's Shylock. These images come straight from the centuries-old anti-Semitic lexicon of

Europe, which characterizes Jews as a disease and as devoid of all humanity, and which reached its peak in Nazi propaganda. The worst accusations
of all, from Yolek's perspective, and those to which he attributes all the
others, are Benya's homelessness and his rootlessness, which Yolek equates
with his lack of conscience. Yolek despairs of Yonatan, "the first of a new
line of Jews whose children and children's children would grow up in this
land to put an end to the malignancy of the Exile. And now the Exile
is back again, masquerading as a rich uncle" (Oz 1985, 192). Benya has
actually *become* the Exile itself, containing in his person all the worst of
the Exile, as defined by European non-Jews and regurgitated by this aging,
heroic Zionist pioneer.

Benya remains forever exiled in his fantastical Florida, ever the lecher-
ous "kike," but the threat of his seduction of Yonatan and, by extension,
of the seduction of the post-pioneering native-born Israeli generation by
the Diaspora, hovers over the novel. Yolek wonders, "What can their lives
mean to them, raised in this whirlwind of history, this place-in-progress,
this experiment-under-construction, this merest blueprint of a country,
with no grandparents, no ancestral homes, no religion, no rebellion, no
Wanderjahre of their own?" (Oz 1985, 225). It is the tension between this
unstable, unpredictable "place-in-progress" and the familiar, beckoning
Diaspora that is so distressing to Yolek. Yonatan, however, yearns not for
the fleshpots of American exile but for a more radical alterity. His flight
from the kibbutz constitutes a rejection of suffocating ideals, obligations
and expectations, and a rejection of life altogether. In fleeing to the desert,
which Yolek considers "a badge of shame, a mark of inequity, a disgrace to
the map of Israel, an evil presence, an ancient enemy," Yonatan chooses
death. Leaving the kibbutz to cross Israel's border into enemy territory is,
for him and for the other kibbutzniks, tantamount to leaving civilization.
Ironically, his choice to proclaim his independence and authenticity this
way only demonstrates the extent to which Yonatan *cannot* escape the kibbutz values he imbibed with his mother's milk and confirms his acceptance
of its spatial hierarchy.

Benya himself never makes an appearance in the present time of
the novel, but Azariah Gitlin is in many ways his double. A European
immigrant, he is passionate and dramatic, stereotypically diasporic in his

fawning yet vaguely menacing behavior and his long-winded, pompous manner of speaking. Structurally, too, he parallels Benya. As Yair Mazor has noted, Azariah competes for Yonatan's wife, Rimona, much as Benya competed for Yolek's wife, Hava (2002, 145). Indeed, as the novel progresses, Azariah *becomes* the protagonist, displacing Yonatan both literally and literarily. Mazor interprets Azariah's place in Yonatan and Rimona's relationship as the point on a triangle, and the end of the novel as a happy compromise by which the three live together in a strange but harmonious arrangement (150). I interpret the situation, and Azariah's character as a whole, as much more ominous.

Azariah enters the novel, and the kibbutz, most harmlessly, on a dark, rainy night, "by way of the muddy tractor road that passed the farm buildings" (Oz 1985, 30). Unlike the hairy blond man he encounters upon his arrival, Azariah is "pitiful" and "skinny," with "a vaguely foreign accent" (31–32). There is "something tense, frightened, and, at the same time, fawning about his whole demeanor, something almost cunningly submissive," we are told (32). His "long, sensitive fingers like those of a girl, the frail shoulders, . . . the restless expression, the green eyes that betrayed some basic fear or despair" converge in a familiar caricature of despised Diaspora Jewishness (40).[11] The novel increasingly implicates Azariah not only as a stranger but as an *invader* of the kibbutz. The narrative momentarily shifts to the stranger's own point of view as he walks through the kibbutz, looking at its homes from outside. While there is no malice in his words, the tone is explicitly strategic:

> There, within, life was flowing truly and unhurriedly such as you have never known it, such as you have longed with all your soul to touch, to be part of, so that you need no longer be the outsider in the dark, but, as if by magic, the neighbor, the friend, the equal and brother of those inside, accepted and loved by all until nothing could stand between you and them.

---

11. Yitzhak Laor discusses extensively Azariah's "exilic" nature, his *galutiyut*. See Laor 1995, 88–89 and 90–91.

How, then, to penetrate the smells, the indoors, the chit-chat, the rugs and straw mats, the whispers, the tunes, the laughter, the feel of warm wool and the sweet fragrance of coffee and women and cookies and wet hair, . . . the rain drumming outside on the lowered blinds. (Oz 1985, 35–36)

The pronounced division between cozy, private internal space and alienating external space in this passage mimics the larger spatial dichotomy that divides the order and security of the kibbutz from the threatening chaos beyond. Azariah's relationship with place neatly inverts Yonatan's: While Azariah desires order, Yonatan longs for disruption; while Azariah dreams of interiors bounded by walls, fences and borders, Yonatan fantasizes of exterior wide open spaces; while Azariah hungers for rootedness, Yonatan craves roaming. Having wandered in his own metaphoric desert and finally arrived at the promised land of the kibbutz, Azariah wants nothing more than to leave behind the travails of exile, while all Yonatan wants to do is flee. Yonatan's return to the kibbutz at the end of the novel constitutes an erasure of the line that creates this oppositional symmetry: having ventured into the desert and sensed the nearness of violent death, he rejoins his wife and Azariah in a ménage à trois, sharing with Azariah the role of husband and father to his wife and their newborn baby. Given this ending, in which Azariah has all but replaced Yonatan as son, husband, and kibbutz member, his wish for acceptance is revealed as something more sinister than an outsider's desire for belonging. His musings on how to "penetrate" the kibbutz, to be magically "accepted and loved by all," to escape the cold, rainy darkness into the warmth of laughing babies and nurturing women eerily echoes anti-Semitic portrayals of the wandering Jew who stops at nothing to infiltrate the very heart of the world of the *goyim*. Intelligent and shrewd, he manages not only to be accepted, but also to find his way out of Bolognesi's shack into Yonatan's bed with Yonatan's wife, even adopting Yonatan's parents as his own. His skin now bronzed, his hair longer and lightened by the strong sun, and his boyish features hardened by a manly scar, Azariah wonders if he ought to Hebraize his diasporic name to match his new Sabra appearance (Oz 1985, 360). He takes to ostentatiously embracing Rimona, "his green eyes glinting with the unspoken arrogance of a male who has taken another male's female and might do it again any time he wants. At last all could see who he really was" (Oz 1985, 360).

This last assertion makes evident that his diasporic shrewdness has not disappeared but is simply masked by the suntan and slowness of the kibbutz. Having gradually usurped Yonatan's position in the kibbutz, Azariah frees Yonatan from his lethargic fulfillment of social obligations and allows him finally to flee into the arms of the desert and certain death. Azariah's upheaval and reconfiguration of the kibbutz's internal order demonstrate the extent to which he has functioned as a destabilizing, dangerous external force. He succeeds where other Diaspora Jews like Bolognesi with his knitting needles and Benya with his comically impotent gunshots could not. Having acquired and honed the requisite masculinity that eludes both Bolognesi and Benya, Azariah is able to discard his Diaspora identity and assert his place at the heart of the kibbutz.

The two-pronged conception of foreignness against which the kibbutz defines its collective identity is represented by those two outsiders, Bolognesi and Benya, and the places with which they are associated in the novel, the desert and America. Their questionable masculinity is no accident; neither is Oz's portrayal of Hava, Yonatan's mother and one of the kibbutz founders, as emphatically masculine. The role of gender in the spatial construction of the novel posits the kibbutz as the domain of true masculinity and the threatening places beyond as emasculating: In the desert, bloodthirsty Bedouin will violently rape Yonatan; glittering America will rape him ideologically. These oppositional poles allow the kibbutz to articulate a distinct identity for itself on the basis of both ethnicity and gender.

The Spectral Poetics of the Ruined Arab Village

Sheikh Dahr, the ruined Arab village on the outskirts of the kibbutz, looms in the novel's background, the ghost of a vernacular place. Reminiscent of A. B. Yehoshua's depiction of the concealed ruins of another Arab village in his famous short story "Mul ha-ye'arot" (Facing the forests) (1963), Sheikh Dahr is merging with the natural place, entangled in its vegetation. Oz's portrayal of this "topos of troubled conscience" (Cleary 2002, 171) engages the memory not only of the *naqba* but also, less directly, of the Holocaust, and suggests that they are linked: Azariah, whose past is haunted by the Holocaust, seems more than anyone else in the group to identify with the specters of the village. When the racist Udi wants to dig up an Arab's skeleton to use as a scarecrow, Azariah warns him: "'If you don't watch it, Udi, . . . one of the birds it scares may be the soul of a dead Arab and peck your eyes out'" (Oz 1985, 134). His dark reprimand suggests an uneasy identification between the Diaspora Jew and the Palestinian Arab, both situated against the Israeli Jew. While it is indisputable that the scene emphasizes the native-born Yonatan's restlessness and the diasporic Azariah's desire "to send down roots," actually Sheikh Dahr does more to integrate the two despite this difference than any other site in the novel. Other places, such as Yonatan and Rimona's home and the kibbutz itself, symbolize life to Azariah and death to Yoni. Sheikh Dahr, however, evokes in both a foreboding sense of abstract and justified revenge biding its time. Oz has written and said more than once that he understands the struggle between the Israelis and the Palestinians as a tragedy, which he defines as "a battle between right and right,"[12] and this scene exemplifies that statement.

It is, moreover, this Arab place that emphasizes Yonatan and Azariah's shared Jewishness. The opposition between Azariah's *galutiyut* and Yonatan's nativeness diminishes when they enter this place, which evokes from them similar reactions, a phenomenon completely at odds with their oppositional character traits. Upon first seeing the crumbling British road around the village, Azariah thinks of the phrase "the wrath of God" (Oz 1985, 122). Yonatan, for his part, remembers being certain as a child that "those dead old villagers were thirsty for blood" (24). On another occasion, he thinks of "their curse hanging over us" (130). He even attributes his urge to flee the kibbutz to the ghosts of the village: "Why all this sadness here unless it's a coded message from the dead who once lived upon this muddy ground?" (132–33). Sheikh Dahr is certainly a "potent memory site," as Cleary asserts, but its primary function is neither to create a hierarchy of Jewish and Palestinian suffering nor to remember the latter for the sake of condemning Israeli violence. Rather, it allows Oz to imbue both

12. See his essay of that title in Oz 2006.

these Jewish characters with the typical Zionist *yore ve-bokhe*[13] ("shoots and cries") consciousness: The Zionist soldier, a man with a conscience, loathes violence but realizes he must act violently to survive; the dilemma causes him to weep while pulling the trigger. Looking inward, he despairs at the violence he feels compelled to enact primarily because he fears his own moral corruption.

Oz Almog discusses this phenomenon in terms of "purity of arms": "The mythological concept of 'purity of arms,' which would become one of the most important symbols of Israeli military culture, was especially meant to symbolize the humanitarian 'pureness of heart' of the Hebrew fighter" (2000, 197). A common trope in earlier Israeli literature, the Israeli who "shoots and cries" refers to men forced to be violent against their nature and haunted by their conscience. Perhaps the best example of this figure in Israeli literature is from S. Yizhar's famous story written in the aftermath of the 1948 War, "Khirbet Khizeh," about a soldier participating in the expulsion of Palestinians from their village during the war. The soldier explicitly compares the Palestinian villagers' exile to that of the Jews (2008, 104–5). This identification with the enemy is, as in Oz's novel, primarily focused on the consequence of violence and injustice on the Israeli's psyche. Sheikh Dahr invokes from Yonatan the heroic soldier and Azariah the weak Jew not thoughts of regret, reconciliation, or renunciation of violence in response to the tragedy that Jews enacted upon its inhabitants, but fear of the ghosts' revenge in the form of a restless

13. The phrase *yore ve-bokhe* most likely originated during the 1982 Lebanon War, but the idea it expresses can be traced back to the 1948 War. Literally translating to "shoots and cries," the phrase refers to those Israelis who announce their repugnance at orders they are commanded to follow but follow them nonetheless; the soldier who "shoots and cries" cries to ease his conscience and purify himself morally, but shoots out of a loyalty to Israel and Zionism. The phrase is intended to highlight the dilemma of maintaining moral purity in immoral or unjust situations. In 1988, the Jewish singer Sy Hyman released a pop song about the first Intifada, "Shooting and Crying," that generated so much controversy in Israel that it was banned by the popular army radio station. In the same year, the Canadian filmmaker Helene Klodawsky released a documentary about two young men, an Israeli and a Palestinian, *Shoot and Cry*.

conscience. It is this shared fear that situates them, finally, as belonging to the same group rather than poised against each other. Sheikh Dahr, a place beyond the kibbutz, heterotopically both inside Israel and outside it, clearly a part of its history and at the same time erased from it, unites Yonatan and Azariah, defining them as Jews in its hostility toward them and its vengefulness against them. It forces them into a common category in a way that no other place—certainly not the kibbutz—does. The "conventional Zionist manner" that Cleary identifies as shaping this scene, then, springs not from what he reads as an insistence that Jewish suffering weighs more than Palestinian suffering, but from the erasure of difference between the victimized Diaspora Jew and the heroic Sabra and their presentation as sensitive, humane Jews subject to a gnawing collective conscience (2002, 171). Despite Oz's acknowledgment of the moral qualms raised by the ruined village, he does not explicitly articulate them, much less resolve them.

Organic process slowly effaces what remains of Sheikh Dahr. The mosque and former homes are invaded by tree branches and weeds; what the war did not destroy, the wild space beyond the kibbutz will erase. This wild space, kept at bay by the kibbutz boundaries, runs rampant in the village, claiming it as its own and serving as a reminder that military triumph is ephemeral: the true force with which the kibbutz continually contends is nature itself. After all, the most intractable enemy of the Zionist pioneers was not Palestinians but the harsh natural conditions of Palestine—swamps, a stubborn soil, and a great expanse of arid desert. Beyond the political implications discussed above, the twisting vines and weeds that have taken over Sheik Dahr represent the land's reclaiming of its own space from the order imposed on it by humans. In its return to nature, Sheikh Dahr illustrates the fate that threatens the kibbutz, and Israel, if its strict boundedness and orderly routine are disrupted, a recurrent theme in Oz's fiction.

In Yehoshua's story, all traces of the village have disappeared, not as the result of a natural process, but because of intentional Israeli efforts to efface it by planting a new forest atop its ruins. The concerted Israeli transformation of the landscape is undeniable. In Oz's novel, the village lies in the outskirts of the kibbutz and the blame for its ruination is partly diverted from the kibbutz residents to nature, which has established a visible stranglehold on the place. Sheikh Dahr is an important setting in this novel not only for its unification of the polar representatives of Jewish spatial identity, Yonatan and Azariah, but also because it embodies the kibbutz's greatest fear: the collapse of carefully maintained spatial order and its reconquest by chaotic nature, a threat more powerful than the ghosts of the village or the Palestinians in general. As Barbara Parmenter argues, the Palestinian relationship to the land never necessitated the type of articulation that the Zionists had to formulate to explain and legitimize their own claim on it (Parmenter 1994, 26–27). This awareness of nature as a force that must be defeated is literalized in the vines and branches that twist through the crevices and cracks of Sheikh Dahr's ruins. Together with the vague moral pangs that this place evokes from Yonatan and Azariah, it reminds them of the fragility of places constructed by humans.

The power of nature on display at Sheikh Dahr is the same force that ultimately drives Yonatan away from the desert and back to the kibbutz at the novel's end. Rejecting the allure of death, that elusive "perfect peace" he had previously privileged over the shackles of order and "civilization," he decides to make do with his previous imperfect existence, alive but not really living. Is a ghastly death in the desert the only alternative to the kibbutz he loathes? While it stems from a superficial desire to reject his father and the kibbutz he founded, his ideals are ultimately confirmed by his interaction with the desert: It is a battle against the desert, not a harmonious life within it; it is a tacit acceptance of its inhabitants' animalistic murderousness, not of their humanity; it is fearful and suspicious, never hopeful and trusting. Oz does not challenge these stereotypes, confirming Yonatan's fears through the warnings of the desert surveyor Tlallim, whose graphic descriptions of the desert's dangers are based on a supposedly authoritative knowledge of it. Upon his return to the kibbutz, none of the problems that drove Yonatan to flee has been resolved. His marriage has become a farce, his father has become a statue, he himself has become a zombie. I must take issue with Mazor's and even Oz's positive interpretation of such an ending as conciliatory and compromising.[14] Yonatan, utterly listless upon his return to the kibbutz, allows himself to be positioned in the same place that initially drives him to self-destructive despair. From his perspective, this is no compromise. This is surrender. Ultimately, the kibbutz's assertion of peace,[15] which leaves the characters at the end of the novel as unnaturally subdued as overmedicated children, is exploded in the last lines of the novel with the narrator's terse description of the toll of the 1967 War.

The Garden as Redemptive Site of Authenticity

The agricultural ethos of the kibbutz and of Labor Zionism more generally shaped socio-spatial dynamics outside agricultural settlements like kibbutzim and moshavim.[16] Even in urban areas, gardens and the act of gardening allowed Israelis to participate in the experience of making the desert bloom. As such, gardening, which was practical and productive, required time spent outdoors in the sunshine, paralleled and complemented the large-scale agricultural endeavors at the heart of Labor Zionism, and instilled Zionist values and praxis within the Israeli self-conception. Modest vegetable patches sprang up among the tents of immigrant transit camps, between urban apartment buildings, and on sunny balconies, where children were often mobilized to care for budding plants. These vernacular gardens brought food to the table and nurtured one of the central components of Israeli identity: closeness to the land. A memorable example of the kind of pride generated by this experience for youth is depicted in Moshe Shamir's 1951 novel, *Be-mo yadav: pirkey elik* (With his own hands: the chronicles of Elik), in which the narrator recalls his younger brother,

---

14. Oz discusses *A Perfect Peace* as "leading to a kind of mystical merger between certain, different people" in its "formation of an unlikely extended family" (Cohen 1990, 186).

15. *Menuha nekhona*, the novel's title, is part of the traditional memorial prayer *El male rahamim* [God full of compassion], recited at gravesides and national memorial ceremonies.

16. For details on the design of gardens in kibbutzim and moshavim, see Almog 2000, especially pp. 168–71.

a prototypical golden Sabra who falls in the 1948 War, as a boy planting radishes and onions in a tiny plot of urban land adjacent to the family's apartment building: "There were good days, too, when there were always radishes at home, both for breakfast and supper, and uncle liked spring onions even more than we did. And all this was ours, produced with our own hands" (1970, 17). One characteristic that contributes to the mythology of Elik is his closeness to the land; the early experience of enthusiastic urban gardening foreshadows his later success at the agricultural school.

In the Western sensibility at the foundation of Amos Oz's writing one of the most common symbolic manifestations of the garden is Eden. Leonard Lutwack notes that the understanding of gardens in literature and culture has ranged from paradisiacal to corrupt, paralleling the extremes of the biblical story of Eden (1984, 36). The banishment from Eden is the most terrible punishment God metes out to Adam, Eve, and the serpent upon discovering their guilt; the other punishments, including painful childbirth, the necessity of toiling to earn bread, and a stubborn soil, are all concretized by the act of departing Eden and create a diametric opposition to the idyll that was the Garden, in which there was no pain, no exertion or labor, and a rich, fruitful soil. If the expulsion from Eden is the first exile, then the Garden itself is the prototype of the idealized home, the object of the yearnings of the modern state of exile. The link between the biblical story and contemporary gardens in Hebrew culture is acknowledged etymologically in the link between the Hebrew word *pardes*, orchard, to the ancient Persian *pairidaeza* and the Greek *paradeisoi* (paradise) (Helphand 2002, 50).

"The garden," observes Lutwack, "with its well-watered trees and pruned plants, represents the reassuring compromise of life contained—an oasis in the desert. . . . It is a piece of the natural world which man encloses in order to hold out alien presences and to cultivate desirable plants" (1984, 48). The idea of the garden as an oasis can be expressed both literally and metaphorically. For example, in Oz's story "*Har ha-'etsa ha-ra'a*" (The hill of evil counsel) (1976), a German-Jewish veterinarian in mandatory Jerusalem plants a garden described as "small, logically planned, uncompromisingly well-kept: [his] dreams had laid out square and rectangular flower beds among the rocky gulleys, a lonely island of clear, sober sanity in the midst of a savage, rugged wasteland, of winding valleys, of desert winds"

(Oz 1978, 14). The garden, like the man who planned and planted it, represents order and enlightenment in its brave resistance of the surrounding desert wasteland.

In a society obsessed with clear borders and demarcations as well as with land itself, the garden provides a comfortable zone that is neither fully "civilized" nor fully wild. It marks the domestication of the land as well as the desire to preserve its wildness to a degree. The dichotomy of domestication and preservation finds a parallel in Israeli landscape design, which is marked by the tension between foreign (usually European) influences and native local ones. Stanley Waterman notes that the landscape architects who immigrated to Israel from Europe, unlike the Bauhaus architects who aimed to shape a new modernity, tried to complement their designs with indigenous flora: "[They] arrived in a country with landscapes unfamiliar to them, with different light and colours to those familiar to them in Europe. . . . [They] often felt that they had to incorporate the local" (2004, 667). The notion that landscape architects felt obliged to "incorporate" local elements into their designs highlights the extent to which they approached the Israeli landscape and their role in the nation-building project from the perspective of self-conscious outsiders. Far from limiting the representativeness of their designs and their applicability to the Israeli experience, this perspective aptly expressed the experience of new immigrants trying to reconcile the landscape they found upon their arrival in Israel with that of both their memories and their expectations.

The tension between the transformation and the preservation of landscape is not, of course, an exclusively Israeli preoccupation. The Israeli manifestation of this tension, however, speaks to the ideological underpinnings of the Zionist project itself and reflects its ambivalence toward the desert and other indigenous landscapes, which were on the one hand considered authentic but on the other hand threatening. "Plants are the quintessence of nature," observes Helphand, "yet they are bound to culture. . . . Plants have their own history and ideological dimension" (2002, 45). The species associated in the Bible with the Land of Israel, such as olives, grapes, pomegranates, and figs, are symbols of an authoritative, "authentic" connection to the land for both Israelis and Palestinians. The debates that continue to preoccupy landscape architects in Israel hinge on the question of whether gardens and parks ought to strive for a more "natural" loyalty to indigenous plants or to introduce new ones; even the question of which plants are actually indigenous has been the subject of heated controversy (91). Such controversies illuminate the political resonance of the garden and landscape design in general in Israel. As Israeli institutions attempted to mold diverse populations of immigrants into a nation with a cohesive national identity, so did they attempt to shape the landscape into a reflection of this identity. The Orientalist idealization of biblical aesthetics, considered indigenous and "authentic," stemmed from the same tense mix of contradictory emotions that inform Jewish Israeli attitudes toward the desert. Whether gardeners chose architectonic or "natural" forms, gardens in Israel as elsewhere are cultural constructs, always a product of human intervention in and ordering of nature.

The eighteenth-century English garden, "wild" and "natural" by design, exemplifies the paradox of the concept of the imitation of nature. An aesthetic reaction against the painstakingly measured symmetry and exactitude of courtly French gardens of that period and earlier, the idea behind the English garden was contrived spontaneity and planned nonchalance. The garden was meant to reconstruct an ideal place, conducive to intense reflection and emotional moments loosened from the constrictions of that society. It was carefully planned to look as unplanned as possible. Yet, just like its rigid French contemporary, its main purpose was to delight human beings, and to this end it was outfitted often with quaint paths and benches for weary amblers. Striving for an idealized Romantic depiction of nature, it reflected the way people imagined nature should look. Roberto Dainotto's observation about regionalist literature encapsulates the potential danger embedded in such seemingly innocuous endeavors: Expressing "the beautiful discourse of what *ought* to be," it is driven by a yearning for an organic "authenticity" and "hostility for what is extraneous and disturbing of the 'natural' order" (2000, 171). It is this pretense of authenticity that Dainotto finds so disconcerting. While the garden that is pruned, weeded, fertilized, and color-coded makes no attempt to hide the role that humans and "civilization" have played in its creation, the place that is falsely wild manipulates the subject into accepting its naturalness and, by implication, its authenticity.

In Oz's novel *Lada'at isha* (To know a woman) (1989), the garden, like the kibbutz, is highly ordered and carefully maintained. The enigmatic ex-Mossad agent Yoel Ravid is obsessed with the maintenance and care of the home he has just rented, and particularly with its garden. A mythological shadow in the pantheon of Zionist gods, Yoel is predictably fair-haired, suntanned, and ruggedly good-looking, the image of the Sabra.[17] Like Yonatan in *A Perfect Peace*, he does not speak excessively, "as though words were personal possessions that should not be parted with lightly" (Oz 1991, 1).[18] His taciturn and closed-off nature is well suited to his new hobby. He spends increasingly long hours planning and preparing his garden for ever-expanding varieties of plants and trees, makes special orders at the neighborhood greenhouse, becomes well-versed in types of soil and fertilizer. Attacking the garden with pesticides and pruning shears, planning every leaf and bud, he is barely aware of the nearby lights of Tel Aviv: "He felt no urge to go into the city. Instead, he sowed sweet peas in the thin soil along the walls of the house" (132). He throws himself into gardening as if trying to exorcise an evil spirit from within. As we later learn that he feels responsible for the death of his colleague, his obsessive gardening is confirmed as a means of redemption and the reassertion of control. The moral goodness associated with gardening in fiction is well documented. Michael Waters notes, for example, that "Dickens often depicted gardening as a potentially redemptive and revivifying activity" (1988, 165). Moreover, he identifies one of the basic assumptions of Victorian literature as "the belief that gardens bring moral and personal benefits to those who care deeply for their gardens" (307). Having chosen to retire early following the death of his colleague, Yoel gardens compulsively, suggesting that doing so may indeed assuage his guilt and reestablish his moral center.

Initially, he plants roses, chrysanthemums, carnations, gladiolas, snapdragons, geraniums—all common enough ornamental flowers in Israel as well as in Europe, Africa, Asia, and the Americas. Yet toward the end

---

17. Laor discusses Yoel as a mythological Israeli figure. See Laor 1995, 102–4.

18. For more on the Sabra's "urge to keep speech to a minimum or to speak simply" as a trait related to authenticity, see Almog 2000, 149–52.

of the novel, as Yoel gazes at the riot of color that the arrival of spring had brought into his garden, he decides to change direction: "Ligustrum and oleander and bougainvillea, and even hibiscus bushes, struck him as boring and vulgar. He therefore decided to do away with the stretch of lawn at the side of the house, . . . and plant figs and olives and perhaps pomegranates. In due time the vines that he had planted around the new pergola would also spread to this part, so that in ten or twenty years there would be a perfect miniature replica of a thick dark Biblical orchard such as he had always envied around the homes of Arab villagers" (Oz 1991, 217–18). Yoel decides to transform his typically suburban garden, with its green lawn and colorful standard garden flowers, into a *bustan*, an orchard or fruit garden. The *bustan* is "a garden of both pleasure and utility, a social setting where food is grown. . . . It is an environment, however, where the pleasures of plants are equal in importance to their productive value" (Helphand 2002, 49). In contrast to the fruit-bearing *bustan*, Yoel's first garden is merely decorative and therefore bourgeois and "vulgar." The *bustan*, "largely a landscape of the past," (50) here is linked explicitly to biblical landscapes. Comparing the passage above with Deuteronomy's description of the "good land" of Israel, "a land of wheat and barley, and vines and fig-trees and pomegranates; a land of olive trees and honey" (Deuteronomy 8:8), we can see that Yoel does not exaggerate his desire to produce a "perfect miniature replica of a thick dark Biblical orchard" (Oz 1991, 218). Yoel's intention to replicate the biblical landscape in the yard of a house he is only renting but is determined to buy can be read as the attempt of the disgraced, foreign-born Mossad agent to assert his Israeliness through the transformation of his place into an exemplary native landscape, which, significantly, Yoel identifies with Arab villagers, those Orientalized, de-historicized native sons. Imitating their landscape constitutes an appropriation of the "authenticity" that historically evoked such mixed emotions among early Zionists like the author and farmer Moshe Smilansky, who simultaneously admired the Arab connection to the land (read in terms of an unbroken continuity from biblical to modern times) and disdained the Arab as the enemy of Zionist pioneering efforts. This passage suggests Yoel's identification with his garden: though he is only renting the house, his plan for the garden spans decades, suggesting his intention to root himself deeply—and, literally, organically—in the place, making it truly his own through his garden. The intimacy he desires with the land, almost erotic in its intensity, also suggests his determination to redeem himself following the ambiguous circumstances of his wife's death: he "knows" the garden as he never knew the woman who was his wife.

The identification between person and plant is not uncommon in Hebrew literature and Zionist thought. In Shulamit Hareven's novel *Ir yamim rabim* (City of many days) (1972), for example, a German Jewish immigrant to prestate Palestine insists on replicating biblical flora in his own Jerusalem garden and attempts to plant a cedar tree, which finally, after much unexpected effort, takes root in the soil. The success of his endeavor symbolizes his own difficult but ultimately successful transplantation to Palestine as a return to ancestral soil. In the early twentieth century, the poet Saul Tchernichovsky spoke to a similar phenomenon in his famous line that "man is but the imprint of his homeland's landscape" ("*ha-adam eyno ela . . .*") (1990–2003).

It is only a few steps from the interpretation that Yoel makes his home his own through his garden to a colonialist reading of Yoel's enterprise. Waters writes that for the middle classes of Victorian England, "exotics were indubitable symbols of triumph and progress—their own and their country's," since they signaled colonial prowess (1988, 123). Notwithstanding Yoel's vision of a garden that comprises emphatically native and historically relevant plants, his careful planning and calculations signal his self-conscious difference from "authentic" Arab natives. Furthermore, his identification of the latter with the indigenous flora makes it "exotic" to Yoel, suggesting a reconfiguration of the colonial enterprise whereby the "colonizer" aims to *supplant* the native.

The telos of Yoel's zealous gardening becomes clear toward the end of the novel, when he goes to visit his murdered colleague's father in Pardes Hanna. The man's home

> was set apart somewhat, near the edge of an orange grove, at the end of a muddy track overgrown with thistles that reached up to the car's windows. After parking, [Yoel] had to force his way through a thick hedge

that had run wild and almost grown together from each side of a path
of broken and uneven paving stones. He therefore prepared himself to
encounter a neglected old man in a neglected old house. . . . To his
surprise, when he emerged from the overgrowth he . . . could see a tiny
but pleasant and extremely clean and neat living room, a Bukhara rug,
a coffee table made from the stump of an olive tree. . . . On the wall he
saw a painting of snow-capped Mount Hermon with the Sea of Galilee
below, wreathed in bluish early-morning mist. (Oz 1991, 228–29)

The neat little home filled with native artifacts and representations of
idyllic Israeli landscapes keeps the hostile wild greenery at bay much as
the kibbutz resists the chaotic wilderness that threatens it. Behind the
house Yoel finds "masses of petunias in flowerpots," and in the kitchen he
finds yogurt jars sprouting marigolds, chrysanthemums, and a sweet potato
plant, all of which seem to fulfill a primal need to send down his own
roots in this splendid house: "It was only with difficulty that Yoel resisted
the sudden desire to sit down on the rush stool and settle here in this
kitchen" (Oz 1991, 229). Before "penetrating deeper into the house," he
steps outside to find henhouses "enclosed by tall cypress trees and with
small squares of lawn decorated in the corners with cactuses growing in
rock gardens" (229). This—not the wild thistles leading to the house—is
the man's garden. Well-ordered and maintained, it seems an appropriate
extension of the old man's house. The obvious and undisputable human
presence is central, representing precisely the type of relationship that Yoel
himself has been trying to cultivate in his own home. His reaction to this
house and garden makes clear that he recognizes there the organic, rooted
authenticity that has eluded him, and which his own obsessive ordering,
planning, and planting are intended to establish. Indeed, in case his stated
desire to "settle" there is not clear enough, we are told that the house's
little kitchen had "won his heart like a promised land" (233).

Since he chooses to reveal the name of the man who sent his son to
his death rather than insisting on the secrecy vital to the Mossad, Yoel
is banished by the old man, who is disgusted with the sympathy that has
displaced Yoel's sense of national duty. Pelted with cries of "Traitor" and
"Cain," Yoel retreats:

It was important to him to avoid the house and its charms and to cut straight through to his car. So he plunged among the overgrown bushes that had once been a hedge. Very soon a bristly darkness, a thick, humid coat of ferns, closed around him. Gripped by claustrophobia, he began to trample on branches, to flail, to kick out at the dense foliage, which simply absorbed his kicks; bending stems and twigs, scratched all over, panting hard, his clothes covered with burrs and thorns and dry leaves, he seemed to be sinking in the folds of thick, soft, twisted, dark-green cotton wool, struggling with strange pangs of panic and seduction. (Oz 1991, 235)

What had initially seemed a sign of neglect and a warning of nature's ability to reassert itself is revealed here as serving another purpose. In this Zionist fairy tale, the warm, tidy home is surrounded and protected by thick brambles to be conquered and destroyed, like those surrounding the castle of Charles Perrault's *La belle au bois dormant* (Sleeping beauty) (1697). The challenge of surviving the wild greenery in order to reach the fantastic house that beckons from within parallels the efforts of Zionist pioneers who had to overcome severe physical and geographical conditions to make a home of an unwelcoming landscape—and then to keep that hostile landscape *at bay*. The never-experienced childhood this fairy tale offers Yoel is more rooted in place than his own fatherless immigrant's childhood, which began with his birth in transit on a boat, neither in the Diaspora nor in Israel. It is this rootedness that he had been striving to create in his own home as an adult, in his obsessive drive for an orderly, neat home surrounded by flora straight from a biblical fantasy.

Yoel's energetic gardening, Oz suggests, constitutes the creation of a native *bustan* that will reassert his legitimacy as an Israeli—an identity that he does not take for granted both because of his background as well as his indirect responsibility for his colleague's death—and allow him to start a new, orderly, carefully controlled life. His Eden is not intended to be a setting for love, or any other potentially destructive emotion, for that matter. To the contrary, it is intended to be a bulwark against such emotions, which he associates with the madness that so fascinated his wife and that presumably led to her death. Alone in his garden, Oz's Adam surveys the outside world and its attendant chaos—the Jerusalem that stole his wife, the Tel Aviv that lures his daughter, the neighbor's house that bewitches and seduces him—with foreboding, wishing only to enclose himself in a rigid, ideologically significant order that might redeem him.

The Embattled Development Town

The Israeli development town, like the kibbutz, was a vernacular place resulting from Zionist spatial agendas, yet it came to symbolize the opposite of the kibbutz values that shaped Israeli identity: its high unemployment was associated with its residents' presumed laziness and sloth, its crime rate with stereotypes of their inherently dishonest sensibility, its barren cultural scene with their supposed apathy. Dusty, hot, and boring, the southern development town was intended to fulfill the Zionist ideal of ingathering and absorption but in reality was inhabited by often frustrated immigrants who quickly became second-class citizens. These towns gave birth to an alternative or "second" Israeli identity.

For the most part, in the early years of statehood, settled Israelis paid no heed to the suggestion of Ben-Gurion and others that they abandon the bourgeois pleasures and temptations of the densely populated coastal plain in favor of an adventurous pioneering lifestyle in the desert. Tel Aviv and Jerusalem, and to a lesser extent Haifa, with their established infrastructure and numerous cultural events, offered convenience and pleasure that few were willing to forego. When new immigrants began arriving in large numbers after the establishment of the state, the least inhabited areas of the state were considered by the government to be the obvious solution to the dilemma of where to settle them. Such a solution seemed to fulfill several important goals. First, it was a way to bring people to sparsely populated areas of the state, mostly in the far north and the south, and to relieve the cities and their already groaning infrastructure and facilities of the burden of absorbing new residents. Second, it constituted a step in the direction of Ben-Gurion's dream of settling the Negev, allowing new immigrants (mostly from North Africa and the Middle East) to participate in the kind of active pioneering Zionism for which the Eastern European pioneers of the Second and Third 'aliyot (waves of immigration)[19] were remembered.[20] Third, as these isolated areas were often near the border, the new towns were considered important to the security and defense of the country. This consideration illuminates the planners' conception of the shared role that would be played by the development towns and the kibbutzim, many of which were established on borders as "guardians" of Israel. "Zionist planners had always been concerned with placing a stable and productive population on frontiers. Together with defense strategists, they preferred civilian settlements to fortresses for securing borders. New towns proved to be a useful concept in realizing that objective" (Troen 1995, 457). Like the kibbutz, the development town was to serve as a spatial force in maintaining order within Israel's borders and repelling the chaotic forces beyond.

Composed almost entirely of immigrants from Arab lands, these towns were intended to exemplify the heterogeneous *kibuts galuyot* (ingathering of the exiles) that characterized the Israeli self-conception. In fact, they became enclaves of ethnic and cultural homogeneity,[21] "spatially isolated from their neighbors and fairly detached, socially, from the larger Israeli society" (Ben-Zadok 1993, 102). The new town policymakers were so preoccupied with the ideological goals of immigrant absorption, geographic

19. The five waves of Jewish immigration, or 'aliyot, to Palestine took place between 1882 and 1939. The First, Second, and Third 'aliyot occurred in 1882–1903, 1904–1914, and 1919–1923, respectively, and were particularly revered as the 'aliyot that brought the *halutsim,* or pioneers.

20. Ben-Gurion draws this parallel explicitly, arguing that "the strength of spirit and the fruits of the labor of the nation's pioneers over the past three generations changed the face of the land while it was still under foreign rule. But their labor and their creation was limited to the northern half of our country, where the land is generally fertile and the rains common and sufficient. The southern half of the nation, called Negev, which constitutes most of the state's land, has stood in its wilderness for the hundreds of years since the Arab conquest; the Turks and the British as well did not attempt to make this wilderness bloom" (Ben-Gurion 2008).

21. Ben-Zadok writes that "the vast majority of the residents are working-class Oriental Jews . . . who originate in the Islamic countries of North Africa and the Middle East" (1993, 93).

distribution, and securing borders that they did not adequately consider the effects that spatial isolation and sociocultural detachment would have on the towns' economic progress and on their inhabitants' sense of themselves as Israeli. Since their policy planning and design did not account for long-term growth or establish mechanisms to ensure economic diversity, development towns suffered from poverty, unemployment, and economic stagnation. The towns' limitations created a situation whereby economic survival was the top priority for the residents. Upward mobility, symbolized by leaving the development town, was complicated in such circumstances. The difficulties were only compounded by the towns' ethnic and cultural segregation from mainstream Israel. In Israeli parlance, development towns became synonymous not only with poverty but also with immigrants, primarily Mizrahi Jews, and their culture. Already in 1955, for example, a report on the development town Beit Shean (whose residents were mostly from Iran and Iraq)[22] asserted that it had become "a backward Levantine city,"[23] an openly racist charge equating the residents' Eastern cultural background with the town's failure. This assertion was made despite the acknowledgment that it was the authorities' failure to invest in infrastructure, education, culture, and vocational institutions that impeded the town's progress (Troen 1995, 450). Sami Shalom Chetrit, a leading Mizrahi activist, intellectual, and poet, has demonstrated the racism that informed the establishment of development towns, which kept Mizrahim "both far from the eye and far from the heart" of the predominantly Ashkenazi Israeli mainstream that referred to them in derogatory terms as "The Second Israel"[24] (Chetrit 2004, 83). Popular films such as *Sof ha-'olam smola* (Turn left at the end of the world, Avi Nesher, 2004) and *Bikur ha-tizmoret* (The band's visit, Eran Kolirin, 2007) depict the marked Mizrahi presence in isolated development towns situated in a

22. Troen 1995, 450.

23. Ruth Bondi, quoted in Troen 1995, 450.

24. Ben-Zadok explains this term as directly related to the development towns, demonstrating the fluidity between the towns and their Mizrahi inhabitants: "Stereotyped as the 'Second Israel,' a housing shelter for the uneducated and economically dependent, the towns could not attract middle-class residents" (1993, 106).

southern desert environment with only the most rudimentary cultural and public services.

In terms of design, the development town is based historically and ideologically in European theories of "new town" planning.[25] Unlike seemingly similar instances of de facto ethnic segregation such as the French *banlieue*, the development town was planned (formally, at least) with the idea of allowing new immigrants to participate in the national narrative. Israeli development towns were planned with ideological considerations, integration, and assimilation in mind, but "no standards were set for planning their ethnic or socioeconomic composition" (Ben-Zadok 1993, 102). Mainstream Israeli society came to blame the development towns themselves and their residents for the dire situation,[26] rather than the well-meaning but misguided planning policies.

From 1948 to 1952, Israeli policy regarding development towns was to rebuild or expand existing historical towns, mostly in the Galilee and Negev regions. Though development towns were established in the north as well as the south, the spacious south became the site of more and larger towns.[27]

25. For a contextualization of the Israeli development town within the broader international phenomenon of "new towns," see Troen 1995, 442–45.

26. For example, Troen writes that "most [development] towns failed to achieve the goals established for them. Rather than becoming centers of population and industry, they became impoverished settlements on the country's periphery offering few prospects for a largely immigrant population" (1995, 455). The tendency to characterize the abject state of many development towns as their "failure to achieve the goals established for them" does not take into consideration that the necessary conditions for the achievement of these goals—opportunities for competitive education and economic growth, cultural involvement, and social integration—were not instituted in the planning stage.

27. In 1989, the Central Bureau of Statistics reported 17 southern towns and 16 northern towns; more significantly, every one of the 16 northern towns has a population of less than 40,000, while four of the 17 southern towns have populations between 40,001 and 75,000; one of the 17, Beer Sheva, has a population of over 75,000 (Ben-Zadok 1993, 94). These numbers attest to the fact that there are more development town residents in the south than the north. Moreover, there is greater spatial diversity in the fertile, more established, and more densely populated north than the south, in the form of greater numbers of economically stable towns, kibbutzim, and moshavim. The development town

After 1952, "new towns were built from scratch" in these areas (Ben-Zadok 1993, 92). The historically relevant towns served Zionist principles in that they strengthened the notion of return to the ancient homeland. The new towns, however, were also considered crucial to the enactment of Zionist ideals, first because they allowed a distancing from colonialism and second because they constituted a spatial manifestation of the New Jew, much as Tel Aviv itself was conceptualized as the first Hebrew city, "a city sprung from the sands" (Mann 2006, 74). In other words, both the saturation and the dearth of historical significance were understood as advantageous to the Zionist conception of space and its manifestation in the new towns.

The fictional town Tel Kedar in Oz's novel *Al tagidi layla* (Don't call it night) (1994) could be any one of a number of southern Israeli towns. The narrator details its most mundane features, providing a meticulous inventory of its shops, restaurants, and other businesses. Tel Kedar is clearly the product of a well-established development town plan. Centered by the requisite war memorial and shawarma stand and flanked by unimaginative districts with buildings in the style of the coastal towns, it constitutes a familiar spatial trope to the Israeli reader. Yet Oz adds another dimension to this flat depiction: almost without exception, all the establishments of Tel Kedar are named for other places. The California Café, the Paris Cinema, the Hollywood Photo Shop, the Champs-Elysées Hair Salon, the Entebbe[28] Falafel Stand, Palermo Pizza—these place-names conjure glamorous images in the heart of this generic desert town. The upscale residential district reflects this escapist aesthetic as well. Its European-style houses and

---

is therefore more of an archetypical spatial configuration in the southern region than in the north.

28. Entebbe holds a prominent place in Israeli collective memory because of the Entebbe hostage crisis. In July of 1976, an Air France flight originating in Tel Aviv and bound for Paris was hijacked by two Palestinians from the Popular Front for the Liberation of Palestine and two Germans. With the support of Ugandan president Idi Amin and his pro-Palestinian forces, they diverted the flight to Entebbe, where they threatened to kill their hostages if their demands for the release of prisoners in Israel and elsewhere were not met. The Israeli Defense Force raided the aircraft, killed the hijackers, and enabled the release of the hostages. The event is remembered as a heroic moment in Israeli history.

carefully groomed gardens represent the townspeople's resistance against the climate, culture, and landscape of their town. The narrator relates that years ago, when the protagonist Theo, a civil engineer, proposed a plan for Tel Kedar that would allow it to exist harmoniously with the desert, his plan was rejected unceremoniously in favor of a more "Israeli" style. For Tel Kedar's nine thousand residents, who originated in thirty different countries, this means not just rejecting the desert surrounding the town, but eradicating it. Their "pioneering efforts" do not seem to be motivated by Zionist ideals, or even by Zionism's ambivalent relationship with the desert. Yet they are nevertheless driven by a Eurocentric, colonialist sensibility that valorizes Western design and conceptions of worldly glamour even when such aesthetics are at odds with their surroundings. The town comprises an ethnically and linguistically diverse populace and an array of modest businesses pathetically and postmodernistically alluding to more exciting places, as it struggles for a cohesive identity that will aid it to resist the desert. The development town deals not with a metaphor or a symbol of the wilderness but with the desert itself. The desert's proximity to the town makes it one of the town's formative factors in spite of and perhaps even *because* of the town's resistance to it.

The text is narrated from three different perspectives, Theo's, his longtime girlfriend Noa's, and an omniscient narrator's. Theo and Noa's road to the development town is not typical. Neither immigrants nor economically challenged, they chose to live in Tel Kedar because Noa is struck by its spaciousness: "Let's go and live in Tel Kedar," she suggests shortly after their return to Tel Aviv from a lengthy sojourn in South America. "It's the end of the world, the desert is like an ocean and everything's wide open" (Oz 1996, 112). Motivated by a sense of romantic adventure and thrilled by the spaciousness that eludes them in Tel Aviv, she easily transposes desert and ocean. Noa, young, bright, and energetic, attaches no special value to the desert that fascinates Theo, a no-nonsense sensibility that Theo envies: "She is so much at peace with herself, with the darkness, with the desert at the end of the garden beyond the two thick cypresses" (10). Whereas for Theo the desert is "ancient," (3) most of the residents of Tel Kedar consider it an empty space signifying the site's a-historicity. Abraham Orvieto, for example, whose son's death has brought him to the town from abroad, comments that Tel Kedar, an unquestionably Israeli town devoid of any biblical or Arab past, is "a miracle" (160, 122). The pseudo-religious term ("miracle") used to describe the establishment of a modest desert town is typical of Zionist language, as we have seen in Ben-Gurion's speech on the significance of the Negev. But the Negev, for Ben-Gurion, is anchored in the Bible. Orvieto's proprietary insistence on Israeli legitimacy and on the a-historical newness of the town strips it of any Judaic significance at the same time that it disallows any Palestinian significance. This denial of historical context parallels the town's own physical-geographical denial of its location at the edge of the desert.

Theo's relationship with the desert is rooted in several prior encounters he has had with it. During his compulsory army service, he volunteered for a reconnaissance task force in the desert in a unit that included a Bedouin tracker named Aatef. Later, as a civil engineer planning the town that would become Tel Kedar, he proposes a design integrated and harmonized with the desert. He recalls the time he spent at the site before the town was built: "For three weeks I roamed all over that bare plateau roasting in the sun at the foot of the cliff from before dawn to after dusk. At night by the light of a pressure lamp I sat in the administration tent sketching through preliminary ideas for a master plan that was intended to get away from the usual Israeli approach and create a compact desert town, sheltering itself in its own shade, inspired by photographs of Saharan townships in North Africa" (Oz 1996, 112). When the plan is rejected, Theo is told that, "when all's said and done, Israelis want to live in the Israeli style. Desert or no desert" (112). Now, living in a Tel Kedar apartment at the edge of town, Theo spends much time silently watching the desert from the balcony. His tranquil, contemplative narrative challenges the passionate rhetoric of "conquering" the desert. Oz's voice of conscience in this novel, Theo is neither blinded by nationalism nor marred by excessive patriotism, not even recognizably Israeli by his name, the vaguely international Theo.[29] Oz creates in Theo a man with independent thoughts and with a

---

29. Theo is probably short for Theodor, which is not a Hebrew name but which is the name of the father of political Zionism, Theodor Herzl.

personal history that allows him to reject the Eurocentric aesthetic that demonizes the desert.

Yet Theo's reverence for the desert accords with at least some elements of the earlier Zionist admiration of it, a concept confirmed by the photograph hanging in Theo's office of Ben-Gurion gazing "resolutely" (Oz 1996, 53, 161, 185) at the desert. Having left Israel and spent thirty years in South America, Theo seems an unlikely Zionist, but his interaction with the desert demonstrates that at least some of Zionism's fundamental ideas still inform his thinking. Like the Palmahniks who wore *kafiyyehs* and adopted Arab slang in imitation of the Arabs whose "authenticity" they admired and whose nativeness they desired,[30] Theo's veneration of the desert is based on an essentialist recycling of Orientalist tropes. "Let's suppose that you see in me what I sometimes see when I look at the desert," he imagines commenting cryptically to Noa (11), suggesting the type of identification that complicates the Euro-Israeli relationship to the Arab East,[31] here spatially manifested in the desert.

Theo's recollections of the Bedouin tracker Aatef, whom he credits with a highly intimate familiarity with the desert, are intended to distinguish Theo from the other characters. Yet several factors contribute to Aatef's reification, implicating Theo in the same Orientalist discourse against which Oz attempts to situate him. First, the nickname Layla (Hebrew: night), which Theo and the other soldiers assign him, not only suggests darkness, impenetrability, and mystery, but also, given the fact that, as Theo recalls, in Arabic it is a woman's name, femininity. Furthermore, the novel's negative-imperative title (literally "don't say night," in the second-person feminine) recontextualizes the word as central to the relationship between Theo and Noa, rather than to that between Theo and Aatef. At the same time that it implies Theo's identification with Aatef, it makes a plea for disassociation. Given Aatef's "natural" bond to the desert and Theo's fascination with it, this plea seems discordant. Yet it is not intended to distance Theo from the desert; rather, it highlights

30. For more on Palmah members' "imitation of the Arab," see Almog 2000, 198–201.
31. For more on ethnically European Israelis and Orientalism, see Peleg 2005.

the difference between the two men's relationship with it. Theo, a soldier-surveyor turned civil engineer, gazes at the desert from the outside with a trained yet unseeing eye, while Aatef, who sleeps with "eyes neither open nor closed," "sees" everything, interacting with the desert not only "naturally" but even *super*naturally (Oz 1996, 117). His animalistic nature is indicated not only by his reptile-like ability to sleep with eyes neither open nor closed and by the "fox-like chin" reminiscent of the nomad in "Nomad and Viper," but also in Theo's explanation of the nickname Layla: "His real name was Aatef, but behind his back we called him 'Night' because the night was as bright to him as if he had the characteristics of a nocturnal creature" (117). In addition to his animal-like traits, a string of clichés confirms Aatef's stereotyped alterity: He can read tracks that other men cannot even see, his wife and daughter were murdered in a tribal vendetta and, like the Arab in Yehoshua's aforementioned story "Facing the Forests," he is voiceless, speaking neither in the novel nor in Theo's memory of him as a whole (117). The only language he spoke, according to Theo, was the language of the desert itself, with which he communed tactilely: "Even on nights when clouds blotted out the stars and the mountaintops he would bend down and pick up a rusty cartridge case, a faded buckle, a dry crust, traces of human excrement on the black scree, a gnawed bone thrown in a crevice, and decipher it with the tips of his fingers" (117). The intimate knowledge he has of the desert and his naturalized presence there suggests that, like the sand and the jackals, he is one of its organic manifestations. Aatef, Oz suggests, is as exotic and incomprehensible as the desert whose language he speaks.

The blind seer Lupo, the Sephardic[32] wolf to Aatef's Arab fox, is another character intended to challenge the concept of an empty and historically frozen desert. At night, Lupo hears the voices of the dead, the desert's forgotten past inhabitants:

At the ultimate limit of hearing the blind man listens to the rustling of the night because he feels that behind the layer of silence and beneath

32. Lupo is Bulgarian (Oz 1996, 57).

the grating of the cricket the howls of the dead are stirring, faint and heartrending, like mist moving through mist. The weeping of the newly dead who find it hard to adapt sounds feeble and innocent, like the cry of a child abandoned in the wilderness. Those longer dead sob with a continuous, even wail, women's crying, as though muffled in the darkness under a winter blanket. While the long-forgotten dead of bygone ages, Bedouin women who starved to death on these hills, nomads, shepherds from ages past, send up from the depths a desolate hollow howl more silent than silence itself: the stirring of their yearning to return. Deep and dull beneath it breathes the groaning of dead camels, the cry of a slaughtered ram from the time of Abraham, the ashes of an ancient campfire, the hissing of a petrified tree that may once have flourished here in the wadi in springtime eons ago and whose longings still continue to whisper in the darkness of the plateau. (Oz 1996, 164–65)

This single passage on Lupo, narrated from an omniscient perspective and appearing within a short, self-contained chapter, suggests his prophetic abilities. The mournful voices haunting him not only establish a resonant historical presence in the desert but also the temporariness of human society and settlement in the face of the desert's timelessness. Here the desert is truly heterotopic, an "other place" containing a multitude of stories and peoples enfolded within layers of shifting sands.

Perhaps the most significant notion emerging from this passage is its conceptualization of the desert as a place of death. Like the desert in *A Perfect Peace*, in this novel it is associated with a disconcerting calmness that belies its potential for violence and its hunger for human life. The mention of Abraham alludes to the biblical 'akeda (the binding of Isaac) and indirectly refers to the ambiguous desert death of the shy youth Immanuel Orvieto, an incident at the center of the novel's plot. Yet the Abraham in this story, Avraham Orvieto, the dead boy's father, does not live in Israel and is absent when he dies after an accidental or suicidal drug overdose. The boy, who jumped or fell off a cliff, is sacrificed neither to God (the Judaic 'akeda) nor to the state (the Zionist 'akeda), but languishes alone in the desert, his neck broken, for a day and a half before dying. The "newly dead" whose weeping Lupo hears sound like "a child abandoned in the wilderness," reminding the reader of the significance of the desert setting of Immanuel's death. The tension between the desert and the town emerges in the context of the boy's death in the repeated mention of Mahler's *Kindertotenlieder,* a decidedly European elegy that, like the chalet-style houses of the wealthy district, seems misplaced in the environs of this emphatically un-European space.

The desert as Lupo hears it is not and never has been an empty space, but Oz's acknowledgment of its multilayered history is motivated by a perceived threat: the ghosts—Bedouin women, nomads and shepherds—want to return from the dead. Oz invokes another familiar text here, Bialik's famous poem "*Metei midbar*" (The dead of the desert) (1902), replacing Bialik's dead heroes with these "long-forgotten" people whose presence in the desert is as natural as the camels, the ram, and the petrified tree that preceded them there. By invoking and then deflating such ideologically resonant texts, Oz relieves the incident of the boy's death of the conventional religious and nationalist significance associated with them, suggesting instead that the seemingly silent desert itself has surpassed the role of both state and God. The desert has been not only anthropomorphized but deified, a notion confirmed by Theo's almost religious veneration of it. Clearly, Oz rejects the myth of the emptiness of the desert through Lupo and Aatef. But he replaces it with Orientalist tropes of the exotic Arab and the eternal, impenetrable, and threatening desert, a force that only wolves and caricatured Bedouin can comprehend.

The interactions of Theo, Aatef, and Lupo with the desert reveal its key characteristics in this novel. But it is the desert's direct confrontation with the development town that provides Oz's most straightforward depictions of the chaos beyond bounded Zionist spaces. No longer relying on the "representatives of the desert," in Nurit Gertz's words, to symbolize its potential violence, here the desert itself is depicted as capable of exerting violence. In earlier stories and novels, the desert was a passive repository for the jackals, Arabs, and other figures threatening "civilization," yet here the desert energetically attacks the town that must constantly fend it off. The pitched battle between them hums in low intensity in the background of the novel, periodically emerging to the surface of the narrative.

In his description of the town as the product of a conventional design scheme, Oz personifies its buildings, flowers, and trees, emphasizing their dependence on human intervention to survive in the desert landscape that is so alien to them. For example, we learn that, "inside iron cages wrapped with sackcloth for protection against the sandstorms, poinciana saplings fed by a drip system look as though they are still uncertain whether there is any point in their existence" (Oz 1996, 24). In addition to the saplings' uncertainty, "the ornamental gardens are forlorn on account of the wind that comes gusting in from the desert, lashing them with dust" (24). The originally white buildings, too, are presumably dejected because of their losing battle against the desert: "year by year the plaster grows closer to the colors of the desert, as though by assimilating to those colors it can assuage the fury of the light and dust. Solar panels gleam on every roof, as if the town were trying to appease the sun's blaze in its own language" (25). The few eucalyptus and tamarisk trees dotting the town, "blighted by droughts and salty wind, [hunch] towards the east like fugitives turned to stone in mid-flight" (25). The relentless sun, the whipping wind, and the sharp dust launch an offensive on behalf of the desert, assaulting the town and evoking its uncertainty, forlornness, and attempted appeasement. Despite the residents' conviction that they are "dressing a wound" when they cover the desert earth with soil brought from far away for their gardens, "the dust constantly makes its way back from the open expanse, straining to reconquer its original terrain. And yet the gardens hang on and refuse to be dislodged" (122).

The veritable war of attrition between the town and the desert manifests itself not just in the town's public space. The wealthy residential district, which encompasses one hundred single-family houses, does not escape the fate of the rest of the town, but, less willing to engage in appeasement, it attempts to deny the desert altogether: "There are no flat, tar-coated roofs here, but red tiles turning grey summer by summer. There are some wooden houses built in Swiss-chalet style, interspersed with others in Italian or Spanish idiom, in a reddish stone brought from the mountains of Galilee, with projections, surrounds and arches, rounded windows and even weathercocks on the gables, sighing for forests and meadows in this desert" (Oz 1996, 25). This escapist Eurocentric aesthetic constitutes the town's most concerted effort against the desert. This is not an attempt to coexist with the desert but to expel it altogether. One character's quip that, in the future, "they'll build Notre-Dame here and the Eiffel Tower, they'll fix us up with a river through the middle, with boats and anglers and everything," is as wistful as the sighing weathercocks (123).

The desert's personification, announced at the beginning of the novel, immediately casts suspicion on its intentions: "From the east, from the mountains, comes a gust of piercing desert wind. Like a cold sharp scythe. The wilderness is secretly breathing" (Oz 1996, 12). The explicit violence associated with the desert here leaves its mark everywhere in the town, as we have just seen. The "fury" of the desert becomes even more pronounced toward the end of the novel, as evidenced by Noa and Theo's nighttime walk. Here we witness the desert's sadistic irrationality: "A fierce southerly wind blew up every now and again and filled the world with millions of sharp specks. . . . Violent gusts periodically shook the bushes at the top of the line of hills, forcing them to bend, wriggle, and stoop in a contorted dance. The piercing sand penetrated to our skin under our clothes, filling our hair, grating between our teeth, hitting us straight in the eyes as if it were trying to blind us. From time to time a low howl crossed the empty plains. And stopped. And started whipping and tormenting the long-suffering bushes again. We progressed slowly southward, as if fighting a way upstream" (194). The town buildings try to "assimilate," "assuage," and "appease" the furious desert, which forces, pierces, penetrates, grates, hits, whips, and torments. Throughout the novel, Oz invariably chooses dynamic verbs and constructions for the desert and defensive or conciliatory diction for the town. The desert is violent, wrathful, energetic, punitive, and the town defends itself, refusing to surrender its conquered territory despite its "fainting lawns" and "poinciana saplings kept alive, as in intensive care, by a drip" (160). Tel Kedar's determined denial of the powerful desert amounts to a transgression, but it is not God's voice that issues out of the wilderness, chastising an errant people and proclaiming its punishment. It is the desert itself that speaks with its own material prowess, lashing out at Theo and Noa with the same weapons that help it encroach onto the town's territory and reclaim it as its own.

While the desert in Don't Call It Night actually trespasses the boundary separating it from the town and, armed with sand and wind, violently announces its presence, it eventually retreats. The town's battle scars—graying plaster, wilting flowers, hunched trees, and tortured bushes—attest to the threat of annihilation more explicitly than in the examples of the kibbutz and the garden discussed previously. If we map Oz's dichotomous spatial relationships, we find that they have evolved quite dramatically. Beginning with the cartography that Yigal Schwartz identifies in "Nomad and Viper," in which an orderly "upper map" inadvertently reveals the chaos of a "lower map," we found that the kibbutz attempts to deny the seeping of the wilderness and its "representatives" into itself. In *A Perfect Peace*, the kibbutz is supposed to be a bulwark of civilization, to which a wayward soul can return after a dangerous flirtation with the desert, but it, too, is prone to penetration and spatial "seeping." The kibbutz's attempts to gird itself against external chaos are challenged by the Diaspora, the abandoned Arab village, and the desert. *To Know a Woman* somewhat ironically privatizes the Zionist spatial enterprise, presenting the garden as an opportunity to assert a carefully planned exoticized authenticity to help ward off various manifestations of chaos: the ambiguity of a wife's death, the guilt regarding a colleague's murder, and the accusations of disloyalty to the state. *Don't Call It Night* purports to abandon the overtly Zionist preoccupations of the other two novels; even though it takes place in a "Zionist space," the characters do not occupy explicitly ideological roles like the kibbutzniks in *A Perfect Peace* and the ex-Mossad agent in *To Know a Woman*. But the desert's stubborn presence and the war it wages on the town suggest that, in some respects, the development town in this novel constitutes the most classical representation of Zionist space.

Conclusion

The Zionist conception of space as divided according to inside and outside borders or boundaries allows for a great deal of complexity within these categories. This complexity, however, does not preclude the exclusionary nature of such a dichotomy. A dialectical construction that defines "outside" spaces by negation (as those spaces that are not "inside" spaces), this categorization of space imbues certain types of place with ideological purpose and significance and establishes others as actively conspiring to dismantle and destroy this hard-earned order. The people associated with each type of space take on its characteristics. They have not only created it, but have also become part of it. As the Zionist endeavor to create a "New Jew" considered the connection between the Jew and the physical Land to be of prime importance, the "inner" place cannot be conceived without the people who helped construct it as such. The "outer" place, too, is important: in its capacity as other space, it is inhabited by those against whom the residents of the "inner" spaces define themselves, whether Arab (Jewish or not), Bedouin, urbanized Diaspora Jew or even animal.

Whether implicit or unequivocal, the spatial relationships in Oz's novelistic world are characterized by a continuously transgressed separation between light and darkness, West and East, native and foreigner—that is consistently articulated in terms of vernacular place. Unsuccessfully attempting to resist the disorder represented metaphorically or literally by the heterotopic desert wilderness, the Zionist places Oz represents in these novels speak to the impossibility of maintaining a Zionist spatiality. However, though criticized, this utopian spatiality nevertheless constitutes the organizing spatial principle in these works.

2

An Architecture of Isolation

Orly Castel-Bloom

> In the morning I sent a fax to the place *HOME*, which is also a key
> on the keyboard.
>
> —ORLY CASTEL-BLOOM, *Ha-sefer he-hadash shel orli*
> *kastel-bloom* (Taking the trend; literally, The new
> book by Orly Castel-Bloom)

As the complexity that exists even within the two seemingly simple categories of "inner" and "outer" space suggests, Jews positioned well within the "inner" space of Israeli society find themselves feeling claustrophobic at times, leading to a rejection of the restricted place categories established by Zionism. Self-proclaimed Zionists such as Oz certainly participate in their fair share of criticism of certain elements of the Zionist project, but their criticism arises out of their desire to repair the ills of a social order that, ultimately, they admire and support.

The characters of Orly Castel-Bloom, one of the most striking and original Israeli authors, cannot adjust to the hegemonic order even if they inhabit "inside" space. Unlike Oz's heroes, they are alienated not because of an individualistic impulse to defy a collective they ultimately believe in and wish to preserve, but because of their inability to attach any real significance to this collective, which results in terrifying isolation.

Castel-Bloom consciously attaches a great deal of importance to the question of place in her novels. As early as 1993, three years after the publication of her first novel, she discussed it at a conference of writers in Italy: "The question of place, in the broad sense of the word, the place where the plot takes place, is very important in the books that I've written. In fact, all the titles of the books are tied to the ground that the protagonists walk on. This ground, if I may express reservations, is not among the steadiest in the world" (Castel-Bloom 1993, 30). This unsteadiness sometimes attains the dimensions of earthquake in her novels. The image of shifting tectonic plates or of broken, fissured ground is an apt metaphor for the fragmentation of Castel-Bloom's characters, who tread this unstable place. Three types of vernacular place prove particularly useful in illustrating this fragmentation: the balcony; "spaces of exclusion" such as asylums, hospitals, and cemeteries; and the city. In her novels, these sites exemplify an architecture of isolation, a spatial system designed to promulgate and maintain collectivity, in the process excluding those who do not or cannot fulfill its demands. Blurring the boundaries between familiar spatial categories, the balcony aims to promote the experience of the collectivist Zionist ethos. Its failure to do so in Castel-Bloom's novels leaves her heroines feeling more alone than ever, robbing them of even the consolation of anonymity. The asylum, the hospital, and the cemetery, places that are supposed to ensure the psychical, physical, and spiritual well-being of individuals, also function as "heterotopias of deviation," to use Foucault's term, enabling institutions and ideologies to maintain their hegemony by isolating aberrant citizens. In these places, individuals find themselves subject to bizarre hierarchies determined according to the symbolic and ideological value of their death or illness. Finally, the city in Castel-Bloom's novels mobilizes the familiar modernist tropes of terrifying alienation as well as elements of postmodernist indifference, resulting in an utterly unstable and disorienting landscape where reality bleeds into fantasy. Castel-Bloom's characters' consciousness of their social isolation results from the alienation they experience in the very places that are intended to unify them. Viewed from the perspective of this isolating vernacular spatiality, national identity and even the basic concept of home itself become little more than fodder for the disconcertingly bleak humor pervading these novels.

The title of Castel-Bloom's first novel, *Heykhan ani nimtset* (Where am I), published in 1990, poses a question that has been present in every novel she has published since. In the short story collections that preceded *Where Am I*, Castel-Bloom had already started exploring the notion of locating the self. Though the question "Where am I?" seems to seek an obvious answer relating to locale, Castel-Bloom presents place as a concept that is ambiguous and highly subjective. The two collections of short stories with which she began her literary career, *Lo rahok mi-merkaz ha-'ir* (Not far from the center of town) (1987) and *Sviva 'oyenet* (Hostile surroundings) (1989), both hint at the need to *locate* something; their titles could be responses to the question that crowns her first novel. The "answers" lead Castel-Bloom to the question "Where am I?", asserting that it is the "I" that must be located, and forging a link between place and subjectivity.

The eclectic group of Israeli authors who rose to prominence in the 1980s generally comprises younger authors who were born in an Israel that was already a formed state with well-worn sentimentality, clichés, and a burgeoning critical tradition. Many of these authors saw themselves as writing against the preceding generation, which was (and, to an extent, still is) considered to be representative of the Israeli experience but that actually represented only a sliver of the wide spectrum of this experience, culturally and socially. These authors began writing during a dynamic period in Israeli history. The emergence of revisionist Israeli historians, the Lebanon War (which was the first war that Israelis demonstrated against publicly and en masse), and the cultural and economic Americanization of Israeli society were some of the factors that converged to create an atmosphere of greater openness, a loosening of ideological strictures, and a readiness to face criticism at a deeper level than before. Thus, novels, poetry, and short stories by Mizrahi authors, women, Israeli Palestinians, and others began to seep into public consciousness. Their writing challenged the perception, propagated in part by the established literary canon, of a more or less homogeneous Israeli identity, offering instead a postmodern conception of a plurality of widely varied experiences of Israel. It is from within this context that Castel-Bloom paints her disorienting literary landscapes.

The Balcony: The Performance of Alienation

The balcony, a ubiquitous structure in Israeli cities and suburbs, is suspended between private and public, between the home and the street. No Israeli urban or suburban landscape is complete without a balcony, where people sit for dinner, beat rugs, drink coffee, read a book, smoke a cigarette. The balcony's floor tiles are often the same as the ones inside the house, creating an impression of continuity from inside to outside space. The balcony thus upsets the spatial binary of private and public space: As "an extension of the home," it encompasses the private realm; as "a public stage to be viewed from the street" (Mann 2006, 167), it asserts itself in the public realm as well, as the vernacular site of *spectacle*. It is crucial to recognize the important distinction between the binary of private/public and that binary of inside/outside. The latter is related to a project of appropriating and demarcating purportedly unclaimed, undeveloped, or wild space and transforming it through manual labor to a place that is owned, developed, and "civilized." The two sides of this binary constitute polar but complementary spatial opposites. On the other hand, the binary of private/public poses a challenge to an ideology intent on creating a cohesive sense of community in a young state, in whose interest it would be to minimize the division.

The balcony can be considered to be "outside" the "inside" space of the apartment, yet it is not truly outside, since it can only be accessed from inside the home and since the street below is the "outside" to the home's "inside." Other attempts to align symmetrically inside/outside and private/public also collapse when subjected to minimal scrutiny: Public space is not necessarily outside, as evidenced by places such as theaters and schools, just as private space is not necessarily inside, but might take the form of a secluded patch of forest or beach. The balcony, however, does not constitute a boundary the space beyond which must be shunned, nor does it define an enclosure. Rather than a line separating the inner space of the apartment from the outer space of the street, the balcony represents a unique type of space that dissolves the separation of an individual from his or her compatriots in the street. Thus, while the *construction* of the inside/outside binary enables a spatial representation of particular Zionist ideals like taming the wilderness, the *dissolution* of the private/public binary, in this case performed by the balcony, plays a similar role in upholding such ideals as cultivating collective identity.

In her study of Tel Aviv and the shaping of Jewish urban space, Barbara Mann discusses how the Zionist valorization of collective identity was manifested in the city's architecture. She writes: "Early visions of the city called for an intertwined relation between public and private space, where customs traditionally associated with the private sphere became idealized in the public realm as a new urban collective identity" (Mann 2006, xviii). The image she uses to elaborate on this intertwining of public and private is that of the balcony, "both a public stage to be viewed from the street, as well as a semi-sheltered extension of the home" (167). More than just a cool spot to read one's newspaper, "the balcony represented a way of thinking about a new relation to space, one where public and private spheres were more interdependent" (167). The gradual closing-off of these formerly omnipresent balconies, Mann argues, reflects the drifting of Israeli society from its original collective ethos to an increasingly privatized and individualist one (167).[1] Some Israelis have transformed their balconies into makeshift guestrooms or graveyards of unused objects. Others, however, maintain the balcony's social relevance and its original purpose by using it as the setting for entertaining or people watching on breezy evenings.

In Orly Castel-Bloom's *Where Am I*, the nameless narrator spends much of her time at home on her balcony or gazing out her window at the street below. References to the balcony abound, situated amongst outright proclamations of disorientation and alienation. Early in the novel, for instance, she wanders through the seedy area of south Tel Aviv, noting its "collapsing balconies," a sign not only of physical neglect but also of the corrupt moral character of the area, where she meets a professional assassin (1990, 14).

Even streets with well-kept balconies contain the potential for violence. The heroine recalls events that occurred when she was younger: "In the street where I lived there was a murder. The murder was at the end of the street. I sat on the balcony and threw things outside. Sometimes I hit, sometimes I missed" (Castel-Bloom 1990, 21). This laconic statement situates a murder at the end of the street and then moves seamlessly to

1. Carolin Aronis, in "The Balconies of Tel Aviv: Cultural History and Urban Politics," historicizes the development and transformation of Tel Aviv balconies from 1909 to the present. She traces their changing architectural characteristics and discusses the building authorities' decades-long resistance to their permanent closure. See Aronis 2009.

the location of the narrator on the balcony. After she and her cousin hit a passerby below with an egg, the enraged man sees them, enters the apartment building, and comes to the door to "beat the two little sluts" (21). The man's violent intrusion into the apartment is a response not only to the girls' childish prank but also to the erasure of the boundary between public and private enacted by the balcony. Since the girls aim their ammunition from the balcony, they are occupying space that is at least partly continuous with the street below. The balcony here fulfills the function that it is intended to fulfill: it creates a space that is both public and private.

Yet the ideological reasoning for such a space loses all significance in this context. The street, the public space with which the private is to mingle, is a dangerous place where violent men tread and where murders are committed. This collective space radiates not a warm sense of community and shared values but rather stark alienation. Only after a gunshot sounds does the street come to life: "The parents ran outside. The whole street ran outside. People came out of all the entrances and ran toward the end of the street. A siren sounded. My cousin and I went outside and down. . . . Everyone talked with everyone. Traffic stopped. Everyone came out of their cars to hear what happened" (Castel-Bloom 1990, 22). The repetition of *hahutsa*, outside, and of *kulam*, everyone, emphasizes the situation, prior to the gunshot, of neighborhood residents ensconced in their private spaces, whether their homes or their cars. The girls, sitting in a space that purportedly breaks down the distinction between private and public space, observe the transformation of the street and are drawn to it, going "outside and down." Yet the circumstances of their participation in this collective scene, and the collective scene in itself, only mock the ideology that encourages collectivity.

Back in the novel's present, in a chapter entitled "*balkon*" (balcony) the narrator muses about her surroundings: "From the balcony I gaze here and there and also here. The solar water heaters, the seagulls, cars driving on the main road. It depends on where you look, and if you know the names of the trees. Knowing the names can warm the heart. Sometimes I feel like spreading my wings and leaving Israel. My neighbors left Israel for Canada ten years ago. Where are they? Where are you? Where did your wife buy the plane tickets? How much did you pay? Where do you live now? Will you return? When I'll leave—I won't return. Am I chained to this place?" (Castel-Bloom 1990, 35–36). The seemingly unrelated statements regarding the view from the balcony, the heartwarming experience of knowing the names of trees, and the possibility of emigrating from Israel bring us back to our narrator's preoccupation with her own place. The collection of objects she observes from her balcony does not include trees, yet she feels compelled to state that, besides also determining what one sees from a balcony, "knowing the names of trees can warm your heart." The detached tone of this observation contrasts starkly with its supposedly "heartwarming" content. Israeli Jews raised on Scouts and youth group hiking and camping trips are familiar with the emphasis these usually Zionist-oriented organizations place on knowing the Hebrew names of trees and flowers.[2] The revival of Hebrew as a modern, secular, spoken language forged a common bond amongst the Jews who came to Palestine and later Israel from different places and spoke different languages, and it also had a political function. The invention of Hebrew words for various components of the native Israeli landscape, part of the broader Zionist process of *kibush ha-safa* (conquest of the Hebrew language), laid the groundwork for appropriation of this landscape as native Israeli. In his lyrical short stories, the Hebrew author S. Yizhar (1916–2006) took care to use the Hebrew

2. For more on the centrality of "knowledge of the land," or *yediy'at ha-'arets*, in the institutionalization of Zionist ideology, see Almog 2000. Almog notes that the 1920s brought the publication of books on the geography and natural history of Palestine that aimed to forge a connection "between knowledge and sentiment—between knowing the land and loving the land" (162). He cites the emergence of "knowledge of the land" (*yediy'at ha-'arets*) books, which were explicitly and passionately ideological in their emotional descriptions of the landscape, as exemplifying the emphasis on an intimate emotional attachment to the physical landscape. *Yediy'at ha-'arets*, which after statehood became *yediy'at ha-moledet*, or "knowledge of the homeland," contained an ideological resonance that was erotically charged: "in Hebrew, 'knowing the land' bore a connotation parallel to the Biblical sense of 'knowing a woman'" (162). Almog notes that *yediy'at ha-'arets* and *moledet* lessons were supplemented by nature hikes, field trips, agricultural work in the school garden and other experiences that allowed students both to participate in and observe the natural and produced rhythms of the landscape. See particularly 161–68.

names of plants and other natural elements, thus aiding to legitimize the tie between the Hebrew language and the land. The narrator's statement about "knowing the names of the trees," immediately preceding as it does her admission that she sometimes dreams of emigrating from Israel, mocks the notion of a native Israeli identity and announces the failure of her integration into a unified and harmonious society. The balcony, the setting for these thoughts, intensifies her alienation rather than fulfilling its intended role and alleviating it, since its view reveals no people, just cars, birds, and solar panels.

As the novel progresses, the narrator's musings on the view from her balcony become even more clearly linked to her alienation: "From the balcony of my home in Neot Afeka you can see birds flying in obedient flocks. October. I see leaves, and balconies. A road and balconies. Fingernails and balconies" (Castel-Bloom 1990, 61). The "obedient flocks" of birds bring to mind Yehoshua Kenaz's novel *Hitganvut yehidim* (Infiltration) (1986), in which an idealistic kibbutznik soldier expresses his admiration for the discipline and collective nature of birds, to which he believes people should aspire. Yet Castel-Bloom destroys any possibility of an ideologically inspired intertextuality through the juxtapositions that follow, which might be logical or might be utterly absurd: leaves and balconies, road and balconies, fingernails and balconies. As in the example above, the element missing from the narrator's balcony experience is human contact. The continuation of this section develops the alienation implicit in the list she provides—birds, leaves, road, fingernails–to comical proportions: "Neot Afeka, when will you be mine. Then I shall rule over you. I'll be the neighborhood queen on the sixth floor. I'll bail out my soul, I'll pay bail" (Castel-Bloom 1990, 61). The echo of "pop Kabbala" or mystical New Age discourse in this plea and the dramatic register in which it is issued leave a distinct mark on this passage, mocking the narrator's clinging attachment to her apathetic place and emphasizing her metaphorical distance from it. Again, Castel-Bloom situates her narrator on the balcony, a spatial construction that is supposed to melt down precisely those boundaries between the individual and the collective, the person and the place she inhabits, but ends up making them only more apparent. The failure of this locale to help the narrator overcome her alienation transforms it from a site of unfulfilled ideological enactment to a tragicomic theatrical setting, in which the heroine cries out to her lover, Neot Afeka, an unresponsive Romeo.

Toward the end of the novel, she decides to go out to the balcony railing and do exercises: "Leg up, leg back, back flip, handstand. Below stood the residents of the neighborhood and looked. . . . In the end—I did a double back-flip and landed a soft landing in the balcony of my house. Thunderous applause filled the neighborhood that always ignored my existence" (Castel-Bloom 1990, 90). This scene begins, bizarrely, with an execution of impressive acrobatics, and ends with an outright accusation of exclusion. As in the scene above, the balcony here, having failed to counter alienation in its merging of private and public space, functions as a stage on which our heroine performs spectacular feats to gain the respect and admiration of her apathetic neighborhood.

The novel's mockery of the purported collectivization of Israeli society emerges not only in the ubiquitous image of the balcony but in thematic details as well. The heroine travels all over Israel during the course of the novel, but no sooner does she arrive at her destinations than she has an urge to turn back around. Immediately upon arriving in Jerusalem, she gets back on the bus to Tel Aviv (Castel-Bloom 1990, 35). Walking in Beer Sheva, she has a similar experience: "As is my custom, I wanted to get back on the bus and return to Tel Aviv, but I was afraid to look strange in Beer Sheva. . . . I walked the city streets. Do they sense my un-Beer Sheva-ness? . . . Foreign to the place" (67). She feels even more foreign in the north of Israel: "In the Dan Bloc no one looked at me on the street, but they didn't flee from me either, and here in the green Galilee, people run away from me as from a dangerous monster" (100). Yet the sense of not belonging does not subside even at home, as she finds when she and her husband return from a trip to faraway Tibet to find that, "instead of causing a flutter of homeliness," the most familiar places have suddenly become hostile (52). It is not the foreign place but their home that threatens them. Thus this novel continues to develop the theme of "hostile surroundings" that emerged in Castel-Bloom's previous work, the short-story collection by that title, published a year before the novel (1989). The heroine's disorientation in *Where Am I* results from the dissonance between the way she expects to experience familiar places, as a person at home, and the way she actually experiences them, as an undesired foreigner. Despite her familiarity with the city streets and their history as well as with "all the holes and hiding places" of her neighborhood, her increasing foreignness suggests that she is far from home (67). The novel ends on a plaintive note, with the narrator making her way "toward the moon, a moon that was hanging at the edge of a hill at the edge of the neighborhood" (113). This pseudo-lyrical ending mocks the narrator's serendipitous search for orientation. That she must go to the edge of the edge to determine where she is only emphasizes that she has not yet found an answer to this question.

In *Where Am I*, while the balcony succeeds in merging private and public space, it fails as a construction of social space. The fusion of public and private, intended to encourage a collective sensibility, in this novel only highlights the exclusion of the narrator from her neighborhood and emphasizes her increasing separation from the place she inhabits. Therefore the balcony becomes the site of a primary separation between person and home-place rather than cementing the relationship between the two. From the close-up perspective of the balcony and the neighborhood in this novel, Castel-Bloom steps back in her subsequent novels, offering a broader view of place.

The protagonist of Castel-Bloom's notorious novel *Doli siti* (Dolly City) (1992), Dr. Dolly, lives in the nightmarish Dolly City, a monstrous urban amalgam of all the cities in the world and, in some ways, a caricature of Tel Aviv. The novel's title seems to answer the question "Where am I?" Yet it does not produce a comforting resolution of the breakdown of subjectivity induced by the misalignment of person and place in *Where Am I*. Quite to the contrary, it amplifies to grotesque proportions the alienation and the violence in that novel and brings its disconcerting mixture of anxiety and apathy to a feverish crisis. This is no usual "identity crisis," however. Since the explorations of place and subjectivity in Castel-Bloom's earlier writing are so intimately linked, the crisis that explodes in *Dolly City* involves both.

The balcony, in this later novel as in the earlier one, functions as a theatrical stage from which Dolly can recite sparsely lyrical lines about her alienation: "Sometimes, even in Dolly City, I feel like a stranger. . . . I want to go home—even though this is my home," she admits early in the novel

(Castel-Bloom 2010, 32–33). Yet the balcony, a stage on which no audience gazes, is also the place from which she sees all that is terrifying about Dolly City. It provides the alienated Dolly with a place from which to regard the grotesque urban spectacle that, in fact, accords with the violence she enacts in her own home. It is not only a stage, but also the opposite—an observation post. Standing in the 37th floor balcony, she looks down at the city and describes its hideousness: "Dolly City lay below me in all its chaos and ugliness. Dolly City, a fragmented city, a cross-hatched city, one motherfucking city" (38). From the balcony, she notes "the trash heaps, the carcasses, the distant ships" (33). She observes the suicides who cross her line of vision as they plummet earthward from above. She sees planes and trains colliding and exploding and endless traffic jams on the ground and in the sky. But since she is situated on the thirty-seventh floor of a four-hundred-story building, Dolly's balcony cannot serve the purpose of integrating inside and outside space. Her distance from the street does not allow for any interaction with people below. While the balcony is intended to create a sense of community by blurring the distinction between private and public space, it fails to do so in *Dolly City* as in *Where Am I*, at least in a positive sense. After Dolly's mother visits her, Dolly runs to the balcony to see her emerge in the street below and suddenly feels an urge to capture her attention: "'Mother,' I screamed, 'mother, mother—' The trains rushed by at the speed of a typhoon" (24). The section break immediately following this short paragraph suggests the narrator's refusal to elaborate on this rare display of emotion unmarked by sarcasm or irony. The last sentence conveys an ominous sensation, however. The juxtaposition of the dizzyingly fast trains below with Dolly's mother, with her tranquil embroidering, her belief in homeopathic remedies like soft peaches against high blood pressure and her affection for Dolly's son, is incongruous (59). Dolly's mother's domesticity contrasts starkly against the nightmarish cityscape, but it is the trains that have the last word, invading the space of Dolly's home and mercilessly drowning out her desperate cries for her mother. In this paragraph the mechanical overtakes the human and invades the domestic, both in the form of Dolly's mother and in the space of her apartment. Rather than allowing her to utter a last word to her mother on the street, the balcony reminds her of the dominance of the machine in Dolly City.

Dolly City retains none of the pretense of collectivity or community that *Where Am I* mocks. In this novel the alienation has been transformed to wrath, and the violence always present just beneath the surface erupts mercilessly. Castel-Bloom conveys this transformation partly by her shift in setting from suburban neighborhood to urban "megalopolis," as Yigal Schwartz has called it (1995), and partly by her portrayal of places whose very function it is to isolate.

Spaces of Exclusion and the Malady of Hypersight

Castel-Bloom's representation of Israeli society in *Halakim enoshiyim* (Human parts) (2002) seems to depart radically from that in *Dolly City*. Abandoning the fantastic-grotesque style and setting that characterize *Dolly City*, Castel-Bloom allows the absurdity of life in Israel during the Al-Aqsa Intifada to speak for itself, opting for a more mimetic portrayal. Despite the marked difference in style between the two novels, they share several common themes. The alienation that finds expression on the suburban balconies of *Where Am I* reappears not only in the overmechanized society of *Dolly City* but also in the fragmented and superficially politicized Israel of *Human Parts*. Moreover, illness, either mental or physical, functions in both novels as a central metaphor for this alienation. It is therefore not surprising that some of the most prominent types of places in these two novels fall into the category of what Alison Bashford and Carolyn Strange call "places of exclusion" (2003, 10) and what Foucault terms "heterotopias of deviation" (1986).

As Edward W. Soja has argued, Foucault's writings on space and spatiality constitute a central factor in his conception of power relations and their link to knowledge (1989, 20). His analyses of the historical development of places such as mental institutions, hospitals, and prisons firmly establish the relationship between place and power as it is expressed in the interaction between the individual and a "normative" collective. Perhaps the most useful theoretical concept that Foucault provides in his discussions on space, however, is the heterotopia, discussed in chapter 1 of this book. In contrast to the intimate "interior" spaces of Bachelard, heterotopic space is social and exterior, "the space in which we live, which draws us out of ourselves," where other sites "are simultaneously represented, contested, and inverted" (1986, 23, 24). Within this spatial subcategory, Foucault distinguishes various types of heterotopia, including the one most relevant to this discussion, the "heterotopia of deviation." Heterotopias of deviation are "those in which individuals whose behavior is deviant in relation to the required mean or norm are placed. Cases of this are rest homes and psychiatric hospitals, and of course prisons, and one should perhaps add retirement homes" (25). These places, Foucault suggests, function as the sites of tension between a hegemonic norm and an individual who deviates from it. In his more detailed and developed historical studies of places such as hospitals and mental asylums, Foucault consistently reasserts this notion whereby these places entail a tension between a collective and an individual or group of individuals. He has spoken explicitly of "spaces of liberty" and "spaces of oppression," emphasizing that the power structures within places enable them to liberate or oppress (2000, 356).

Heterotopias of deviation correspond on several levels to "spaces of exclusion" and "spaces of isolation." A space of exclusion is any place that has been constructed expressly to cure, correct, protect, punish, prevent, or purify through confinement. The implicit aim is political: "Institutions of confinement, then, have long aimed both to clean up the streets, as it were, *and* to rehabilitate and normalize those confined in the interests of a hegemonic social order" (Bashford and Strange 2003, 7). This definition confirms Foucault's insistence that power relations determine the practice and policy of such places, whose purpose is to restore the social, political, or biological order violated by the deviant individual.[3] Keeping in mind

3. Though they are used more or less interchangeably by Bashford and Strange, exclusion and isolation designate acts that may be related but are not identical. The etymology of these terms gives a sense of their different nuances: The English "isolation" derives from the Latin *insula*, island; "exclusion" comes from the Latin *excludere*, from *ex-*, out, and *claudere*, to close. Isolation implies a complete detachment, a lack of contiguity with anything, while exclusion implies a relation in which one element pushes out or closes off the other. The concept of exclusion provides a better sense of the tension between two forces, the excluder and the excluded, and it also gives a nod to the in/out opposition—in the case of spaces of exclusion, the exclusion is achieved by closing *out* a person. Heterotopias

the ironic centrality of these often marginal places to the maintenance of hegemonic order, we shall see that asylums in *Dolly City* and hospitals and cemeteries in *Human Parts* function, respectively, as sites of resistance to or reflection on the alienating social order. Moreover, the tension between inside and outside reaches an ominous pitch in these texts: inside the asylum, asserting one's individuality assures its destruction; inside the hospital, the collectivity of disease and disaster abolishes one's isolation only superficially. Yet outside these places, the disintegration of the collective fails to redeem the individual, who remains powerless and isolated.

Spaces of Exclusion (1): The Asylum

It may seem obvious that asylums, quintessential "places of exclusion," exclude the people inside from the larger, outside world and also that they are generally isolated. They are often not only socially and metaphorically marginalized but also physically and geographically detached from a larger place, a town, a village, or a city. In the past, fences often marked the edges of these places, which were themselves edges. In mental asylums until the 1930s, "fences isolated the insane from the outside world, from the dangers that awaited them and from the voyeurs, but equally separated the violent and the peaceful, the trusted and the unpredictable within the asylum" (Finnane 2003, 94). Over the course of the twentieth century, the image of the asylum changed (94). The acceptance of psychiatry as a legitimate medical science, the existence of psychiatric wards in general hospitals, and changes in attitudes toward mental illness have made the mysterious, dungeon-like asylum an all but obsolete institution, a relic of classic horror films. Yet even with this relative "normalization,"

---

of deviation can be said to correspond to spaces of exclusion, though the terms themselves emphasize different elements of these places. While the latter emphasizes the response of the hegemonic force to the deviant individual, the former illuminates society's judgment of the individual as deviant. A more significant difference is that heterotopias of deviation stress the relationship between these and other, related places, and take interest in the way these places affect their relations with other places.

the asylum or the psychiatric ward exists to address a deviation from the norm of mental health. Located in a strangely contradictory metaphorical space that is simultaneously at the margins and in the center of society, the asylum isolates perceived deviation in order to eradicate it, thus ensuring the continued humming of normative social function. The asylum functions as the site for the battle between the unified and coherent reality that reigns outside and that the asylum tries to maintain, on the one hand, and a fragmented, chaotic conception of *realities,* espoused by the subversive impulses of mad characters confined in the asylum, on the other.

As Foucault insists, the heterotopia of deviation—and any other place, for that matter—does not in and of itself enact freedom or oppression. The asylum, like other places, allows for particular types and methods of interaction that reassert and strengthen existing power relations. In the prison, these relations are enacted by the prisoner and the warden; in the asylum, they are enacted by the doctor and the patient. The asylum patient and the madness that brings her to the asylum in the first place both have crucial roles within the power structure established there, a structure that upholds that of the society beyond the asylum walls. In literature, characters who question their society's assumptions rather than accepting them may find themselves incarcerated in asylums. Their quest for truth, threatening to other characters, is perceived as insanity, and the asylum, isolating and oppressive, becomes for these mad characters the place where they see the truth ever more clearly.

Dolly City relies on this familiar trope but also complicates it, leaving the questions of Dolly's madness and of "truth" itself unresolved. The line separating the insane asylum from the world outside is both confirmed and collapsed, as we note when Dolly announces that "the world [is] a hospital for the mentally ill" (2010, 94). She mentions asylums several times in the novel, always as matter-of-factly as if she were discussing a supermarket or bank (places that she never mentions). She thus creates the impression that the asylum is a definitive and familiar feature of Dolly City's vernacular landscape. It is instructive, in this light, to examine the few instances when Dolly is actually inside the asylum.

"The idea that madness can produce extraordinary insight is not a revolutionary one," notes Lillian Feder in her ambitious survey of madness in literature (1980, 281). She warns of the error of valorizing insanity as liberated truth-seeking rather than disease, and of the idealization of the asylum as a "temple of consciousness" that makes such an endeavor possible (286). Yet madness in literature, as well as its place, the asylum, function as metaphors, all the more powerful for their recognition of the intense isolation of mental illness. Barbara Tepa Lupack links madness in contemporary American literature to the individual's effort to challenge a social order that is alienating and inhumane. She observes several characteristics of literature of madness, noting these texts' "blighted backdrops and landscapes of nightmare," their messianic protagonists, and the presence of war, "a symbol for the even larger, ongoing violence in the contemporary world as well as for the destructive technologies that seek to make humanity obsolescent. . . . Underscoring the struggle of the individual against the repressive, impersonal, technological, dehumanizing forces of contemporary society, these novels suggest that insanity may be one of the few sane alternatives available in a mad world" (1995, 4–5). Against this bleak background of violence and excessive mechanization, the individual feels increasingly powerless and disconnected. Dolly City, a textbook example of such an urban wasteland, functions as a veritable incubator for Dolly's madness, as she relates: "I tried to ignore the terrible din of the metropolis, the clatter of the machines, the screeching and rattling of the traffic, which behaved as if Dolly City belonged to it. Cable cars, steam engines, express trains, ships, trams, airplanes, automobiles, trucks, motorbikes—they all crossed each other's routes, colliding with each other, freaking me out, making me frantic" (Castel-Bloom 2010, 38). Dolly's consciousness of the city's adverse effect on her mental state parallels her awareness of her own difference from others in Dolly City, and of the revolutionary potential of this difference. Describing the main political parties, Bureaucracy and Procedure, she notes: "Luckily for me, I managed to avoid falling into any of these groups—I learned to keep a low profile. I learned that the trick is simply to pretend to be asleep, and so clandestinely undermine" (78). By challenging the established social order, Dolly attempts to defy the increasing instability enacted by the city itself, which creates a din so great that it causes her to question her own perception of reality. She relates that, every time she wonders if the noise is real, "I got up to make sure. To make sure again. And again, and again. Until I was absolutely, absolutely, absolutely certain that the trains I saw down below, the colliding cars, the commotion of the modern world, were really and truly there" (51). From early in the novel, Castel-Bloom signals the destabilization of Dolly's already questionable mental state through her decreasing self-control and autonomy of action, triggered by her growing sense of uncertainty. The most obvious factor that contributes to this destabilization is Dolly City itself, a metallic, smoggy, deafening, overwhelming urban monster.

Her own perception of herself as a doctor, an identity she embraces fully and unquestioningly (whether or not she is really trained as a doctor remains ambiguous), also contributes to her rapidly deteriorating sense of autonomy. Her obsessive need for visual proof of her diagnoses constitutes her one defense against the only disease she recognizes in herself: the "disease of infinite possibilities, the determination of doubt" (Castel-Bloom 2010, 51). This line of defense itself, her sense of sight, becomes so overly developed that instead of alleviating her uncertainty it only worsens her disease, further destabilizing her.

As Foucault notes, the relationship between the doctor and the patient, or the doctor and the disease, is mediated by the gaze: "The eye becomes the depository and the source of clarity" (1994, xiii). The act of seeing, intensified in this novel, transforms Dolly from a physician, who observes symptoms to diagnose a disease, into something more like a clairvoyant, who sees disease where others cannot. For Dolly, the gaze promises a clarity that remains just out of reach, prompting ever more penetrating gazes to counteract her uncertainty. Juxtaposed with the blindness of those around her, Dolly's "hypersight" allows her to see that which remains hidden from the eyes of others. It becomes the symptom of her perceived madness.

Dolly's realization that her city is critically ill with cancer constitutes a turning point in the novel. As a doctor, she feels that she must do something to cure the city, even though she seems to be the only person able to see its tumors: "I saw cancerous growths on the blonde women's faces, on the barrels of tar, on the wheels of the buses, on the telephone poles, on the trees, on the wheels of the cars, on the newspapers—wherever I looked, malignant, terminal, spreading tumors danced before my eyes"

(Castel-Bloom 2010, 62). This section, with its remarkable emphasis on *seeing*, links Dolly's gaze explicitly to the existence of the tumors. The act of looking implicates Dolly, actively involving her in the tumors' existence. The emphasis on sight and seeing continues throughout the passage and warrants quoting at some length:

> As a doctor, I knew that it was my duty to treat these tumors, to cut them out, to do something—but I was helpless. Overcome with despair I fell to the ground and closed my eyes, which kept on wanting to open and see the truth—the metastases multiplying in front of them. For half an hour I lay there on the pavement, I could have seen under the horses' tails if only I'd opened my eyes. . . . Everything leapt up and hit me in the eyes, the metastases were taking over the world—it was their finest hour. . . . I tried everything, God is my witness that I tried to help the cellars and the wine barrels, the drunks and the cripples, the welfare coupons, the purses and the cats. They were all equal in my eyes and they were all very sick. . . . I bought myself a few chocolate cookies and sat down on a bench to finish them off. I ate with my eyes closed, in order not to see those cancerous worms again. (62–64)

Acutely aware of her role as a physician, yet unable to cope with the responsibility that it entails, Dolly closes her eyes to avoid a confrontation with the images that assault her. Like the "loquacious gaze" of Foucault's doctor, Dolly's "hypersight" allows her—and her alone—to observe "the poisonous heart of things" (Foucault 1973, xi).

In caring for her son, however, Dolly's gaze becomes more than loquacious—it becomes downright vociferous. Riddled with doubt, she trusts only her eyesight to determine his health, even buying binoculars in the hopes that "maybe I'd see something I hadn't seen before" (Castel-Bloom 2010, 75). She operates on him repeatedly and unnecessarily, opening and closing him "like a curtain" to examine him visually from the inside out: "I decided to cut him open. . . . I wanted to check and see with my own eyes that everything was really in order. . . . His internal organs were revealed to my searching gaze" (60, 31). Her obsessive concern for the boy exemplifies her loss of autonomy and her increasing desperation: "How long can you let your eyes work overtime, flipping through images until you can't see straight anymore?" she wonders (49). Controlled by her urge for certainty, she depends on her doctor's gaze—on her "treacherous eyes"—to dictate her actions and determine a reality that even she begins to question (72).

Dolly is not only a doctor. She also becomes a patient, finding herself committed to a mental asylum twice during the course of the novel. The blurring of the boundaries between these two identities, doctor and patient, in the asylum constitutes the greatest threat yet to Dolly's autonomy. She reminds her psychiatrist there of her unique situation: "I understand that these people are your patients. . . . But my case is different. Even if I am crazy—I'm not like them. I'm special, if only because of the fact that I'm a doctor myself" (Castel-Bloom 2010, 125). Yet her attempt to assert her individuality in the asylum fails. Desperate to normalize Dolly, the psychiatrist tries to convince her that she is actually *not* the doctor she claims to be. In this asylum, the psychiatrist diffuses rebellion by persuading aberrant individuals that nothing is wrong. When Dolly tries to assert her individuality in this insistently conformist space, her psychiatrist immediately strikes down this attempt. For the first time, Dolly is subjected, as a patient, to the probing gaze of a doctor who tries to root out the threat of her refusal to conform and to realign her within the existing social order.

Despite the psychiatrist's friendly banter with Dolly and despite the patients' interaction with one another, Castel-Bloom reminds us how ominously exclusionary this place is when Dolly's son leaves: "He ran out of the ward, rang the bell, the armored door opened, and for a split second a few sunbeams filtered in" (Castel-Bloom 2010, 125). Inside, she is separated not only from the outside world by the walls and doors, but also from the other patients. Locked away in a guarded, sunless place, Dolly must cope with the denial of her very identity as a doctor, her only certainty.

The first time Dolly is placed in an asylum, she escapes, asserting that "the role of loony bins in the world [is] to provide something to run away from" (Castel-Bloom 2010, 62). Later, she castrates a misogynistic psychiatrist who had institutionalized her, prompting him to jump out of a window to his death. The second time she finds herself in a mental hospital, she unwittingly undergoes treatment. Her arrival at the asylum seems spurred by a murder she has just committed, but the psychiatrist who evaluates her never refers to this or to Dolly's many other acts of violence. Rather, she desperately tries to convince Dolly that she must acknowledge that she is not really a doctor and that she does not really think the world is infected by cancerous tumors. Dolly, too, attributes her confinement in the asylum to the fact that she sees cancerous tumors on all her surroundings, rather than to the violent manner in which she has tried to eradicate them: "What have you done to me? Why did you clean the metastases out of my eyes?" she asks desperately (126). Dolly poses a danger to society not because of her violent acts, which align with the norm of Dolly City as a whole, but because she alone insists that her society needs to be cured of a potentially fatal illness. Her certainty that cancerous tumors cover her surroundings, her determination to cure the world of cancer, her desire to *fix* the world, all threaten the order, or disorder, of things outside. She is confined in an asylum until she accepts that everything she considers objective truth is only an illusion. The asylum aims to reduce Dolly's "disease of infinite possibilities" to just one possibility, only one reality, in which Dolly City, and, by extension, Dolly, is perfectly healthy.

Dolly clearly considers her "cure," the restoration to normalcy that renders her no longer able to see the tumors around her, a cause for frustration. Upon waking up in the asylum and realizing that "they'd done something to [her]," she is "horrified to feel a very sharp stab of sorrow" (Castel-Bloom 2010, 123). She has lost her ability to see clearly. This loss, because of the important role of seeing in Dolly's practice of medicine, supports her psychiatrist's efforts to convince her that she is not a doctor; the loss of her "hypersight" equals the loss of her identity as a doctor and as the one who has diagnosed her society's disease. At the same time that Dolly loses the trait that made her a doctor, that reality is assaulted by the psychiatrist in the asylum, who asks her, "Tell me, are you still convinced that you're a doctor who studied in Katmandu?" (127). Dolly, on the brink of losing her own identity, resists this loss by slyly switching roles with the psychiatrist. Rather than answering the questions that the psychiatrist poses to her, she begins to question the psychiatrist, evoking the latter's desperation by announcing, "I think I can confidently say that you're completely normal" (128). She refuses to relinquish her identity as doctor, reasserting it by turning the psychiatrist into the patient and suggesting that it is the psychiatrist whose normalcy should be questioned.

Dolly's hypersight provokes revolutionary impulses that threaten the social order; the asylum attempts to safeguard this order by eliminating her heightened sense of vision, thus silencing the "loquacious" doctor's gaze that drives her to act against disease. She manages to resist this forced blinding by upending the prescribed power hierarchy of the asylum and reasserting herself as a doctor rather than as a patient. Despite its ultimate failure, this act constitutes an attempt at resistance, at reaffirming Dolly's identity, and, on a larger scale, at insisting that her society remains ill.

Other examples of spaces of exclusion in *Dolly City* confirm the notion of such places as sites of resistance. Whether a women's prison, a German orphanage, or a battered children's shelter, spaces that exclude and isolate certain people for their own or for others' protection display the hypocrisy and injustice of their society. The ubiquity of these types of spaces (particularly the "many insane asylums," as Dolly points out [Castel-Bloom 2010, 151–52]) in Dolly City suggests that the hegemonic power is threatened by the very society it claims to represent. In Dolly City, the deviant *is* the norm, and any attempt to articulate or challenge the situation is thwarted. The psychiatrist in Dolly's asylum disputes everything she is certain about, from the tumors blighting her surroundings to her personal history and identity. This challenge reconfigures Dolly's very relationship to her society: If she is not a doctor and Dolly City is not ill, then what is her role there? Released from the asylum presumably because she submits to her psychiatrist's impatience—"Enough with the bullshit already"—she does not seem to have internalized the psychiatrist's lectures on the health of her surroundings (128). Immediately upon her release, she wanders in the "indifferent streets" of the city; shortly thereafter, the French air force attacks Israel, raising to new levels the violence and chaos in Dolly City, and giving Dolly, who works in a war hospital, a new sense of purpose.

Dolly's resistance against the hegemonic social order enforced by the asylum is subtle. Yet, in this novel, it is not only Dolly's experience in the asylum but also the fact that there are *so many* asylums in Dolly City that designate it as a site of resistance in that "blighted landscape." The more insistently unified and homogeneous the society, the more places of exclusion it needs to safeguard its dominance. Accordingly, the novel's end finds Dolly hospitalized, at age 45, in a "shelter for the elderly" (Castel-Bloom 2010, 157).

Dolly City designates not only Israel but also a more general conception of modern society. Certain elements of the place, however, do refer specifically to Israel and to recognizably Israeli institutions and places. It is generally accepted that Castel-Bloom's critique of Israel is no less than scathing in this novel, yet this understanding is based on her representation of Dolly City itself. As we have seen, though, it is not just the nightmarish city that reflects the failures and fissures of Israeli society, but also the places created within this landscape to counter those who would defy it, change it, or simply succumb to its horrors. Unwittingly, these places intensify their patients' alienation from society, making it more tangible than ever and driving their will to resist it.

Spaces of Exclusion (2): The Hospital

Much as the asylum is the space in which the hegemonic order attempts to maintain itself and stifle rebellion in *Dolly City*, in *Human Parts* the hospital and the cemetery create a purported collectivity that ultimately reflects the hypocrisy and superficiality of this order. Early in the novel, Castel-Bloom acknowledges these two places as crucial vernacular sites in the new geography of a terrified yet benumbed Israel: "In the cemeteries they began to bury the corpses one on top of the other, and the undertakers worked day and night digging graves in the ground or building them above it. . . . The doctors and nurses stayed at the hospitals around the clock on emergency shifts and they hardly had time to rest" (2003, 24). In a novel so concerned with the arbitrary nature of death and dying, it is not surprising that the setting shifts so frequently to these two types of places. Yet they acquire an additional symbolic value here. The hospital is not just the place where people are cured or die. It is also the place that brings people together either in the common experience of the mysterious Saudi flu or in the aftermath of the shared shock of a terror attack. Moreover, it erases the social and economic boundaries that figure so prominently elsewhere in the novel. The wealthy Liat Dubnov must sleep in the corridor of the crowded hospital for several days until a room becomes available, even while she dreams of her luxurious apartment.

The structure of the hospital itself as it is described in the novel is worth noting. After hearing the details of Liat's death, Adir, her brother, tries to find his way out of the hospital. He

> walked out of the ward, went down in the elevator, left the old build-ing, and entered the various wings of the Suoraski Medical Center. He became increasingly lost in the long corridors of this labyrinthine hospi-tal, to which more and more wings had been added over the years, above ground and below ground, some of them finished and others still being built. . . . [He] continued to wander into all kinds of wards and depart-ments, from observation to hospitalization, from in-patients to outpa-tients, from Wing 3 to Wing 2. At last he asked a nurse who walked past him how to get to the parking lot. . . . In the parking lot he forgot if he was parked on lower level two or lower level three. . . . He found his car at the entrance to lower level four and started the engine. (Castel-Bloom 2003, 40–41)

A Kafkaesque array of bureaucratic layers and divisions, the hospital dis-orients physically as well as emotionally. Its cold, impersonal nature, its constant flux and growth, its sheer size—all these qualities make the hos-pital seem oppressive. Yet it also reassures the characters: when Adir fears that a bomb might have exploded in the café where his girlfriend Tasaro is meeting a friend, Liat calms him, saying, "where would they bring the wounded if not here" (Castel-Bloom 2003, 28). Despite the undertone of Castel-Bloomian sarcasm in this statement, it is true. People die in hospi-tals, but they are also cured there. In the novel, Liat dies in the hospital, but other characters leave after a period of hospitalization. The hospital's ability to be at once terrifying and reassuring, dangerous and safe, the place of disease and the place of cure, reflects the contradictory nature that Foucault attributes to heterotopias.

Although the hospital, being the place where people are whisked to safety after being diagnosed with illness or surviving a terror attack, cre-ates an atmosphere of security, it necessarily requires its patients to relin-quish a measure of their freedom. Foucault considers the modern hospital a space of isolation, replacing the crowds that used to populate such institutions with "a collection of separated individualities" (1995, 201). The hospital can be an inhospitable place for an ill person. In *The Birth of the Clinic*, Foucault writes that "[the disease] must not be fixed in a medically prepared domain, but be allowed, in the positive sense of the term, to 'vegetate' in its original soil: the family, a social space conceived in its most natural, most primitive, most morally secure form" (1994, 18). The home, the place where the family lives, is the "original soil" to which Foucault refers. The last day of Liat's life, spent in her hospital bed, is marked by intense loneliness. Of course, it is not surprising that the hospital, a place of disease and dying, makes people feel uncomfortable and frightened. As Foucault asks, "Can one efface the unfortunate impression that the sight of these places, which for many are nothing more than 'temples of death,' will have on a sick man or woman, removed from the familiar surroundings of his home and family?" (15). Liat, as is expected, misses her home and experiences the "loneliness in a crowd" to which Foucault refers. Yet there is a peculiar quality to her longing. She imagines herself in bed in her beloved apartment, "taking refuge inside herself, and simply sleeping, next to the wall, hiding from the world, and not caring about anything" (Castel-Bloom 2003, 30). Later, the narrator reveals that "[Liat] never set foot outside her apartment except to go to her therapist and to the health club. . . . The rest of the time she stayed with her books, her dictionaries, and her crumbling calendars" (44). Clearly, at home, in her "original soil," she is isolated too, surrounded by words and text, not by family and friends. Adir remembers that she "lived like a recluse, for days on end she didn't answer the phone, and above all she liked being alone, with her books, in the apartment on Amos Street" (75). That Liat is "single on principle" is the first thing we learn about her, after her hair and eye color. As other characters recall her "narcissism and snobbishness" (55), the feelings of superiority she harbored and the distance she maintained from her peers become readily apparent. Her wealth and the luxurious lifestyle it affords her set her apart from the other characters and from the majority of Israelis, a distinction she embraces and flaunts. The hospital does not create her loneliness; it reveals it. Ironically, then, it is the forced nature of the hospital's collectivity that makes her feel lonely, because she has become one of many: one of many patients, no longer autonomous but dependent on the doctors and nurses and the functioning of the hospital as a whole for her well-being.

In a separate episode, another character, Liat's childhood friend Iris Ventura, must rush her daughter to the emergency room for fear that she has contracted the Saudi flu that has killed Liat. As she waits in the hospital for her daughter's condition to stabilize, "Iris felt very lonely. . . . She felt as if she was at the nadir of loneliness, a solitary soul in a wasteland of herself" (Castel-Bloom 2003, 120). Despite her personal circumstances, which are very different from Liat's, Iris's time in the hospital evokes a similar "loneliness in a crowd," forcing her to confront her reality in an alien, threatening space far from the familiarity and distractions of home. It is important to note the relative rareness of such overt declarations of naked emotion in Castel-Bloom's prose.

As Foucault asserts, then, the displacement from one's home to the potentially fatal space of the hospital can be traumatic. Yet, while he relates this to the removal from one's natural and organic place, the implication in this novel is that the hospital is the place of truth, a "temple of consciousness," to adopt the term Lillian Feder uses in the context of asylums. The many distractions of one's familiar settings—Liat's calendars, Iris's financial woes—lose their significance in the space of the hospital, which levels and equalizes those within it, whittling their concerns and thoughts to the very basic and primary one of survival. Since the hospital affords no place for the truth to hide, loneliness emerges unhindered. In this novel in particular, which strives for a more realistic portrayal than any of Castel-Bloom's previous novels, and which depicts Israeli society at a time of great crisis, the hollowness of the collectivity and unity deemed so important to national survival signals fatigue. Even though it takes place during the Intifada, this novel is concerned, first and foremost, with internal Israeli issues—racism, prejudice, hypocrisy, and poverty within Israel. These divisions, which continue to afflict Israelis even during times of great external political and natural disasters, affect those throughout the socioeconomic spectrum. By providing a space of equalization, the hospital momentarily does away with those divisions, only to reveal the loneliness at the core of these people's existence in the times when they most need genuine human interaction.

Spaces of Exclusion (3): The Cemetery

In his essay on heterotopias, Foucault lingers on the cemetery, "certainly a place unlike ordinary cultural spaces," noting that the nineteenth century brought with it "the individualization of death" and the corresponding idea that "everyone has a right to her or his own little box for her or his own little personal decay" (1986, 25). Accompanying this "individualization," however, was the fear of death as disease, a fear that extended to the geographical location of the cemetery itself and brought about the shift of cemeteries from the center of cities to their edges: "The cemeteries then came to constitute, no longer the sacred and immortal heart of the city, but the other city, where each family possesses its dark resting place" (25). Though Foucault is discussing Christian European cemeteries, his observations illuminate the strange paradox of the cemetery as simultaneously a marginal and a central component of the community that it serves.

Cemeteries in Israel are maintained by the religious authorities and function according to *halakha*, Jewish law, which stipulates that cemeteries must be surrounded by a fence; they may contain only Jews; and women and men can be buried in adjacent plots only if they were related or married. One significant feature of Jewish cemeteries that has been retained in Israel, and which has garnered much public attention, is the surrounding fence. The Jewish cemetery, located at the border, just outside the city, also creates a border of its own. The fence symbolically embraces those buried within the cemetery and shuns those who, according to *halakha*, cannot be buried there. The significance of the cemetery fence is manifested in Hebrew parlance and in practice. For instance, someone who is "*me-'ever la-gader*," or on the other side of the fence (from the perspective of the living), is someone who has died. On the other hand, someone who is buried outside the cemetery fence or wall is someone who has committed an act at odds with *halakha*. An instance of such an act is suicide. In the Israeli context, the practice of burying non-Jews outside the cemetery fence has instigated uproars when fallen Russian Israeli Defense Force (IDF) soldiers were refused burial within the cemetery walls since their status as Jews was questioned.[4] In the eyes of the Israeli public, the implication of burying someone outside the cemetery walls is clear: it constitutes a rejection of that person from the community, which is deemed eternal. The Russian soldiers' cases garnered so much media and public attention because they had fallen while fighting for Israel. As many Israelis considered them to have made the ultimate sacrifice for the state, they believed that the religious question of their Judaism was secondary or could be waived in light of the circumstances of their death, which superseded the question of birth to determine whether or not they were really part of the Israeli collective. That is, their Judaism is not as important as the fact that they sacrificed their life for Israel; *that,* not the traditional religious community, is the relevant collective. As the circumstance of their death determines the fallen soldiers' Israeli identity, this identity must be acknowledged through burial within the cemetery walls.

Nationalist ideology (or exclusion from it) is expressed not only in terms of the cemetery's organization and borders, but also in the behavior of the mourners while in the cemetery. In her book on mourning in Hebrew literature, Hannah Naveh writes that in the prestate and early statehood periods, a restrained manner of mourning was considered to contribute to a culture antithetical to that of the Jewish Diaspora: "This official [mourning] pattern culturally marginalized ethnic mourning customs, particularly those that originated in Eastern lands [*artsot ha-mizrah*], but also those that originated in Eastern Europe and which were considered especially 'diasporic'" (1993, 147). Naveh points out that the customs practiced by communities that failed to fully assimilate into Israeli culture and society were more likely to have survived, generally evoking disdain from those who had assimilated and adopted the "stoic," distinctly masculine mode of Israeli mourning (147). The institutionalized rejection of traditional Judaic forms of mourning in favor of new, distinctly

4. For more on the controversy surrounding the question of non-Jewish Russian Israelis and their burial as fallen soldiers, see Siegel 1998, 61–63.

Israeli ones transformed the Jewish cemetery in Israel into a site of cultural homogenization.

In the context of collective versus individual identity, the term *kever yisrael*, usually translated as Jewish burial, reflects an interesting duality. *Kever yisrael* contains two main components: first, the cemetery must be a Jewish cemetery, meaning that Jews and gentiles do not share the same burial space; and second, the deceased owns his grave. The obligation to maintain a collective Jewish identity does not preclude—and indeed is *balanced* by—the necessity of individual ownership, a phenomenon traced back to Abraham's purchase of the burial cave of Makhpela, the Cave of the Patriarchs.

The Israeli cemetery has had to find ways to adopt certain characteristics of Jewish cemeteries while maintaining its own commitment to secular democratic values. Maoz Azaryahu and Yoram Bar-Gal have written about what they call "Zionist cemeteries," a category in which they include kibbutz and military cemeteries as particular examples of cemeteries where the tension between the collective and the individual determines everything from the planning and design of the layout to the shape and size of the gravestones themselves (1997). They write about cemeteries in general that they are "sacred spaces" and "hallowed premises" (105). Israeli military cemeteries, they assert, are "sacred sites of patriotic Israeli culture" (106). This conflation of the religious and the national suggests that the cemetery, poised between these two realms, is a liminal space, as Adam Newton notes in his discussion of cemeteries in *The Elsewhere* (2005). Azaryahu and Bar-Gal write: "As hallowed premises, the cemetery lies outside of the realm of the mundane, yet it is firmly incorporated into societal space and temporal rhythms of the community" (1997, 105). That is, the space of the cemetery itself is sacred and secular simultaneously, much as it is both central and marginal, individual and collective. These seeming contradictions support Foucault's assertion of the cemetery as a heterotopia, confirming his characterization of it as a contradictory space that is in relation with all other spaces at the same time that it resists them. Unfortunately Azaryahu and Bar-Gal do not offer a clear definition of "Zionist cemetery" or a distinction between Zionist and Israeli cemeteries. Instead, they announce the kibbutz cemetery and the military cemetery as "quintessential Zionist cemeteries" (106). Their main concern is the discord between socialism and Judaism in the kibbutz cemetery and nationalism and Judaism in the military cemetery, which they relate to the tension between the individual and the collective in these spaces. "The kibbutz cemetery and its gravestones," they write, "may be termed the meeting place between collective values and those that belong to the individual, the personal plane" (113). For them, the individual aligns with Judaism and the collective with the secular in Israeli cemeteries.

Strangely, they write in the same article that the Zionist cemetery is a "landscape of equality" (Azaryahu and Bar-Gal 1997, 122) at the same time acknowledging that, because nonkibbutz cemeteries in Israel function according to Jewish law, "the location of the grave was an essential means of exclusion" of non-Jews (120). For them, the kibbutz's removal of religious constraints from the practice of burial reflects the egalitarian ideals of the kibbutz, and the fact that military cemeteries abide by Jewish burial law makes them inherently unequal. Yet the myth of kibbutz egalitarianism has been widely contested by women, Mizrahim, and Israeli Arabs, and the inequality that they argue existed in kibbutzim is reflected in the kibbutz graveyard as well. Meir Shalev's novel *Roman rusi* (Russian novel/affair; translated as *The Blue Mountain*) (1988) hinges on a narrative in which a young orphan on a cooperative settlement defies its ideology by growing rich off the adjacent cemetery, in which anyone with enough money to buy a plot can be buried. The elders fume, considering his act a desecration of their values, which are revealed to be nothing if not exclusionary. They want only members of the cooperative to be allowed in its cemetery. Like the other spaces in this section, the cemetery actively instigates a sense of belonging or exclusion not only for the dead but also for the living. A space that is supposed to cultivate a sense of collectivity amongst Israeli Jews (partly through the exclusion of those who do not fit in ethnic, religious, national, or cultural terms), it ultimately heightens the alienation and social detachment of its visitors.

The importance of the cemetery in cultivating a sense of collectivity in Israel, however, is not limited to the kibbutz cemetery's reflection of socialist egalitarian values or to the military cemetery's insistent uniformity and solemn ceremony. In her writing about the Old Cemetery of

Tel Aviv, Barbara Mann notes that the death of a single individual was understood as a collective experience.[5] Her examples, famous political and literary figures, were men who helped to create the sense of a collective national Hebrew culture in prestate Palestine and in the early years of Israeli statehood.[6] Their deaths, like their lives, were potently symbolic. At a time when the future of this collective was so tenuous, suggests Mann, these figures' deaths were experienced by the entire community, bringing it together in collective mourning not only for the figure himself but also for his accomplishments and contributions to the community as a whole.

Several decades later, the Israelis of *Human Parts* continue to experience death collectively, reflecting the unnerving fragility of their future. This sense of instability and uncertainty creates a morbid hierarchy of death, determined by the value of an individual's death in terms of the collective. Thus Adir, trying to compose his sister's death notice, laments that she died of the Saudi flu and not of a terror attack, which would have allowed him to write a more passionate and dramatic announcement (Castel-Bloom 2003, 42). Liat herself, after finally checking into the hospital, continues to feel "like a second-class patient compared to the victims of the terror attacks," wasting the nation's resources on herself when terror victims surround her (30). Adir busies himself "checking attendance" at her funeral and, dismayed at the small number of mourners, resigns himself to "a quiet, intimate funeral" that reflects her self-involvement in life (76). At each ceremonial gathering after Liat's death, fewer people show up. The funeral in this novel is a patently political event, as is evident from the president's role in the novel: after each terror attack, he visits wounded survivors in the hospital and consoles bereaved families at the cemetery, finally collapsing and requiring hospitalization

5. See Mann 2006, chapter 2: "The Zionist Uncanny: Reading the Old Cemetery on Trumpeldor."

6. Mann writes: "The Trumpeldor Cemetery therefore has a unique relation to modern Hebrew culture's historical attempts to be 'at home' in Palestine, being the resting place of key figures in early Hebrew culture, including Max Nordau, Ch. N. Bialik, Ahad Ha'am, and Meir Dizengoff. It is, in other words, a virtual mapping of modern Hebrew culture" (2006, 34).

himself. Those who die in a terror attack become national heroes, martyrs who have made the ultimate sacrifice for the state and therefore are honored ceremoniously in the presence of state officials, much like fallen soldiers. Issues that are not connected with national security, such as poverty and disease, take a backseat to the terror attacks, against which the populace feels helpless and around which it rallies. In other words, the experience in Mann's Old Cemetery was a response to the uncertainty of the community's future through its shared cultural sensibility, whereas in the cemetery of *Human Parts* characters respond to a similar uncertainty through a shared sense of victimization.

The scenes that take place in the cemetery demonstrate the impoverishment of a collectivity that tries to sustain itself through shared fear and shared tragedy. Castel-Bloom in effect desanctifies the space of the cemetery and the ceremony of the burial. At Liat's graveside, Iris's cell phone rings suddenly to the tune of "Diva," the Israeli pop song that won the Eurovision song contest. As she digs through her bag to silence the phone, she looks at the outraged mourners: "They all looked so holy to her with the skullcaps on their heads, some of them made of cardboard" (2003, 81). Following this sarcastic observation, she flees to another gravesite, her hand in her bag, and draws the attention of a security guard at an adjacent funeral, who orders her to empty her bag and put her hands up: "This is a high security area," he tells her (83). Later in the service, she declares tearfully that Liat was "pure gold," a sentiment that contradicts her earlier feelings about Liat. The gravitas of the cemetery, a space whose secular holiness is confirmed by the presence of the president and other officials and by its role as the final resting place for Israel's martyrs, is deflated through sarcasm and the display of hypocrisy.

The cemetery is, to use Foucault's words, a "strange heterotopia" because it is at once individuated and collective, a space in which the individual dead are separately compartmentalized and marked but that is "connected with all the sites of the city, state or society or village, etc., since each individual, each family has relatives in the cemetery" (1986, 25). The cemetery is a touchstone for the members of a community, a shared space that, like the hospital, equalizes the unequal in their shared and insoluble awareness of the inevitability of death. Finally, its fence makes the final determination of belonging, eternally banishing those outside the collective and embracing those within it.

The City and the Irrelevance of Boundaries

Orly Castel-Bloom's spatialization of social and political relations is perhaps most pronounced in her depiction of urban spaces in Israel. The cities in *Dolly City* and *Human Parts* not only reflect but actively engender the deep rifts in Israeli society. Their own disunity contrasts against the modernist Zionist conception that space serves a particular ideological function, specifically, the creation of a sense of belonging. By turns spaces of alienation, indifference, wrath, and disintegration, these cities clearly have a role greater than the setting for the misadventures of her heroines. The most striking feature of Castel-Bloom's representations of the city in these novels is the rejection of standard boundaries and categorizations. From the performance of alienation on the balcony and the forced exclusion in heterotopias of deviation, we move now to the city and to the various levels of disunity it exposes and, more crucially, *creates* within Israeli society. These disunities, the result of a sustained rejection of the most fundamental attributes of urban space, react against the limitations of the Zionist conception of space but stop short of actually suggesting an alternative.

Dolly City, perhaps the most fascinating city in Hebrew literature, contains all the elements of modernist cities. Technologically advanced, crowded, and polluted, it causes the heroine, Dolly, to feel anonymous and alienated. "Sometimes," she reflects, "even in Dolly City, I feel like a stranger. I look at the traffic jams, I listen to the ding-dong of the big clock tower, the gong of the Chinese restaurant, but in spite of it all I begin to tremble, I want to go home—even though this is my home" (Castel-Bloom 2010, 32–33). A few pages later she relates that "from time to time various pieces of furniture would fly out of the skyscraper windows, and sometimes my line of longitude would be crossed by suicides whose screams were swallowed up in the terrific noise of the trains and cars and airplanes" (35). Clearly, the alienation of Dolly and others in Dolly City is directly related to the city's overwhelming technology, in typical modernist fashion. Dolly's wrath, too, points to a rational moral or ethical framework that organizes her conception of how the world is and how the world ought to be. Far from being an indifferent speck floating in a moral wasteland, Dolly is opinionated and often enraged. Her determination is channeled into several missions: uncovering the Pan-T Airline conspiracy that resulted in her father's death; protecting her son; and healing Dolly City of cancer. Despite the sarcastic undertone that characterizes what seem to be her most honest revelations, Dolly's teleological endeavors, along with the wrath that often accompanies them, suggest a distinctly modernist conception of the world that demands moral edification and yearns for a reality that is less bleak and lonely.

However, these features of Dolly City do not account for the overwhelming evidence that Dolly City is also the ultimate postmodern space. Grotesquely mechanized, allowing impossible simultaneities, and promulgating constant motion, Dolly City represents anything but rational planning. David Harvey articulates the difference between modern and postmodern urban design in terms of the distinction between a unified, teleological conception of the purpose of the city and a disjointed, purely aesthetic one. Whereas modernism espouses "technologically rational and efficient urban *plans*," he writes, "postmodernism cultivates, instead, a conception of the urban fabric as necessarily fragmented" (1990, 66). Dolly City is postmodern in its constitution of modernism to the extreme. The fragmentation of Dolly City exemplifies modern planning that has spun out of control and is at its most dysfunctional. The technological presence is inefficient because there is simply too much of it: "Cable cars, steam engines, express trains, ships, trams, airplanes, automobiles, trucks, motorbikes—they all crossed each other's routes, colliding with each other" (Castel-Bloom 2010, 38). History loses significance in this lumping together of technologies like the steam engine, associated with the Industrial Revolution, and the airplane, an invention of the twentieth century. The result is chaos, an urban space that amalgamates the various stages of the city's development, as represented by its vehicles. This incongruity represents a temporal montage that complements the city's geographical duplications: if there is a Henrietta Szold Street in Tel Aviv, there will be one in Dolly City as well; if there is a Gare Saint-Lazare in Paris, there will be one in Dolly City too (93). This urban monstrosity has developed beyond efficiency; its means have subsumed its ends. Similarly, the main political parties' infrastructure has taken over the issues, as is clear from their names, Bureaucracy and Procedure. These standard components of typical modernist portrayals of the city—bureaucracy, mass transportation, fragmentation—typically lead to one of two reactions on the part of the modernist hero, as Robert Alter has shown: anxiety or exultation (Alter 2005, 111). Dolly, however, decidedly unexultant, exceeds anxiety in her aggressive reaction to the city. After a period of violent anger, she becomes apathetic, abandoning her quest to heal the city: "I no longer felt the urge to open [it] up and take it out before it spread. I said to myself: Honey, just drop it" (Castel-Bloom 2010, 107). Walking through the city, Dolly continues to see its tumors, but they no longer arouse any kind of emotion. She walks listlessly, the ultimate anti-*flaneûse*, apathetic to her surroundings, which, in turn, are apathetic to her. In an overtly mirroring moment, Dolly describes "the ploughed streets of Dolly City, . . . the indifferent streets, . . . the fountains pissing in an arc" (131). She decides to urinate into the "pissing" fountain, thereby contributing her own indifference to that of the city. She no longer laments her inability to remove the city's tumors, and, while she still recognizes the city's illness, she feels no urge to heal it nor does she offer or seek any other alternative. Whereas she had previously epitomized the mad figure in Munch's famous painting, she has become its hollow imitation, blasé even on the verge of suicide: "I opened my mouth like in *The Scream* by Munch" (155).

The mixture of modernist and postmodernist characteristics in *Dolly City* is consistent with postmodernism, which, by its very definition, includes juxtapositions of different and even contradictory elements. The postmodern aesthetic, John Docker writes, is "inclusive, contradictory, extravagant, excessive" (1994, 88). He observes this tendency in postmodern architecture, which "freely includes the modernist as one of its possible elements and perspectives" (87). Dolly exudes a clearly modernist anger about the state of the world, but she does so without supporting a specific hierarchy of values, positioning Dolly City squarely on the seam between modernism and postmodernism.

Dolly City resists other, less abstract boundaries as well. Castel-Bloom deconstructs the border between public and private space, notably between the street and the home. Dolly relates that her high-rise apartment was designed by a Bedouin architect "who'd possessed a tremendous sense of space" (2010, 35). Bedouin, nomads who inhabit temporary desert dwellings, do not conceive of home as enclosed, rooted, and static. This presumably effects a distinct understanding of space more generally, on which Castel-Bloom capitalizes using irony: the open nonurban space with which the Bedouin is most familiar is literally out of place in a high-rise apartment in the middle of the city. The very idea of a sense of space in Dolly City seems ridiculous. Without romanticizing the rural or pastoral way of life, Dolly's ironic observation suggests that all the familiar spatial categories have been shuffled and reconfigured in Dolly City, a place where Bedouin design skyscraper apartments and imbue their tiny interiors with a "sense of space" that exists only as a myth in this urban crunch.

The boundary between home and street collapses with finality when Dolly comes home to find that a clan of Kurdish refugees has occupied her apartment. Rather than exploding at this invasion, she asks with uncharacteristic politeness to be allowed into her own home: "'Excuse me,' I said, 'many years ago I used to live here. Can I just come in for a minute and look around? Thank you so much'" (Castel-Bloom 2010, 68). She enters and observes that "the Kurds were sitting in the Jacuzzi and using my shampoo" (68). Having explained that "everybody in Dolly City knows that you can't argue with the Gypsy or the Kurdish refugees or with Asians either," Dolly does not try to eject the refugees from her apartment. Their occupation of her apartment suggests an ironic inversion of the Israeli displacement of Palestinians and the occupation of Palestinian lands. In occupying her home, the refugees bring the street into the home and Dolly out to the street, which becomes her home. The public and the private lose their distinction, and the emplacement of the refugees inevitably enacts the displacement of Dolly. "So—we found ourselves in the streets, me and the child. We slept, like most of the homeless, in filthy niches, in buses, in abandoned train coaches" (78). Her forced exile leaves Dolly closer to the city than ever, sleeping in its crevices and occupying its trash heaps. Having descended from her four-hundred-story skyscraper, Dolly finds herself scraping the earth of Dolly City.

The interchanging or inversion of standard conceptions of home and street, inside and outside, private and public is accompanied by the reconfiguration of physical conventions of the city. Dolly City's phantasmagoric geography plays on existing urban norms but exaggerates or decontextualizes them to the point of grotesquerie. Geographically, the city itself comprises all the streets of all the cities of the world. Yet, while Dolly makes clear that the city is part of Israel and contains elements of Tel Aviv, she distinguishes it from this most urban of Israeli cities. When her mother dies, Dolly wryly reports, she leaves half her property to Dolly's son, "on condition that he didn't, on any account, live in Dolly City, but only in Tel Aviv" (Castel-Bloom 2010, 139). In its fragmented simultaneity, Dolly City incorporates several key elements of postmodern urban space, most notably simulation and pastiche.[7]

In addition to these characteristics, though, Castel-Bloom imbues Dolly City's geography with the fantastic. Looking down at these places with which she is presumably familiar, Dolly experiences Certeau's transformation into a "solar Eye, looking down like a god" at New York (1984, 92). She scrutinizes the map of Dolly City late in the novel, marveling, "for the first time in my life, I looked down on things from above" (Castel-Bloom 2010, 120). Strikingly, she sees not the city's streets, not its buildings, not its roads, but its "Wells of Despair," "Lakes of Fear," and "Swamps of Boredom" (121). This peculiar cartography, whereby the landmarks of Dolly City are defined not by its *physical* geography but by its *psychological* geography, offers a different conception of place than the one that typically establishes spatial contours, laying bare the irrelevance of the norms of recorded spatial configurations and confirming that what matters is how Dolly sees the place, not how the place *purportedly is*.

Of course, the most infamous instance of fantastic cartography in this novel is not limited to Dolly City but encompasses the Land of Israel in its entirety, which Dolly carves in the flesh of her son's back. The map itself is a more or less accurate rendition of the biblical Land of Israel,

---

7. For more on simulation, see Baudrillard 1994. For a critical examination of postmodern pastiche, see Jameson 1991.

including "all those Philistine towns like Gath and Ashkelon," the Sea of Galilee, the Jordan River, the Dead Sea, Lebanon, the Jordan Valley, Kiryat Shmoneh in the North and Arad in the South (Castel-Bloom 2010, 37, 98). The map, though originally carved by Dolly to reflect her own political leanings as well as her sovereignty over her son, surprises her by reverting to the 1967 borders, defying her control and, like the map of Dolly City, indicating the absurdity of spatial representation. Nevertheless, all the places that Dolly includes in her living map are real and recognizable, unlike the places on the map of Dolly City, which are rendered in the language of fairy tales and imbue the place with more than the standard postmodern fare of simulation or imitation. Yet the city itself, like Dolly's Israel, also includes Henrietta Szold Street, Gare Saint-Lazare, and presumably every other street and place. This disconcerting and disorienting mix of pure simulation on the one hand and pure invention on the other is another example of how this novel defies conventions of fictional representations of the city by refusing to choose between fact or fantasy, re-creation or creation. The bizarre climate and progression of time in Dolly City add to its perplexing geography. "It was August, snow was falling softly," Dolly reports, and hops into a taxi to Ben Gurion airport, where "the sun beat down . . . with calm tyranny" (29). Later she relates that "Another April came to an end, the fifth in succession, and February arrived" (111). These climatic and temporal details reinforce the strong undercurrent of fantasy that informs the representation of Dolly City and that is juxtaposed alongside its familiar and recognizable components.

The neighborhoods and quarters of Dolly City are notable for their perverse functionality and amplified urban decay. The Jewish ghetto of European cities becomes in Dolly City an anti-anti-Semitic quarter, "where the holocaust survivors crucify a different goy every day" (Castel-Bloom 2010, 97). Lillienblum Street boasts a black market where men stand around engaging in shady activities: "They've all got $-shaped, crooked mouths from all the times they've hissed the black market rate of the dollar out of the corner of their mouths" (108). The way to the sea is lined with "garish prostitutes" (13).

The only place in Dolly City that contrasts with this distinctly and exaggeratedly urban setting is the abandoned building at the edge of town where Dolly befriends a caricatured Zionist pioneer named Gordon. He grows organic vegetables in a sad little garden there and in other places in Dolly City. He spends six months wandering through Dolly City with Dolly before he decides to leave. "'Dolly City,' he said, 'is not a place to put down roots or start a farm. It's not a place. It's an ugly, disgusting, stinking, filthy, boring, depressing town'" (88). Despite Dolly's unhappiness, and though she agrees with him that "Dolly City was indeed one big grave," she describes herself as "overcome by melancholy" by his decision to leave (88). Dolly's experience with Gordon, who subscribes to the fundamental ideals of Labor Zionism, provides her with some reprieve from the cold urbanity of the city. Yet, though Gordon's interests are in the land, their setting is not pastoral or rural, but still inescapably urban, a fact that assures their failure. Despite their isolation, he and Dolly are still in Dolly City. His garden is makeshift, and their lives, Dolly pointedly repeats, are miserable. As soon as he leaves, Dolly returns into the thick of Dolly City. The contrast between the urban and the agricultural here exists only theoretically. The retreat is fleeting because it cannot be grounded, or "rooted," to use one of Gordon's favorite terms, in the proper place.

Castel-Bloom's rejection of boundaries in this novel is most striking in her depiction of the relations between people and place. Gordon, eager to merge with the place, shoots up chlorophyll instead of heroin. At a striptease, he is fascinated by the fig leaf covering the dancer; when she removes it, he is interested only in chewing the leaf. He babbles to Dolly about roots and the earth, proclaiming that he is not afraid to die because he does not fear Mother Earth: "Like the fruits of the earth, Dolly, when I ripen—I'll drop from the tree like a guava on the Eve of Sukkot" (2010, 82). Castel-Bloom's portrayal of Gordon is clearly meant to satirize the historical Zionist figure A. D. Gordon (1856–1923), best known for his "religion of the earth" philosophy. His reverence for the land is here transformed into Gordon's obsession and his inability to distinguish between himself as a human being and the fruits and vegetables he cultivates; his ultimate aim is to merge with the earth, with the place itself. He fails to do so in Dolly City because the place is so dehumanized and inorganic that he finds nothing to identify with. Rather than abandon his cause, he leaves Dolly City for Mexico City, his ideals about closeness to the earth intact but no less an object of Castel-Bloom's mockery.

Like Gordon, Dolly's son transcends the boundaries of his own humanity to merge with the place. In his case, however, the merging is forced on him by his mother. When Dolly carves the map of the Land of Israel on his back, she not only politicizes him and their relationship, as is clear from the updates she provides about his withdrawal to the pre-1967 borders, for example, but also links him permanently to the place itself. His flesh is wounded and cut in service to the place. Yigal Schwartz has discussed this scene as an exemplary instance of the Zionist version of the *'akeda* (1995). The concept of sacrifice is clearly present, and in stressing that this is a particularly Zionist reenactment of the biblical story Schwartz implies the importance of the connection between the person and the place. The place is physically inscribed on the person, growing and changing with him, but permanently marking him. Dolly's son will never be able to escape the Land of Israel, regardless of how far he travels.

Dolly herself is the character in the novel most clearly and closely linked to place. "Dolly" is not a Hebrew name, and "Dolly City" is transcribed from the English words into the Hebrew in the novel. The fact that Dolly and the city share this unusual name is never confronted in the novel, but one puzzling scene does briefly acknowledge the commonality. An optician asks Dolly what her name is, and when Dolly tells her, she replies, "Dolly. Is that short for Dikla?" (Castel-Bloom 2010, 76). Dolly responds that "it's an acronym," a mysterious claim that Castel-Bloom herself has made. The optician's question reminds us that Dolly City is in Israel, since the name Dikla is a common Israeli name (deriving from the Hebrew *dekel*, palm tree). Yet it also raises confusing questions. If this optician is in Dolly City, then she presumably knows that it is called Dolly City. Yet, rather than questioning the fact that Dolly has the same name as the city, she immediately tries to connect the name to a Hebrew counterpart. Why does she not recognize the connection between Dolly and Dolly City? Is it possible that Dolly City is Dolly's private name for the city? Might she experience the city differently than other people, and therefore assign it a different name? The riddle remains unsolved. What is clear, however, is that there is a forceful link between Dolly and her city, an implication of possession, though it is not clear whether Dolly possesses the city or vice versa. The relationship might be imagined as a reflection, insofar as Dolly herself thinks in such terms: "[Madness] takes over the soul as rapidly as our forces occupied Judea, Samaria, and the Gaza Strip in 1967. After madness takes over and settles in the territory of the human mind, the mad cows come into the picture. . . . And if a state like the State of Israel can't control the Arabs in the territories, how can anybody expect me, a private individual, to control the occupied territory inside myself?" (95–96). Comparing the occupation of the soul and the mind to geographical, physical occupation, and then referring outright to the "occupied territory" inside herself, Dolly establishes the possibility that the phenomena that inform spatial practices reflect human behavior. Dolly's sharing of the city's name suggests that, like the city, she is overwhelming and overwhelmed, mad, and fragmented. As Avraham Balaban points out, the lack of a center in the postmodern metropolis parallels the lack of a centered "I" in the protagonist (1995).

Castel-Bloom's representation of urban space changes significantly from *Dolly City* to *Human Parts*. The later novel reestablishes the conventional boundaries blurred or deconstructed in *Dolly City*, but offers no more of a solution to the problems it illuminates and ultimately only reaffirms the indifference to which Dolly succumbs. Therefore in reestablishing some of the boundaries obliterated by *Dolly City*, Castel-Bloom demonstrates that neither conception of the city—the one that rejects these boundaries and the one that acknowledges them—can adequately respond to the apathy created by the urban experience.

In *Human Parts*, Castel-Bloom relies on the associations her readers have with extra-urban Israeli places such as the cramped, marginalized *ma'abara* (immigrant transit camp) and the idealized, salt-of-the-earth *moshav* (semicollective agricultural settlement). The geography of the cities in *Human Parts* is by no means fantastic like that of Dolly City, with its Wells of Despair. Netanya, Jerusalem, Lod, and, most notably, Tel Aviv, are recognizable in the later novel; the boundaries between cities, neighborhoods, and types of places are clearly defined. Israeli readers recognize the wealthy north of Tel Aviv, the poverty around the Netanya central bus station, the anxiety-inducing foreignness of Jerusalem. Castel-Bloom delineates precisely the units of the city, from street to neighborhood to the city as a whole. This precision, in contrast to the chaos of Dolly City, the representation of which is defiantly unconcerned with mimesis, suggests that in the decade between the publication of the two books Castel-Bloom's critical approach shifted, bringing her from a distanced, allegorical critique of Israel to one that is more subtle in tone but more directly confrontational in representation.

One example of her careful representation of the city is the streets and street names that proliferate in this novel. Already on page 11 the narrator informs us that Kati Beit-Halahmi lives on Micah Reisner Avenue in Lod; we soon learn that Liat lives on Amos Street; Kati washes stairs in the buildings on Halalei Egoz Street; Iris's parents had an apartment on Nordau Street in Tel Aviv, and she later lived on Dor Dor v'Dorshav Street in Jerusalem and Jeremiah Street in Tel Aviv. Kati, the poor Kurdish Jew, finds herself in north Tel Aviv for the first time, and, as she walks through the streets meditating on her impoverished childhood fantasies of this relatively affluent neighborhood, she is struck by the fact that all the street names have only first names, not recognizing them as the names of prophets: "Beit-Halahmi advanced into Micah Street and was very surprised. She herself lived in Micah Reiser Avenue, and here they called him only by his first name. It must be something to do with 'protectzia,' with having connections, she thought. . . . She went onto Malachi and from there to Ezekiel, and she thought what is this, all first names only? And by the time she reached Joel Street, she stopped thinking about it" (Castel-Bloom 2003, 149). When Kati runs into Iris (whom she does not know) on the street, she asks her why the street names are only first names, and why these people get special treatment, and Iris, bewildered and impatient, responds that "'They get special treatment because they were prophets. It's from the Bible. In the Bible, there aren't any last names, or actually there are,' she quickly corrected herself, 'but not like now'" (151).

The emphasis on the street names, many of which are prophet or other biblical names, is not Castel-Bloom's innovation. In *Mikhael sheli* (My Michael) (1968), Amos Oz's Jerusalem, for example, is replete with ideologically and historically resonant street and other place names. Hana Wirth-Nesher has discussed the significance of his use of these names, asserting that "the names of the streets and landmarks seem to defy all attempts to return Jerusalem to a city of mere citizens and pedestrians. In fact, the city seems to demand that the simplest actions be situated on an allegorical map" (1996, 53–54). Castel-Bloom, on the other hand, uses these charged names to accomplish precisely the opposite. Particularly in Kati's inability to recognize the names as names of important prophets, it is clear that these names are as meaningless as the numbers and letters that constitute the street names of so many American cities. They do, however, allow the reader to follow the characters' itineraries, or, as Certeau might say, to "map" their walks through the city: "[Iris] decided to go on walking around for a bit before going home. . . . She walked along Micah Street, crossed Micah Lane and Dizengoff Street, continued east along Malachi Street, reached Ezekiel Street, and after passing Obadiah, found herself completely by chance outside Adir's building" (Castel-Bloom 2003, 118). These distinct place names create what Certeau terms a "disquieting familiarity of the city" (1984, 96), at least for the reader. But the familiarity is divorced from the meaning behind these place names. The "poetic geography" that Certeau attributes to place names, which he locates "on top of the geography of the literal, forbidden or permitted meaning" of these names (1984, 105), plays an important role in Oz's My Michael, as Wirth-Nesher argues, but is utterly hollow in this novel. If, as Certeau insists, walking is a poem, an act of spatialization and enunciation, then Iris's walk is a poem of banality. It also, however, vivifies the city and Iris's presence in it, allowing the reader to accompany her and experience the lack that she experiences through her wanderings. It is a certitude that provides a questionable comfort, suggesting that the geographical emplacement of these prophets from the unemplaced Bible might have confirmed the immortalization of the prophets' names, but at the cost of their signification, leaving them as empty shells.

The prophet street names, a scarlet thread woven throughout the novel, tie together the various characters and reveal, more than anything else, their relationship to the city. Kati's absurd contemplation about the street names toys with the conceptual categories of Zionist and Jewish, placing Tel Aviv in the realm of the sacred generally reserved for Jerusalem, and Lod in that of secular Zionism. At the same time, the historical and religious significance of these prophets is reduced to their names, valuable only in their potential as game-show questions worth money. Empty linguistic signifiers, they are ultimately as meaningless as the wooden plank reading "Dachau" in Dolly City. Yet they nevertheless establish a sense of recognition for those who are familiar with Tel Aviv.

It is not only the street names but also the associative value of various Israeli neighborhoods that contribute to Castel-Bloom's literary cartography in this novel. Kati's neighborhood in Lod, itself notorious for poverty, high crime rates, and low education levels, is called Ganey Aviv, Spring Gardens, and was intended to be the nicest neighborhood in Lod, "but things didn't turn out that way" (2003, 18), since the native Israelis moved elsewhere and Russian immigrants replaced them. The Russian presence in Ganey Aviv, and Kati's reaction to it, demonstrates Castel-Bloom's refusal to grant her characters a reprieve from hypocrisy. Even those with whom the reader is most likely to sympathize are guilty. In the context of Kati's emotional discussion of herself as a victim of Ashkenazi racism, she reveals her own prejudice against Russian immigrants and implies that the neighborhood has gone to seed because of them.

Tasaro, the Ethiopian beauty, hates to visit her family in Netanya and leave behind "her new life, the Israeli one," even for a few hours (Castel-Bloom 2003, 178). North Tel Aviv, where she lives with her affluent white boyfriend Adir, is the place that she hopes will enable her to forget her other places—both Netanya, where her family lives, and Ethiopia, where they all came from. Tasaro thinks of the place where her family lives in Netanya as "the ghetto" (164) and is eager to leave quickly after her obligatory visits. Netanya, a seaside city with a large population of North African Jews, is very different from Tasaro's north Tel Aviv neighborhood, which is predominantly Ashkenazi and upper middle class. The central bus station, in particular, where Tasaro began her Israeli adventure, is known for its drugs and prostitution. Irritated that her brothers and mother are stuck in Netanya and, by extension, unable to make their way into Israeli society, she has forgotten that it was her beauty that enabled her to overcome the invisible barriers between the cities and neighborhoods in order to attain her present place. Kati's origins in Ramle are assigned a similar signification. When her husband wants to "put her in her place," he brutally reminds her not to forget where she came from—"the slums of Ramle" (104).

Jerusalem, too, has a place in Castel-Bloom's urban hierarchy. Boaz, Kati's husband and a former taxi driver, is confounded by Jerusalem's entangled, unfamiliar streets, which literally ensnare him within their tentacles. The discomfort that he feels in Jerusalem stems not only from his unfamiliarity with its streets but also from the sense that Jews are innately supposed to know their way around Jerusalem: "He felt that this was some sort of sin, as if every Jew must be able to find his way around the mazes of Jerusalem. As opposed to a Jerusalemite, who if he gets confused in Tel Aviv or another city, you have to help him" (2003, 251). His inability to familiarize himself with this city that is imagined to be inherently Jewish makes him feel guilty, and he wants nothing more than to return to Tel Aviv, which makes no demands of him as a Jew. After an hour of trying to extricate himself from the streets of Jerusalem, Boaz is murdered on the outskirts of the city. It happens just after he spots the yearned-for green sign pointing toward Tel Aviv, which is *literally* unreachable.

Those characters who do feel a sense of belonging in Tel Aviv are aware of the status this lends them, even if it is imagined and not practical in any way. Iris, the struggling single mother, consoles herself about her poverty by feeling superior to the "non-native" Tel Avivians she encounters in the city (Castel-Bloom 2003, 73). Disdainfully, she calls them "immigrants," thus staking her claim in the city where her life is so difficult—as opposed to Jerusalem, where she lived in a palace with her ex-husband. Castel-Bloom portrays—and deconstructs—through Kati the mythology of north Tel Aviv:

In her childhood, in the Ramle immigrant transit camp, "North Tel Aviv" was a very important place, where very very big bosses lived. Firstly, they're Ashkenazis, she was told, secondly, they're educated, they know Hebrew and at least six other languages, thirdly, they're not in the least shy, because they've got nothing to be shy about, and therefore they're also taller, because they've got more money and they eat better.

In the Ramle camp, people talked a lot about North Tel Aviv. They said the North Tel Avivans had everything. Toilets, baths, showers—strong water pressure from all the taps, kitchens with fridges and gas stoves and ovens. (147–48)

Kati's memories of the Ramle stories of north Tel Aviv clash with the reality she encounters when she visits her makeup teacher there: "She stepped into the apartment, and this was the first time in her life that she saw a North Tel Aviv apartment from inside. This was not how she had imagined a North Tel Aviv apartment looking as a child in the immigrants' camp in Ramle: stuffy and stinking of cigarettes, every wall painted a different color, and sometimes the same wall painted a number of colors, as if they couldn't make up their minds what color to paint it" (Castel-Bloom 2003, 152). The repetition of "North Tel Aviv" in this and the preceding quotation makes clear that this is a concept that needs no elaboration. Upon her visit there, the mythology that had informed Kati's understanding of the geographical barriers between socioeconomic and ethnic groups in Israel falls apart; nevertheless, north Tel Aviv represents everything that Ramle and its immigrant camp strive for—a place that is not only a locale but also a metaphorical location at the top of the Israeli social hierarchy. The *ma'abara* in Ramle represents the opposite pole, the bottom of the ladder, the place that people want to leave and where they dream about other places.

Besides the north/south division that marks Tel Aviv with distinct socioeconomic and ethnic associations, this novel emphasizes the characters' urban spatial experience using a typically modernist medium, mass transportation. The many episodes that occur in this novel in taxis and buses create the potential for community and communication, but ultimately only confirm the characters' detachment. In most cases, however, the characters do not despair at their state of being alone in an urban crowd but in fact isolate *themselves*, privatizing the public space they occupy by using cellular telephones and thereby denying their isolation. When Iris takes a taxi after earning money for a temporary job, for example, she "assumes the air of an upper class lady, temporarily in need of assistance from the common man," (Castel-Bloom 2003, 112) keeping silent despite the driver's attempts to strike up conversation. She reflects that "in days gone by, when she was very poor, and counted the pennies so that she would have enough for the Laundromat, and did the drying at home, [she] would join in every conversation going, if only to assert the fact of her existence to herself and others. She needed to be answered in order to feel present. But now? She wanted people like this taxi driver . . . to know their place and be conscious of the gap between them" (114). Certain that money has replaced the need for social interaction, she prefers to enact the illusory social differences separating her from the driver rather than cultivate a sense of community. Her silence alone, however, does not sufficiently distance her from the taxi driver, so she calls Adir (the ex-boyfriend who dislikes her intensely) on her cell phone during the quiet spell that descends when the driver realizes her lack of interest in him. The cell phone, like the opaque barrier separating limousine drivers from wealthy passengers, ensures her privacy and finalizes her refusal to interact with the driver. Creating a private space within the communal realm of bus and taxi, Iris and other characters resist both the anxious modernist alienation and the possibility of human interaction afforded by public transportation.

Conclusion

Whether fantastic, realistic, or a combination of both, Castel-Bloom's representations of the city demonstrate multiple levels of isolation and disintegration at the core of the urban experience. Yet her characters' interactions with the city, wavering between anxiety, wrath, and indifference, reflect the impossibility of stable spatial relations. Her most recent novel, *Tekstil* (Textile) (2006), which moves between an affluent north Tel Aviv neighborhood and the United States, continues to develop this unstable spatiality, particularly in its ambivalent representation of Israelis in America. In addition to the city, other places examined in this chapter evoke disorientation: the ambiguous spatiality of the balcony, precariously balanced between the private and the public; the forced isolation of places like the hospital and the asylum; and the desanctification of the cemetery. This disorientation, an unintended consequence of the drive to maintain a precarious collectivity, catalyzes the breakdown of the carefully planned social order in which the organization of space determines who is included in society and who is excluded from it. The possibility of national identity in general and of Israeli identity in particular collapses when Castel-Bloom's characters find themselves performing their exclusion before empty spaces or hostile crowds. Quarantined in hospitals and asylums to restore them to appropriate social function, they become hyperconscious of their aloneness, a state of being that provokes terror in the context of a society whose ruling ideology valorizes collective identity. The cemetery is the site charged with the final decision on matters of communal belonging or exclusion, the final determinant of Israeliness. Barred from familiar categories of identity, Castel-Bloom's characters attempt to tread the unsteady and disorienting ground she lays out for them, refusing to define themselves according to fictitious homogeneity but despairing at their failure to find an alternative.

The No-Man's-Land
of the Israeli Palestinian

Sayed Kashua

> "Understand," says Judat [a Palestinian], "that in living here, in
> the West Bank, I constitute an international problem. The whole
> world talks and argues about me. No one talks about him [the Israeli
> Palestinian]. I am free in my soul, I know that I can say what I feel
> toward you and the occupation with a full heart. He can't. He is too
> tied up with you."
> —DAVID GROSSMAN, Ha-zman ha-tsahov
> (The yellow wind)

The Place of Israeli Palestinians

In his poem "Thirteen Ways of Looking at It," Anton Shammas expresses
a multi-layered uncertainty: "I do not know. / A language beyond this, /
And a language beyond this. / And I hallucinate in no-man's-land" (1979).
Shammas sketches the site of his struggle to come to terms with the inco-
herence of his identity as a Palestinian citizen of Israel,[1] and as an Arab

---

1. The question of nomenclature is fraught with political and ideological implications, and reflects the in-betweenness of Israeli-Palestinian identity. The terms most commonly used in the mainstream Israeli media and public discourse are 'aravim yisraelim,
Israeli Arabs, and 'arviyey yisrael, Israel's Arabs. The main problem of both terms, which
points at the delicacy and complexity of the question itself, is that they replace the culturally and nationally specific noun "Palestinian" with the generic "Arab." The difficulty

poet writing first in Arabic and then in Hebrew. It is a site where a hallu-
cinating poet wanders in the liminal zone between two languages (*safoth*).
It is also a site that invokes, through the poet's masterful use of biblical
Hebraic constructions (*me-'ever mi-ze*) the ancient scenes of conflict that
defined the Israelite nation.[2] Shammas, a Christian Israeli Palestinian,
emphasizes his uneasy bond to Jewish history and culture not only by
demonstrating his familiarity with it through biblical allusion, but also
by situating himself within the biblical conflict zones to which he alludes.
Playing, as he is apt to do, with the two meanings of the word *safa*, language and lip (in Hebrew, *safa* refers to the "river's lip," or riverbank, as
well as the face's lip), Shammas demonstrates the link between place and
language; yet, writing between these lips, places, languages, he defies this
link, thus finding himself in a space between places, a ghostly zone. While
Hebrew literature written by Palestinians is replete with images of "in-
betweenness," as Lital Levy notes (2008, 350), Shammas's no-man's-land
coalesces issues of language, place, and conflict, and thus presents itself as
a particularly apt metaphor for the situation of Israeli Palestinians.

"The whole world talks and argues" about the Palestinian refugee, the
one whose authenticity is not doubted, the one who is *wholly* Palestinian. This Palestinian, the one who has no state, no citizenship, no rights,
considers himself freer than the Palestinian who *does* have all these, the
Israeli Palestinian who continues to live in the same village or town where
his family has lived since before 1948, who has Israeli citizenship and the
rights associated with it. The Palestinian's assertion to Grossman that he

---

is compounded by the split within the Palestinian nation, part of which lives in exile
and defines itself as Palestinian (whether living in another country or in the Occupied
Territories), and the other part of which remains at home but defines itself sometimes as
Israeli, sometimes Palestinian, sometimes both and sometimes neither. In an attempt to
acknowledge these nuances, I shall use the term "Israeli Palestinians" in this chapter,
though I am fully aware that some might reject this term as well. The difficulty of finding
a term that would be acceptable even to the people whom it aims to designate only attests
to the complexity of this identity.

2. Thanks to Esther Raizen for her insights on the use of biblical grammar in this
poem.

is "free in [his] soul" seems ironic considering Israel's efforts to impede his freedoms, particularly basic spatially related freedoms: the freedom to establish a viable Palestinian nation and the freedom to move in place. The Palestinian experience of place and space has been explored exhaustively in Palestinian literature and film, almost always in terms of overtly political expression. To name a few, the writings of Mahmoud Darwish, Ghazzan Kanafani, and Edward Said on exile, and the films of Elia Suleiman and Hany Abu-Assad on the effect of the Israeli occupation—particularly the *mahsom*, or roadblock—on daily life exemplify the Palestinian preoccupation with these two spatial themes of homeland and restricted movement-in-place. The negation of his basic spatial rights has focused the world's eye on the Palestinian, making him an identifiable, even an iconic figure. The Israeli Palestinian, on the other hand, has not been forced to relinquish his spatial rights. Through an intricate and sometimes absurd color-coded system that classifies identification cards, license plates, and maps, he is allowed to continue living in his home, and to move about the country relatively freely. Yet Judat, the Palestinian interviewed by David Grossman, insists that it is *he* who is truly free and not the Israeli Palestinian, who is "too tied up" with Israeli Jews (2002, 125).

The notion of being "tied up" is at the center of my analysis of Hebrew works by Israeli Palestinian authors. How does the bond between Israeli Jews and Israeli Palestinians affect the latter's relationship to place? What does this relationship to place reveal, in turn, about Israeli Palestinians' self-identification? One Israeli Palestinian author's literary representations of the *mahsom*, the house, and the village, considered through the prism of Shammas's metaphorical no-man's-land, illumine the spatial dynamics of the bond between Jewish and Palestinian Israelis. In Sayed Kashua's novels, these three sites function to disrupt and deny the movement that is purportedly the privilege of free citizens. The isolation and instability encountered by Orly Castel-Bloom's heroines in the previous chapter are intensified in Kashua's characters' daily experience of social, cultural, and spatial in-betweenness, to the point that, metaphorically or literally, they cannot move. The characters' paralysis asserts the fallacy of their designation as Israelis even as it denounces the futility of their identification with Palestinians and Palestinian nationalism. These vernacular places concretize the metaphor of in-betweenness expressed even in the term "Israeli Palestinian" and offer a geographical allusiveness to both sides of Israeli-Palestinian identity. The presence of the Israeli Palestinian between Israelis and Palestinians suggests that the two sides may reconsider a relationship that is often uncritically cast by both as antithetical. Homi Bhabha, in articulating the location of an international postcolonial culture, offers the concept of Third Space to account for its hybridity. He writes that "we should remember that it is the 'inter'— the cutting edge of translation and negotiation, the *inbetween* space—that carries the burden of the meaning of culture" (1994, 56). Yet the Israeli Palestinian encounter with in-between places, far from offering a fertile and fluid Third Space of identity formation that may help "elude the politics of polarity," foregrounds the uneasy and often paralyzing tension they impose on the Israeli Palestinian (56). Rather than eluding "the politics of polarity," these places confirm it by bringing about a performance of identity based on internalized social assumptions and expectations. The novels of Sayed Kashua, the most visible figure in what has been dubbed the "third generation" of Israeli Palestinian Hebrew authors, illustrate this process forcefully (Kayyal 2008).[3]

The *shetah hefker*, or no-man's-land, of Shammas's poetry vividly portrays the complex idea of in-betweenness. Like the spaces between the French and German trenches during World War One, Shammas's no-man's-land is more than just a space of in-betweenness. Exposed and unprotected, it endangers all those who would venture within or across it, and therefore remains generally untouched—a land where no man wants to be. It is a space traversed only for the purpose of encroaching on the other and asserting, usually violently, the difference and opposition between the two sides. As Arabs writing in Hebrew, Shammas and Kashua are men in no-man's-land, wandering this space to try to make sense of, if not to reconcile, the differences. Yet it turns out that a man wandering no-man's-land

---

3. Mahmoud Kayyal posits Atallah Mansour as a representative of the first generation and Shammas as a representative of the second.

risks becoming, himself, "no man," able to move neither here nor there. The Hebrew phrase for no-man's-land, *shetah hefker*, literally "a territory of abandonment," connotes even more explicitly the terrifying impossibility of moving beyond this hopeless space where one has been left behind. Within this framework, Kashua's representation of vernacular places can be related to the experience of persistent, formative, and paralyzing in-betweenness.

Approaching Israeli-Palestinian identity from the perspective of intertextuality, Levy focuses on allusion in Hebrew poetry by Israeli Palestinians as an expression of their "poetics of in-betweenness," which can be imagined in terms of border, interstice, or crevice: "The borderline," she suggests, "can be an apt metaphor for the situation of writers whose home is characterized by the intrusive, oppressive presence of borders and barriers and whose command of both languages enables them to transcend, in some sense, these dividing lines" (2008, 345, 349). Two other scholars, Rachel Feldhay Brenner (2003) and Gil Hochberg (2007), have confronted the question of the Israeli-Palestinian "bond" affirmatively, proposing that the link between Arabs and Jews in general can be conceived of as the basis for a shared future.[4] Such an interpretation is productive and revelatory, a breath of fresh air in the heavy discourse promulgating eternal and innate enmity between Arabs and Jews. Yet it is crucial not to lose sight of the fact that this bond, though it may bring Israeli Palestinians and Jews closer, also restricts the freedom of the Palestinians it binds and relegates them to inferiority on a daily basis.

Kashua was born in 1975 in Tira, an Israeli Palestinian village in the central district of Israel, and now lives in Beit Safafa, an Israeli Palestinian

---

4. Brenner writes: "In contrast to the deeply entrenched perception of unbridgeable cultural, social, and political divergences between Arabs and Jews, this study shows that the two literatures affirm a complex yet indissoluble affinity between the two communities" (2003, 3). Hochberg writes that her book "aims at challenging the dominant ideology of separation that informs the current relationship between Arabs and Jews in Israel/ Palestine" (2007, ix).

neighborhood southeast of Jerusalem. He has worked as a journalist for the Jerusalem weekly *Kol ha-ir* and has a regular column for *Haaretz*, where he has made a name for himself as a sharp and sardonic observer of Israeli society. His satiric sitcom *'avoda 'aravit* (Arab labor), about a young Israeli-Palestinian couple living outside Jerusalem, is broadcast on Israeli television. He published his first novel, *'aravim rokdim* (Dancing Arabs), in 2002, and was awarded the Prime Minister's prize in 2004, following the publication of his second novel, *va-yehi boker* (Let it be morning) (2004b). Mahmoud Kayyal, one of the few scholars to have published on Kashua so far, is primarily interested in whether or not his (and other Israeli Palestinians') work can be considered part of the Palestinian canon, despite the fact that he writes in Hebrew. The counterpoint, which has been exhaustively discussed mainly in terms of Shammas, asks whether or not Israeli Palestinian literature can be considered part of the Israeli or Hebrew canon. I operate from the assumption that the works of Kashua and other Israeli Palestinians writing in Hebrew can and should be considered part of the Hebrew and Israeli canons without denying their concurrent place in the Palestinian canon. The question of language has played a prominent role in these debates. Since some Israeli Palestinian authors, such as Emile Habiby, write in Arabic, thereby aligning themselves with Arab culture despite their Israeli citizenship, those who write in Hebrew find themselves in a more ambiguous space of identity. The question of which canon or nation can make a more legitimate claim for the inclusion of the latter, however, while illustrative of their in-betweenness, is not the immediate concern of this chapter.

At the center of Israeli-Palestinian identity, and of Palestinian identity in general, is the land. That spatial concepts dominate Palestinian discourse and the Palestinian narrative is not at all surprising, considering that the event that is etched most deeply in the collective Palestinian memory is the mass displacement effected by the *naqba*, the catastrophe, of 1948. The most important and definitive element in this narrative is the concept of being in the land. Two examples of this trope are the notion of *sumud*, steadfastness, often imagined in terms of the Palestinians' organic relationship to the land, "like an old olive tree deeply rooted to the ground";[5] and that of return, which includes reclamation of the lost place. Both these tropes resonate with the Palestinian people as a whole, but the situation "on the ground," so to speak, differs widely among Palestinians scattered throughout the world. In considering their disparate spatial experiences in the most basic terms—whether they live inside Israel or outside it—articulating a shared relationship to the land becomes difficult if not impossible. Edward Said acknowledges the substantial difference between the Israeli Palestinian and the Palestinian experience of space, pointing to the tension as primarily one of interior and exterior, inside the homeland or outside it, in exile. All too familiar with the experience of exterior, Said is also well aware of the disadvantages of being *already inside* the place for which the Palestinian collective yearns and in honor of which it has constructed an intricate poetics of return: "Being inside is a privilege that is an affliction, like feeling hemmed in by the house you own" (1999, 53). This Palestinian dyad of inside/outside differs fundamentally from the one I examined in the works of Amos Oz in the first chapter of this work, in which "inside" reigns order and peace while "outside" lurks chaos. These realms in the Palestinian case are paradoxical: inside is the object of the dream, but it "hems one in"; outside is the product of nightmare, but it is clear and well-defined. Being outside, while undeniably painful and trying, allows one to function within the familiar trope of longing for home. Being inside offers no familiar relationship to place, because the same land exists within a changed political and social configuration. The contradictory idea that inside is simultaneously privilege and affliction is at the core of the Israeli Palestinian experience of space. Ami Elad-Bouskila writes about the ambivalent attitude many Palestinians felt toward those who had remained inside and become Israeli citizens after 1948. These "inside" Palestinians (Arabic: *filistiyyin al-dakhil*, an appellation sometimes used in the Arab world) "were marginal to the Arab states and indeed to other Pal-

---

5. This oft-invoked idea of the relation of *sumud* to rootedness is quoted here from the website of a 2006 exhibition of photographs by James Prineas, entitled "The Spirit of Sumud." See Prineas 2006.

estinians; they gained stature only after 1967 and especially 1969. . . . This division also holds for Palestinian writers" (Elad-Bouskila 1999, 9). These "inside" Palestinians are no longer shunned by Palestinians and the Arab world. But their position inside the land establishes a substantial difference between them and the Palestinians living in the Occupied Territories or elsewhere in exile. Susan Slyomovics, like Said, writes of the distinction between exiled Palestinians and Israeli Palestinians as a tension of outside versus inside, and associates these spaces with captivity and prison camps (inside) versus exile (outside) (1998, 170). Within this ambiguously privileged "inside," a veritable no-man's-land, Kashua's characters struggle to participate in the most basic processes of self-definition: to find a place and to articulate an identity.

Mahsom/Roadblock: The Performance of Identities

The *mahsom,* or roadblock,[6] as perhaps the most visible and ubiquitous spatial marker of the occupation after the separation wall, has become a fundamental component of Palestinian landscape and experience.[7] It has become so vernacular that the Hebrew term for roadblock, *mahsom,* has, like other Hebrew words related to the jargon of occupation, penetrated the Arabic of the Occupied Territories. The term springs from the root *het-samekh-mem, hasam,* which is the basis for the verb *lahsom,* to bar or obstruct; *mahsom* means, literally, that that obstructs. The *mahsom,* which serves to obstruct and slow movement, is a dreary site of much tension for Palestinians waiting to pass it. Said Zeedani writes that "Checkpoints lay a siege around you" (2005, Part III). The restriction on movement they

6. The most literal English translation of the Hebrew *mahsom* is "roadblock." The term is also sometimes translated as "checkpoint," a term that emphasizes the bureaucratic, rather than the geographic, aspects of the barrier. In this chapter I use mostly the Hebrew *mahsom* (plural: *mahsomim*) to avoid confusion, since some citations refer to "roadblocks" and others to "checkpoints."

7. According to the Israeli women's group MachsomWatch, which sends volunteers to observe *mahsomim* and to report human rights violations there, Israel controls roughly 600 *mahsomim* in the West Bank.

enforce is related to the uncertain borders of Israel/Palestine itself. Derek Gregory observes that the *mahsom* is part of "a frenzied cartography of mobile frontiers rather than fixed boundaries" (131). That the *mahsom* is a liminal, complex space has been noted and elaborated by several scholars, particularly in the field of film studies, since it has become one of the most important symbols in Palestinian cinema. Nurith Gertz and George Khleifi write of the cinematic focus on the *mahsom* as one example of Palestinian directors' use of a particular spatial detail as a synecdochal representation of a whole Palestine (2005, 325). Anat Zanger argues that the *mahsom* is a "transition space" that, like airports and frontier posts, traps people in a "spatiality designed for maximum control of people's movements" (2005, 41). She analyzes it in terms of Gloria Anzaldúa's borderland, "a vague and undetermined place created by the emotional residue of an unnatural boundary" (40). Even in the few examples provided here, the *mahsom* has been variously described in terms of borders, boundaries and frontiers, all terms that articulate a space that is *between* other spaces.

The *mahsom* is a space of transition; it delays or denies movement; it makes visible the hierarchy between the Israeli soldiers, the "owners" of the space, and the Palestinians waiting to pass through. Yet one *mahsom* may differ substantially from another. As Kotef and Amir note, the *mahsom* in the Occupied Territories began as a temporary structure but became gradually entrenched: "What started as a cement cube on a dirt path, behind which the soldiers stood, was expanded, developed, and solidified, evolving from a provisory obstacle into a permanent and elaborate construction" (2007, 981). Elsewhere, the *mahsom* is more easily dismantled and moved as the Israeli Defense Force (IDF) sees fit. The most important difference, however, is geographical. In the Territories the *mahsom* purportedly demarcates Palestinian space from Israeli space, thereby imitating a border.[8] Within the Green Line, however, it may be scattered throughout Israeli territory. Instead of blocking the movement from Palestinian spaces to Israeli spaces, it disrupts the movement *within* the Israeli space, suggesting that

8. I write "purportedly" because, as Kotef and Amir observe, most of the checkpoints are actually located inside the Palestinian territories (2007, 974).

the area beyond the *mahsom* is a purely Jewish-Israeli space that can be corrupted by the presence of the Arabs who wish to go there. This relates to the "inside" of the town or the kibbutz discussed in chapter 1, which is threatened by the dangerous "outside" in Oz's stories and novels. As Zanger points out in her discussion of checkpoint as border, the checkpoint "separates purity and impurity, similarity and difference, and inside and outside. But at the same time as they connect, borders also sunder. They insist on purity, distinction and difference, but facilitate contamination and mixing; and they are imaginary, fluid, and always in the process of change" (2005, 40). Besides announcing the desirability of the "pure" space beyond it, the space it bars, the *mahsom* in Israel deepens the already substantial instability of the demarcation of space through its mobility. Since "outside" and "inside" are easily shifted, the contours of the no-man's-land between them become increasingly blurred, defying delineation.

Zeedani emphasizes the *mahsom*'s effect of cutting off the Palestinian gaze at the land: "Checkpoints mean that the rest of the country with its space and landscape recedes into the distance and the background. It becomes off limits, too remote and unreachable. Your desire to see it is being frustrated; your right to see and enjoy its landscape is indefinitely suspended" (2005, Part III). The *mahsom* not only blocks the Palestinian gaze, but also allows the Jewish Israeli gaze to penetrate ever deeper, since a primary function of the roadblock within Israel is to render Israeli Palestinians more visible. Soldiers conduct multiple levels of surveillance: they look at faces (what in the United States is called racial profiling); they glance at license plates; they inspect identification cards. These means of surveillance allow an immediate, ethnically based classification of the people passing through the *mahsom*. Of course, the Palestinians who are citizens of Israel have the yellow license plates and blue identification cards that Jewish Israelis have, not the white, green, or blue license plates and orange identification cards that Palestinians have. The pronounced role of visibility (and the lack thereof), together with the clearly delineated categories of identity and the associated and predictable roles they assign (Palestinians: submissive or defiant; Israeli Jews: abusive or benevolent) lend the *mahsom* a theatrical air. The bureaucratic determination of identity according to the colors of objects and documents contributes a Kafkaesque absurdity to the enterprise of surveillance carried out at the roadblock. This absurdity, however, constitutes the day-to-day reality of Palestinians and Israeli Palestinians.

These elements of the theatrical and the absurd have been represented in several Palestinian films that center on the *mahsom*. Indeed, there are so many such films that they constitute a genre in and of themselves, and have been analyzed in several scholarly studies.[9] In his film *Yadon ila-heyya* (Arabic: Divine intervention) (2002), Elia Suleiman, perhaps the best known Israeli Palestinian director, portrays most explicitly the road-block's absurd theatricality. A repeated scene shows two Arab lovers, from opposite sides of the *mahsom*, sitting in a car near the structure itself and silently holding hands. Facing the barrier, they watch from behind the windshield as the slow procession of cars and people winds past the IDF observation tower and the soldiers checking documents. At times, the gro-tesque soldiers decide on whim to force drivers to switch cars, to sing and dance, to hand over a coveted jacket. The lovers watch from afar, detached spectators of a theater of the absurd in which they, too, must participate when they are on either side of the *mahsom*. The woman takes matters into her own hands when, one day, she walks through the roadblock with her head held high and sunglasses concealing her eyes, past the gawking, paralyzed soldiers and the observation post, which collapses in her wake from the sheer power of her defiance. Thus she asserts her right not only to move freely but also not to be surveyed (hence the sunglasses concealing her eyes, and the collapsed observation post), while the stunned soldiers, unable to stop her, can only watch as she passes them. Suleiman replaces one absurd performance with another, thus overturning the power struc-ture of the occupation by using its own aesthetic.

Kashua's *Dancing Arabs* documents the absurdity of daily Palestinian life on multiple levels. For example, it utilizes an absurdist poetics in its reworking or negation of the *bildungsroman* genre: instead of establishing the moral and emotional maturation of the unnamed protagonist whose life it follows from childhood to adulthood, it suggests that each new phase

9. See, for example, Gertz and Khleifi 2005; also see Zanger 2005.

or turning point he encounters *stunts* his growth and further destabilizes his already precarious identity. Upon his acceptance into an elite Jewish boarding school in Jerusalem, his family rejoices, certain that the school will pave the way for his success in Israeli society. His shift from the familiar Arab world of Tira, his home village, to the exclusive and foreign Jewish world of his school, however, cultivates in him a hyperconsciousness and, eventually, a fragmentation of self.

One of the salient events that drive him to this state takes place at the *mahsom* at Ben-Gurion Airport, a memory he revisits twice in the novel: "There was one time when they picked up on the fact that I was an Arab and recognized me. So right after that I became an expert at assuming false identities. It was at the end of my first week of school in Jerusalem. I was on the bus going home to Tira. A soldier got on and told me to get off. I cried like crazy. I'd never felt so humiliated" (Kashua 2004a, 91). The setting of this awkward situation, in which the protagonist and his friend are forced off the bus in front of the other passengers and are expected to reboard after the bus returns from the airport, thrusts their identity as Arabs into the public eye. The events effectively announce their Arabness and prompt their expulsion from the public space of the bus, forcing them to perform the identity that has been imposed upon them by the state. That he chooses to describe the experience as one of recognition or identification (*zihuy*) implies a certain familiarity, despite the fact that he has never seen this soldier or these passengers; their "recognition" of him refers to their recognition of The Arab as stereotyped by Israeli society and internalized by the protagonist. When his identity is revealed, he knows it is immediately conflated with the Jewish Israeli conception of the archetypal Arab.

Following the humiliation of this incident, the protagonist decides that from now on *he* will determine the terms of his identity, and he begins to don masks. Public places become spaces of performance, opportunities to prove his Israeliness before a Jewish audience. Literalizing Judith Butler's conception of identity as *performed* rather than *essential*, he endeavors to remove all traces of Arabness from his appearance, behavior, and speech, in effect eliminating his Arab self: "I have almost no accent. You can't tell by looking at me. I've got sideburns and Coke-bottle sunglasses. Even

the Arabs mistake me for a Jew. I even speak Hebrew with the housekeep-
ing staff" (Kashua 2004a, 202). He wears his costume convincingly, and,
well aware of the implications of his performance for his Arab identity, he
sardonically relates his successful passing: "That's what I've always wanted
to be, after all: a Jew. I've worked hard at it, and I've finally pulled it off"
(91). Most striking is his constant awareness of his role-playing, and of the
Jewish Israeli collective as the audience he must convince with his performance. Waiting for his wife in the hospital waiting room, for instance, he
looks disdainfully at the Arabs all around him: "Just don't let anyone think
I'm one of them or that I'm like them. Just don't let them call out my wife's
name when it's her turn, or announce it on the PA system. . . . [My wife] is
capable of talking to me in Arabic even inside a crowded elevator or at the
entrance to the mall, when we're being processed through the metal detec-
tor. She plays with the baby in Arabic in public places"[10] (203–4). Public
space—the waiting room, the elevator, the mall, the park—provides an
opportunity to test his Jewish mask.

Yet the *mahsom,* the place that exists solely for the purpose of unmask-
ing him, poses the greatest challenge and becomes the ultimate stage, and
the IDF soldier his most intimidating and powerful critic, the one with the
most penetrating gaze. After his humiliating experience at the roadblock,
the protagonist hones his acting skills and perfects his mask. He begins
shaving his mustache, learns to pronounce the letter *p* properly, buys new
clothes, and makes sure to have Hebrew cassette tapes in his Walkman
and Hebrew books on the bus with him. His audience is mollified. He is
not "recognized" again for years.

For the protagonist's father, the *mahsom* symbolizes not the test of his
Israeliness, but an opportunity to defy it: "'Nobody ever told me to get off,'

10. His wife, a graduate of the Hebrew University of Jerusalem who speaks Hebrew,
"doesn't give . . . a second thought" to his fears of being recognized as an Arab (Kashua
2004a, 203). It is interesting to note that, unlike him, she is a refugee whose family is not
originally from Tira but wound up there after the destruction of their village. Though
they both carry blue ID cards, this difference in their identity (native/refugee) parallels
and arguably accounts for their dissimilar attitudes toward "recognition" and assimilation.

he said. 'They didn't notice I was an Arab. Every time the soldiers told an Arab to get off, I'd get up and shout, 'Take me off too, I'm an Arab!' and I'd hold up my ID card and wave it proudly'" (Kashua 2004a, 101). He, too, performs, but his performance is intended to trumpet rather than conceal his true identity. Nevertheless, an undercurrent of pride at the fact that he was never recognized as an Arab emerges from his narrative. The real challenge, he suggests, is to reveal the Jews' foolishness by passing as Jewish and then *announcing* the trick, not in the act of passing. The father and son's antithetical attitudes toward the *mahsom* reflect broader differences in their self-conception, which cannot be attributed to the protagonist's youth since they persist and even deepen as he matures. In contrast to his intrepid father, who was arrested at a roadblock once on his way to a demonstration, the son does all he can to avoid recognition at the *mahsom*. "I took that bus line hundreds of times after that," he recalls. "Each time, I'd feel the fear again. It didn't let up until we'd passed the airport. . . . I felt sorry for the Arabs who were taken off, and I thanked God they hadn't picked on me" (101).

The incident at the *mahsom* turns out to have been one of his most formative experiences. It awakens his recognition of the hierarchy of space in Israeli society. Subsequently, he realizes that his own identity as an Arab is entangled in this spatial hierarchy and that he is fated to engage in a complex lifelong endeavor of self-effacement and masquerade. The *mahsom* itself participates in the greatest performance of all: it operates under the pretense that it separates two sovereign states, with recognizable, fixed, and mutually agreed borders, with officials representing the two states on opposite sides of the roadblock; moreover, it purports to protect its own citizens while subjecting certain ones to intense fear and humiliation. This performance of spatial legitimacy allows the *mahsom* not only to impede movement from place to place; situated between a space understood as "pure" and another as "corrupt" and potentially corrupting, it also becomes the defining geographical metaphor of the interstitial experience of Israeli Palestinians, who must choose, as they approach the roadblock, whether to reveal their Arab identity or conceal it and attempt to assume a Jewish Israeli one. The *mahsom*, then, paralyzes the movement of Israeli Palestinians literally, and it also arrests the development of their independent identity (whether Palestinian, Israeli, or a hybrid), subjecting them always to define themselves according to their dialectical relationship to Jewish Israelis.

The Violable Village House and Israeli-Palestinian Kitsch

The Palestinian house, particularly the Palestinian village house, holds a special place in Palestinian literature. Susan Slyomovics writes that

> Palestinian poetry of the land describes trees, plants, and soil, but in the foreground is always the Palestinian village house. In poetry, each part of the house—stone walls, storage bins, threshold, courtyard, and terrace—is described in loving, concrete detail. Architectural details emerge from every line of verse to make real those familiar things that have been given different and alienating functions. The Arab house continues to exemplify Palestinian identity, steadfastness, and resistance by its very presence linking itself to the domestic, everyday life, thereby speaking of every Palestinian home. (1998, 176)

The lyrical, detailed descriptions of the Palestinian house offer a unifying spatial metaphor to help cope with and resist the loss of homeland, portraying it as the archetypal home with room for all in the collective Palestinian family. In stark contrast to the tin shacks and tents of the refugee camps, the unwelcoming apartment buildings of Israeli cities, and the foreign brick or wooden houses of the diaspora, the sturdy stone house gives the impression of indestructibility. The ubiquitous symbol of the house-key in Palestinian literature and popular culture has become the portable synecdoche-within-a-synecdoche, an expression of the larger symbol of the house, signifying a promise to return to the stone house and its patiently waiting lock, which represent Palestine itself. Both the house and the key as symbols assert endurance and persistence.

Edward Said observes a far bleaker role for the house in Palestinian literary representations: "Each Palestinian structure presents itself as a potential ruin," he writes. "The theme of the formerly proud family house (village, city, camp) now wrecked, left behind, or owned by someone else, turns up everywhere in our literature and cultural heritage" (1999, 38). Said's melancholy observation intends to illuminate the vulnerability of the Palestinian house, which submits to a variety of actions: it is wrecked, abandoned, appropriated. The passive construction he uses to describe these events demonstrates the house's helplessness in the face of greater powers, the unnamed subjects of these verbs. The notion that every Palestinian structure contains a "potential ruin" suggests that these structures are all on the brink of obliteration, but implicit within the image of a ruin, particularly in this context of literary representation, is the notion of preservation. Indeed, the lexicon of symbols of the Palestinian narrative includes no few "ruins," traces that preserve the past in collective Palestinian memory. The success of the Palestinian house-key as a mobilizing symbol for the rallying cry of Palestinian refugees' right to return, for instance, is based on its capacity to remind the world that this key once fit into a lock of a door of a house in a village that no longer exists. The key is the only remaining trace of the village, and stubbornly proves its existence. Moreover, the picturesque appearance of the decades-old key, which is usually large, old-fashioned and made of iron, arms it with the irrefutable authority of the past. In this respect, the idea of a "potential ruin" implies that, even in the face of threatening destruction and forgetfulness, these structures manage to resist annihilation and to maintain a fragmentary existence and a hope of return and redemption. Anton Shammas's poem "halakhti ad sof ha-geshem" ("I walked to the end of the rain") tells of the house that manages to cling to his memory when everything else, including his childhood village, has been washed away by rain: "I recite names that I knew, in the melody of calm forgetfulness. / And only the house in which I was born follows me like an untamed child" (1979, 15). The interpretation of the house as preserving ruin and persistent reminder can be connected to Slyomovics's reading of the house in Palestinian poetry, in which painstaking poetic documentation preserves the house that may exist only in a potentially treacherous memory.

While the house as ruin is, for Said, characteristic of Palestinian houses in general, his acknowledgment of the particular experience of Israeli Palestinians evokes a different metaphor, of the house that "hems one in." Kashua, in his portrayal of the Israeli Palestinian house, literalizes this metaphor, but adds an important twist. The houses in Kashua's novels are passive, acted upon by threatening forces, failing to provide protection and safety for their inhabitants and actually leaving them feeling cornered and constricted. Significantly, his protagonists seek protection not only from Israeli Jews, in the guise of fanatical settlers or IDF soldiers, but also from other Palestinians, fellow villagers and even neighbors, who, driven by their own "hemming-in," resort to violent penetration of the private space of others. Kashua's house becomes a porous place vulnerable to invasion by the very people it is supposed to embrace as a unified extended family—other Israeli Palestinians.

Unlike the houses in Palestinian representations, Kashua's house is not reconstructed out of the fragments of a sometimes unreliable and idealizing memory. Instead, the description is firmly rooted in the present moment, transforming traces of the past and hints of the future into kitsch. In *Dancing Arabs*, for instance, the narrator, on a visit to his parents' house in the village, describes it thus:

> Our house is ugly. There are electric wires sticking out of the living room wall, and a bell that never rings. Next to it is a clock made of gold-covered plastic, inspired by a lion's mane. Hanging next to the clock is a deer's head, also made of plastic. There used to be two sabers, too, but they broke long ago. Three brown wooden plaques hang unattractively on the wall across from me, with the inscription *Allah* in black lettering. On the wall to the left, there's a painting by Ismail Shammout with the inscription *Uda* (Return), and next to that is a picture of a mother and a baby with a flight of ravens hovering over them. (Kashua 2004a, 210)

Unapologetically unsentimental, this description either mocks or remains indifferent to objects linked to the most important symbols of Palestinian identity. It ridicules the gaudy artifice of objects intended to signify a close connection to nature (a golden leonine clock, a plastic deer's head). The broken sabers denote an outdated and ineffective military strength; the religious plaques evoke not spirituality but aesthetic displeasure; and the painting filled with the promise of return, a somewhat ironic concept in this house of people who never *departed*, is nothing more than an item in a catalogue of the unsightly. Describing the room of his wife's young-est brother, who still lives in their parents' home, the narrator notes, "It used to be a storeroom for oil and olives, and it had an oven too. . . . He covered the bare walls with red scarves of Hapo'el soccer team, and with pictures of the Chicago Bulls, Michael Jackson, Fairuz, and Lenin, and with Land Day posters, like the one of a man sitting under an olive tree holding his blond grandson, who's covered in a *kaffiyeh*, and the inscrip-tion WE'RE STAYING PUT" (Kashua 2004a, 215). American and Israeli stars and athletes are mingled here with symbols of Palestinian identity, such as the Land Day posters. Any hierarchy that might place the latter at the top of the young man's cultural and intellectual priorities is lost in this postmodern mishmash of political statements (nationalism and communism), athletes (American and Israeli), and superstars (Western and Eastern). Most significant, however, is the fact that this superficial display of the youth's fragmented identity replaces the simple, functional aesthetic of the former storeroom. The posters and banners plastered over the bare walls that once housed only olives function as a palimpsest, par-alleling the transformation and fragmentation of the Israeli Palestinian village discussed later in this chapter.

Shammas historicizes the changed aesthetic of the walls of the Israeli-Palestinian house in his essay "Kitsch 22." In this context, he invokes Milan Kundera's definition of kitsch as the attempt to find favor with the majority by embracing accepted opinions, an effort that is expressed through "the language of beauty and emotion" (1987, 24). He character-izes the Israeli Palestinians' situation as one of "kitsch 22": Israel asks its Arab citizens to consider themselves Israeli, but when they attempt to do so the state makes clear "that their participation is only social, and that they must find the national content of their identity elsewhere" (25). When they do seek it elsewhere, they are blamed for "undermining the founda-tions of the state," and can therefore not be considered Israeli (25). He links this situation to the transformations over three generations of liv-ing room walls in Israeli-Palestinian houses: from the father's serene white walls hung with functional-aesthetic objects close to the ceiling; to the "kitsch attack" on the walls of the son's house, "the house of the orphans of '48," in the form of neighborly gifts he feels obliged to hang; and finally to the grandson's walls, "a real kitsch festival" and ultimately "a transgression of Arab aesthetic laws" (24–25). According to Shammas, the exposure to majority Jewish-Israeli culture brought about an aesthetic uncertainty and confusion for Israeli Palestinians, who began decorating their walls with "cheap reproductions (often depicting a crying child) or tapestries describing imaginary gardens in imaginary places, or uniformly decorated carpets, a distant, melancholic echo of the Alhambra walls" (24). That is, the clash between the contrived tranquility of an idealized Arab past (designated by the symmetrical arabesques of the Alhambra) and an imaginary European future (represented by the Swiss mountains on a living-room tapestry) reflects an ongoing tension experienced by Israeli Palestinians. Confronted with Eurocentric Israeli culture and negotiating competing aesthetic systems, the Israeli Palestinian invokes the Swiss mountains to demonstrate his appreciation of Western beauty, and the arabesque to prove the worthiness of his own culture—but it is the classical Arab home, now lost, that most accurately represents his identity and his culture. Much as the house-key and the stone house represent Palestine itself, Shammas asks us to consider his historicization of the aesthetics of the Israeli-Palestinian house in broader terms, as reflecting the impossible struggle of the Israeli Palestinian seeking a true cultural home in Israel. Returning now to Kashua's houses, it is clear that neither the description above nor the previous one of the parents' house evokes any real sense of "homely-ness."[11] Rather, they demonstrate the extent of the narrator's alienation from the tacky, incongruously juxtaposed objects on the wall, from popular expressions of Palestinian solidarity, and finally from the most intimate space of his childhood. He recognizes the kitsch for what it is, but he finds nothing to replace it.

Kashua does not portray these houses, like the Palestinian poets Slyomovics discusses, in order to assert the fact of their persistent existence.

11. For more on the "homely" and the "unhomely" sensations evoked by different homes, see Blunt and Dowling 2006. Blunt and Dowling link these sensations to experiences of belonging and alienation. Homi Bhabha, in "The World and the Home," uses the term "unhomely" to describe the uncanny and disorienting experience of home in the postcolonial context.

Nor does he attempt to document a culture in ruination, as Said observes in Palestinian literature, through the portrayal of the house as "potential ruin." Kashua's village house is whole, not fragmented; it can be physically inhabited in present reality, not only in memory or the imagination. It functions not only to protect and shelter, but also to assert the continuity of the family, the parents' sense of responsibility for their children and their families, love of one's childhood village (the land as well as its people), and the embrace of tradition. Thus when Kashua's houses fail to protect, the failure reverberates not in terms of a lost past and a determination to regain it in the future, but rather in terms of a collapsed present, a deceitful past, and a hopeless future. Said and Slyomovics refer to remembered houses filled with the yearning for return; Kashua portrays lived houses that are revealed to preclude any possibility of a future or of home. Since his protagonists' relative mobility as blue-ID-card-carrying Israeli Palestinians allows them to *choose* to leave their village home and reside elsewhere, when their alienation drives them back to the village house, it leaves them feeling more vulnerable and isolated than before. After all, the inadequacy of a Tel Aviv apartment as a haven for its Israeli Palestinian inhabitant is to be expected, but the failure of the village house is no less than terrifying, implying that no house can be a home for these characters. Gertz and Khleifi's discussion of the "shrinking of Palestinian space," in general, and the connection they identify between the loss of public (national) space and the loss of private space, refer to cinematic spatiality, but are applicable to literary representations of space as well (2005, 331). The interstitial existence of the Israeli Palestinian reemerges, then, in the tension between tradition (family, community, people) and individual desire (privacy, a release from obligations), a tension that nearly literally brings down the house.

The childhood house in *Dancing Arabs* is established from the onset as having not only a rich family history, but also as a setting in the historical struggle against Israeli Jews. The grandmother's stories and superstitions, particularly regarding the house's dialogue and collaboration with nature, color the protagonist's relations to the house when he is a boy, and demonstrate the divergent attitudes toward the relationships of nature, house, and nation from one generation to another. "My grandpa . . . was a hero, a strong man who had fought against the Jews, but he died at the entrance to his own home just as he was picking some grapes," he relates. "Grandma says Grandpa is a *shahid,* and there are anemones growing in the spot where he bled"[12] (Kashua 2004a, 22). The house, unable to protect the grandfather as he died on its threshold, transforms the grandfather's blood into flowers and memorializes the site of his death. The "local space" of the home intersects with the "national space," to use Gertz's terms. In another instance of natural phenomena playing a role in the national struggle as well as protecting the house, Mother wants to cut down the eucalyptus trees outside the house, which make the house's entry filthy with dirt. "Grandma said that cutting them down would be a disaster, because eucalyptus trees contain a *wali,* a holy spirit who guards the home and the village. She told us how Grandpa's father, Sheikh Ahmad, used to stand beside the eucalyptus trees and talk with the rebels in Jaffa and in the mountains. He would warn them against the Jews, telling them where they were hiding and which route was safest" (25). The eucalyptus trees outside the house symbolize the grandfather's resistance efforts against the Jews, a fact that is directly yet inexplicably related to the holy spirit that resides within them and protects the house. Despite this combined natural and supernatural protection, the protagonist, as a boy, decides with his brothers to dig trenches all around the house, "so we could stand there when the shooting started" (26). When the family visits friends in Ya'bad, in the West Bank, they see bullet holes in the walls of their home. "It really scared me," recalls the protagonist, "because it had never occurred to me that a bullet could actually make a hole through the wall and get inside the house" (26). In the friends' house (situated "outside"), the war is not marked by anemones and eucalyptus trees but by bullet holes. Shocked as a boy that bullets can penetrate a house, the narrator assures himself that "it wouldn't happen to us . . . because our doors were made of wood" (27). His belief in the protective capacity of the house remains unshaken despite this display of vulnerability.

12. This image recalls Esther Raab's poem, "*Pirhey aviv ve-ha-ben ha-met*" [Spring flowers and the dead son], about a youth who has fallen in war, whose sacrificed blood is symbolized by brilliant red anemones (1964, 99).

The vulnerability of the house is exceedingly political in *Dancing Arabs,* which refers to IDF soldiers searching Grandmother's home for weapons (Kashua 2004a, 10); British soldiers ransacking the house and defecating in the big olive jar (32); Israeli police uprooting floor tiles while searching for weapons and drugs in a neighbor's house (209); and other instances of penetration, invasion, and dismemberment of houses. The protagonist's wife begs him to leave Beit Safafa, a Jerusalem neighborhood near "the scariest Jews," the settlers of Gilo, and to move back to Tira, to the house-shell that awaits him, precisely because she feels vulnerable and is certain that they would be safer in a home in the village (157). Trying to convince him to make the move, she says, "At least in Tira you don't hear shooting or helicopters overhead, and they don't disconnect the electricity every time they shell Beit Jala" (157). The statement highlights the sensation of transparency within that home, always open to the noise of war and to the whims of the Israeli Jews who can simply switch off the electricity at will. Lacking a sense of privacy and control over their own space, they consider leaving for the relatively independent position of owning a house in a place where they would not feel like an isolated minority, far from the invasive tentacles of the Jews.

Let It Be Morning reconfigures this dilemma, making it a central concern for another young couple that has just left an increasingly hostile Tel Aviv for the safety and familiarity of Tira. In this second novel, however, the forces that invade the house often blur the simple line between Jew and Arab. Inter-Palestinian relations dominate the plot's foreground; the occupation hovers in its background. Yet it is clearly the occupation and its ramifications that spur the deterioration of relations among the Israeli Palestinian villagers of Tira. *Let It Be Morning* opens with the protagonist's return to his childhood home after a ten-year absence. The young man has left Tel Aviv, significantly, because, unlike his wife, who was "willing to put up with graffiti calling for her deportation, for her death," sprayed on the walls of their apartment building, he was frightened (Kashua 2006, 17). As an Israeli Palestinian living among a Jewish majority, he feels exposed and vulnerable, so he decides to return to his home village, to the large new house his parents have constructed for him, to a quieter and safer life among other Israeli Palestinians.

The house in this novel lacks the mythological elements that characterize the house in *Dancing Arabs*, but it, too, is emphasized as the heart of the family and the touchstone of generational continuity. The main house belongs to the prodigal son's parents, who have built "house shells" for three of their four sons in the hopes that they will return to the village to live near them. The house shells represent the modern manifestation of the *hamula*,[13] or extended family, structure that characterized traditional Arab village life: "In Palestine, members of a *hamula* (clan) are descendents of and share the name of an eponymous ancestor, and in pre-1948 Palestinian villages, members of the same hamula were also bound together territorially by land held in common and adjacent living quarters" (Slyomovics 1998, 137). The shells are also the expression of the parents' hopes for proximity to their cosmopolitan sons. "Fifty steps separate my parents' house from the one where I am about to live," the narrator observes, and recounts his parents' efforts to prepare the house for him. "That's the way it is around here: good parents build homes for their children" (Kashua 2006, 9–10). Two months after his return to the village, he notes that "actually, the two houses we were born in, my wife and I, have become the focal point of our lives. And we're not the only ones. Everyone here is like that" (86). In-laws, parents, brothers—these people and their homes converge to create a community within the larger community of the village, providing a sense of support and combating isolation but also, for the protagonist, stripping the private house of its privacy and denying individual needs and desires. In the first week of his arrival, he stays at his parents' house while the work on his own new house is completed. Kashua provides mundane and almost clinical details of the house's construction, thus emphasizing its newness—a marked departure from conventional poetic representations of Palestinian houses, which, as Slyomovics observes, emphasize objects testifying to rootedness in the past and steadfastness for the future. The protagonist initially imagines a self-imposed isolation in the not-yet-completed house: "I won't even have to

13. For more on the *hamula* and its role in the traditional Palestinian Arab village, see Slyomovics 1998, especially 107–9 and 137–39.

leave the house at all. I'll just sit here at home, oblivious to everything," he thinks. "At least I have a big house to bury myself in" (11). Yet he quickly finds that the anonymity he had hoped to attain there is impossible; the house is prone to continual penetration.

At first, this penetration is mild, the necessary condition of living according to traditional social codes. The protagonist's nosey aunts' unannounced visit, for instance, annoys him and his wife, but they both understand the unwritten rules of the place to which they have returned, and graciously serve and entertain the aunts. Yet more serious events test the house's capacity to act as haven. When the village is suddenly and inexplicably cut off and reserves of food, water, and supplies dwindle, the house, instead of protecting its inhabitants, is penetrated violently by neighbors and other villagers. The "shrinking of space" that Gertz and Khleifi identify in the cinematic context and that Said expresses through the metaphor of the "house that hems one in" becomes literal. Maddeningly for the narrator, though it is the actions of the distant but ever-present IDF soldiers that spark the panic-driven house invasions, those who are penetrating the village homes are other Israeli Palestinians. First, the protagonist realizes that someone has climbed to the roof of his and his brother's home and stolen the remaining water from their tanks (Kashua 2006, 195). As the situation worsens steadily, the nocturnal phantoms that sneak onto the roof to steal water are replaced by hordes of hungry neighbors who, in broad daylight, try, and eventually succeed, to enter the house and strip it of the family's food stores. In one of the most powerful passages in the novel, the protagonist describes his and his brothers' efforts to keep their neighbors out of their parents' house after a neighbor witnesses his wife shaking a bottle of baby formula. As the crowd amasses and attempts to approach the entrance to the house, the brothers realize that they must use force to keep the trespassers at bay. They grow violent in response to the threatening mob, pushing, cursing, charging the crowd and threatening them with improvised weapons and brutal words. The prying neighbor who started the argument draws a veritable lynch mob, a throng of people certain of their entitlement to the contents of their neighbors' house. The scene culminates in vigilante justice. When the thugs who have taken charge of the village arrive to restore order, the narrator admits that there is food in his own house. He relates what follows: "As soon as they hear this, the crowd starts running as fast as they can toward the new houses behind my parents'. . . . [They] break into a wild gallop. . . . We hear the sound of the door breaking. . . . Children and adults run out with big smiles on their faces, carrying sacks of rice, sugar, salt, coffee and flour. They break into my brother's house, too. . . . I sit down on the front steps and look at the people. Most of them I recognize. They're from our neighborhood, after all, some of them close neighbors" (224–25). This scene represents the "shrinking of space" beyond the Israelis' unexplained closure of the village from and to the outside world. The protagonist realizes that the space in which he hoped to "bury" himself and escape the tribulations of political tensions as well as interpersonal dealings had shrunk to nonexistence because it can be appropriated at will—it is not truly his. The distinction between the interior and the exterior of the house blurs and private space effectively disappears as the crowd breaks down the door. All the villagers face the same situation of uncertainty and fear, yet the others are quick to rise against him and his family for self-preservation. The breakdown of the boundaries of public and private space reflects the broader collapse of relations between the village community and the narrator.

The "shrinking of space" manifests itself in both novels, and particularly in the second one, on two levels. The first is the broad political context to which Said refers: Both the protagonists consider leaving their homes in the predominantly Jewish cities where they live and returning to their childhood villages because of increasing hostility toward Arabs. Regardless of their citizenship and their right to live where they please in Israel, they find their Jewish neighbors less and less tolerant of their presence. The space of their acceptance, they determine, cannot be a space with a Jewish majority; their Israel shrinks to the space of their childhood village. The second level of spatial shrinking, which dominates the second novel, is manifested in the invasion of public space into private space, and the disappearance of the latter altogether. The protagonist can move freely neither in Israeli cities nor in his own house. Significantly, in both novels the protagonists end up homeless, lacking the most basic protective capacities of a house: In *Dancing Arabs,* he becomes a "settler," squatting in friends' dorm rooms, and ends up sharing his grandmother's room at home, his own room having been taken over for other purposes. In *Let It Be Morning,* the house that yields so easily to hostile fists disillusions the protagonist, who determines to leave the house and the village because of this incident, only to find himself unable to return to Tel Aviv. Clearly, the house, for Kashua, serves as a microcosm for the broader concept of home-space of the Israeli Palestinian, a vulnerable space subject to the decisions and desires of others. While Kashua's houses, like the houses in the poetry to which Slyomovics refers, exemplify the identity of those who inhabit them, his Israeli Palestinian manifestation of this phenomenon is ominous. Rather than celebrating the close bond between the community and the individual, Kashua's representations suggest that this bond smothers the individual and leaves him prone to violation. For his characters, these houses, unlike those remembered or dreamt of by their exiled compatriots, signify not community but isolation, not safety but vulnerability.

The "Inside" Village and "Inauthentic" Palestinianism

Said writes about the Palestinian village as "the center of life" (1999, 88). Slyomovics concurs, calling the village an "Arab vernacular" (1998, 38). Its centrality in the collective memory of exiled Palestinians has imbued it with political meaning as well. Slyomovics cites Ted Swedenberg's assertion that the village is one of the most important national signifiers in the Palestinian struggle against Israel (xx). In literature, the return to the fertile, intimately familiar childhood village is a prominent theme, a particular manifestation of the broader theme of return to the homeland. Levy notes the expression of this theme in poetry by Israeli Palestinian poets, arguing that for Shammas the move from the traditional village to the Jewish city constitutes an "exile from childhood" that makes it impossible for him to truly return (2008, 382). Other critics have focused not on the theme of *returning* to the village but on the difficulty of *leaving* it. Batya Gur compares the village in Kashua's first novel to the *mahsom,* writing that it impedes the protagonist's successful integration into mainstream Israeli society: "Every detail in this book— . . . the anxieties at intersections that he will be identified as an Arab—reveals the tragic conflict linked to the identity of Israeli Arabs who want to break through the *mahsom* of the village" (2005, 394–95). Gregory, on the other hand, argues that Israel has institutionalized the besiegement of Palestinian villages within Israel, making it difficult to move freely beyond them (130). In a similar vein, Zeedani writes that Israel has transformed every unit of Palestinian space, including the village, "into an island separate unto itself, into a large prison" (Part I).

It is not surprising to read the sad statistics supplied by Gregory and Zeedani and to arrive at their conclusion about the paralyzing effect of Israeli policies on Palestinian villages in Israel. Kashua's portrayal of the besieged Tira in *Let It Be Morning* stands as an extreme and quite literal example of this paralysis. In that novel, the protagonist has returned to his childhood village of Tira, hoping to find some peace in his new house. One morning, the village is inexplicably surrounded by IDF tanks that violently deflect all attempts to leave the village. The villagers helplessly watch their food and water diminish; with no electricity or phone service, they are suddenly and utterly cut off from the outside world. Yet even before the IDF surrounds and closes off the village, the narrator's wife points out that her relationship to the village, as a woman, differs from his, and that she detests "this stifling, bleak village that has nothing to offer her" (2006, 18, 87). She perceives the village as limiting and provincial, and the family's move from Tel Aviv to Tira creates considerable tension between husband and wife: "My wife didn't like the idea of returning to the village. In fact, she hated the idea, and she hated me all the more on account of it. More than anything, she hated the village" (16–17). The narrator makes the decision to leave Tel Aviv, where he feels threatened by hostile graffiti; yet he, too, is not thrilled to return to "this lousy village," which demands that he relinquish his cherished anonymity (11). When the tanks surround the village and barbed wire appears across the roads leading inside and out, the stifling is no longer abstract. No one can enter or exit the village, and the inhabitants retreat into their homes to await some explanation or reassurance as the village around them explodes into crime and disarray. This paralysis is literal and palpable—these people cannot move—and it constitutes the heart of Kashua's plot.

The more subtle dynamic of the village, however, and the one that reveals more about the self-conception of Israeli Palestinians, involves the relationship between the Israeli Palestinian village and its "outside" counterpart. Several critics have noted the role of memory and the past in the habitation of the "outside" villages. "While Arab houses become Jewish-owned in Israel," notes Slyomovics, "simultaneously, Arab villages outside Israel are imaginatively recast as Palestinian" (1998, 83). She cites Nawwaf Abu al-Hayja's concept of "twins" to discuss these "deterritorializing ruptures in time and place that are precariously restructured by Palestinian exiles. Exiles entwine and twin disparate and separate places. . . . Former dwellings are imaginatively reconstructed elsewhere" (83–84). The role of Palestinian poets and writers, for Slyomovics, is to reconstruct the place through eloquent and detailed descriptions of place, to allow for a "return" in memory and the imagination (84). Similarly, Barbara Parmenter observes that Palestinian refugees have reconstructed their home villages in the space of the refugee camps, duplicating their "inside" villages on the "outside": "Re-creating certain aspects of home imbues the camp with form and meaning otherwise absent in exile" (1994, 67). She cites Mahmoud Darwish's story of his conversation with an Israeli soldier after the 1967 War: "He told me that when he entered one of the refugee camps he found that its residents were living exactly as they had lived in their former village. They were distributed just as they had been. The same village and the same streets. The soldier was irritated. . . . Nineteen years had passed and they still said: 'We are from Bi'r al-Sab'!'" (67). The exiles, having superimposed the "form and meaning" of their home village onto the camp, confirm their connection to that place with the assertion "We are from Bi'r al-Sab'."

Imagining the village as "twinned" reveals fascinating nuances of its prominent role in the establishment of a unified, *authentic* Palestinian identity. The village "inside" allows its inhabitants to retain their connection to the land, but the village "outside," which had to sacrifice this connection and to develop a narrative about this loss, is considered more authentically Palestinian. In what can be understood in relation to an ironic reconstitution of the Jewish relationship to the land, a crucial theme of the Palestinian national narrative became yearning for the lost land and dreaming of return. The notion of actually residing on it was inevitably complicated by the requirement of civic, political, and cultural intimacy with the Israeli oppressor.

The "inside" village differs fundamentally from the camps and villages described by Slyomovics and Parmenter. The village inside Israel is truly rooted in its place, having survived the *naqba* and the fragmentation of the Palestinian nation. Its inhabitants have lived there for generations, and it overflows with their memories and stories. Yet the Palestinian narrative is centered on and formulated around the concept of *return*. The extent to which Israeli Palestinians can participate in such a narrative is, of course, severely limited. One of the undercurrents in Kashua's novels is the Palestinian discourse of authenticity. Suffering and displacement define the experience of the Palestinian refugee and entitle him to an uncomplicated identity. The relative comfort and privilege of Palestinian citizens of Israel, rooted in their home villages, precludes such clarity. The Israeli Palestinians in Kashua's novels consider themselves less Palestinian than their compatriots in refugee camps, whose lives are characterized by suffering and whose identity is grounded in memory rather than in the proximity to a Jewish Israeli culture that alternates between seduction and hostility. This consciousness is as defining as their alienation from mainstream Jewish Israeli society. Both phenomena find expression in Kashua's portrayal of the village as a space continually imitating other spaces, not in an assertion of identity but in a desperate attempt to integrate its disparate and often opposed elements.

The "outside" Palestinians, those whose identity is not diluted by Israeli citizenship, are sometimes portrayed as ghosts. In *Dancing Arabs*, the protagonist relates how neither he nor any of his classmates in Tira could answer the teacher when he asks what Palestine is; when asked if any of them had ever seen a Palestinian, one student said "he'd once been driving with his father in the dark and they'd seen two Palestinians" (Kashua 2004a, 104). The figure of the "Palestinian," having faded in the child's consciousness to a ghostly trace, symbolizes the broader forgetfulness that threatens Israeli-Palestinian identity. The angry teacher replies, "'We are Palestinians, you are Palestinians, I'm a Palestinian! You nincompoops, you animals, I'll teach you who you are!" (104). As a child, the protagonist does not know what PLO stands for and "can't even draw a flag" (18). These recollections of ignorance imply that the protagonist is not worthy of the identity that others embrace proudly and without ambivalence. If he is, indeed, a Palestinian, then he is a different kind of Palestinian—an inauthentic one. Not only are he and his friends and siblings ignorant of concrete signifiers of their identity, but they also have a clear sense of *separation* or *difference* from those who they perceive as Palestinian, a perception that is based on place. When the family goes to the West Bank village Ya'bad to visit friends, the protagonist notes that "the war in Ya'bad was very real, not like the one in Grandma's stories," emphasizing his personal distance from the "real" war, and suggesting that he is therefore not a "real" Palestinian (26). His father confirms the dissimilarity when he asserts that "we were different. . . . He'd say that the people in Ya'bad and their children were heroes. They weren't spineless nothings like us" (27). As a boy, the protagonist would hurry to buy the morning groceries before the arrival of the *Gazazweh*, the workers from Gaza, whom he hated "because everyone hated them. . . . You'd only see them early in the morning when it was still dark outside, because they weren't supposed to be moving about in the daytime. They came to buy food, and then they'd vanish as if they'd never been there, as if there were no Gazazweh in the world" (19). Ephemeral, voiceless, and distant, the Gazan workers represent a distinct, threatening identity with which the protagonist cannot identify. The two figures walking on a dark road, the Gazans hated by the villagers, the men who are inexplicably threatening to the young protagonist—they are the ones who can presumably draw the flag and explain the meaning of PLO—they are the ones, in short, who are *authentically* Palestinian. Significantly, they are also shrouded in mystery, unknowable and unspeaking. Since they must move beneath the gaze of Israeli surveillance, they are seen only under cover of darkness in the village, a fact that casts doubt on their very existence and makes the concept of "Palestinian" almost mythological for the young protagonist.

Kashua's village itself reflects this distinction between the mysterious but authentic Palestinians and the Israeli Palestinians in its fragmented spatial duplications. The spatial palimpsest mentioned by Slyomovics, in which traces of formerly Palestinian places are visible beneath newly Israeli places, has been represented in Israeli literature, most notably in A. B. Yehoshua's famous story "*Mul ha-ye'arot*" (Facing the forests) (1968), which tells of a Jewish National Fund forest that burns to the ground to reveal the remains of an Arab village that it replaced. Parmenter invokes the palimpsest to describe a different spatial reconfiguration, of the refugee camp on which refugees impose, to the best of their abilities, the structure and organization of the village they fled or were forced to leave. This duplicated village serves as spatial resistance to the displacement experienced by the refugees and to the forgetfulness that threatens to tarnish their memories of home. The image of their home village as it was when they left it becomes the true representation of the Palestinian village home. Of course, what these duplications do not take into account is that the original village, if it still existed, would not remain frozen in a single historical moment, as it remains frozen in the collective memory that preserves it.

The real space of quotidian life, the Israeli Palestinian village is never frozen like the remembered place, but dynamic. It is not reconstituted or duplicated. It is the original village, the one from which the Palestinians were not expelled, the one from which they did not feel compelled to flee. Yet as we have seen, the Israeli Palestinian's presence on the land is what foils his authenticity as a Palestinian. Those who suffer, who live far from the land, who are impoverished and stateless—they are the true Palestinians. This confused and confusing identity, suspended between a clearly Israeli one and a clearly Palestinian one, gives rise to a new identity that is not so much a hybrid but more a superficial collage of various components identified with "authentic" Palestinian and Jewish Israeli identity. The Israeli Palestinian village, where Palestinians continue to live, experiences the changes that the "authentic" duplicated village does not. The narrator of *Let It Be Morning*, who left the village after high school, returns to a very different place. For him, the transformation, characterized by Western consumerism, brand-name fetishism, showy technology, and a new personal aesthetics, represents the seeping of the Israeli culture of Tel Aviv into the village. He drives past the local high school on his way to his in-laws' house, watching the students congregated outside

> looking different from what I'd expected. The boys look like Israeli high school students. Their clothes are so different from what we used to wear at their age, which was only ten years ago. Everyone wears

jeans, everyone has gel in their hair, and their shirts are the latest fashion. When I was their age, we all dressed the same, in clothes that were
made in the village, cotton pants and blue shirts. . . . The number of
girls wearing a veil is even more surprising. I don't remember a single
girl wearing a veil when I was at school. . . . I don't really feel like I'm
going back to an old familiar place. I'm going home, to a new place.
(Kashua 2006, 15–16)

The students still congregate, as they always have, outside the school.
However, the surface features of the familiar scene—the clothing, the
hairstyles, the attitudes—have changed. It is not just the superficial elements of Tel Aviv culture that have invaded the village. External signs
of increasing religiosity, a harking back to a different sense of tradition
(which was never part of the village as it used to exist), appear in the form
of the girls' veils. Watching the displacement of the village culture that
he remembers, he is as nostalgic as an exile, yearning for a place that no
longer exists except in his memory.

As Tira descends into chaos and the rule of law, already tenuous,
dwindles ever more in *Let It Be Morning,* the chagrined narrator relates
that gun-toting gangsters and hoodlums have appointed themselves the
authorities in this new state of emergency, increasing the influence they
had already begun to enjoy prior to this new state, when they "protected"
businesses in exchange for hefty sums. Most disturbing to him is their
cynical use of nationalism as the banner beneath which they seize power,
and their replication of "authentically" Palestinian behavior to justify
their might. The ubiquitous television sets that beam infinitely duplicated
scenes of Palestinian heroism give rise to a literal duplication by the Tira
gangs. Their violent behavior and their unlawful takeover of the village
are legitimized by their claims of authentic Palestinianism.

A few of the older women shout with joy at the sight of the armed men,
as if they were warriors about to liberate the village from a siege. . . . All
of them have a criminal record, they are members of a gang that steals
cars and pushes drugs, the kind of gang that have become an inseparable part of the local scene. Now the women are shouting and treating
them like war heroes. Their attempt at imitating well-known Palestinian

themes is pathetic. What can they be thinking? And just what organization do they belong to? . . . What exactly does the nationalistic consciousness of those people consist of? (Kashua 2006, 203)

In effect, the thugs attempt to duplicate the power structures necessitated
by statelessness and the lack of an infrastructure and a legal system, a situation all too familiar to "outside" Palestinians, which has now been effected
in Tira by the withdrawal and stranglehold of the Israeli authorities. The
thugs are simply responding to the village's new configuration, filling a
vacuum of uncontrolled space. While the refugee camps and exilic villages "outside" the land replicate the Palestinian villages left behind on
the "inside," this Israeli Palestinian village imitates the power structure of
the Occupied Territories.

Such spatial flimsiness reflects the uncertainty of Israeli Palestinian
identity as a whole. Kashua's protagonists feel like unwelcome guests in Tel
Aviv and like strangers in their village, which itself is caught between the
ostentatious Western material culture of Israel and the imitation of what
is perceived as authentic Palestinian existence, the suffering and violence
of exile. In *Let It Be Morning*, the villagers' acquiescence toward this new
development demonstrates their eagerness to participate in an authentic
Palestinian narrative that has been denied them because of the uncertain
privilege of their Israeli citizenship. When, at the end of the novel, their
village is included in a newly created independent Palestine, however, the
unceremonious stripping of their Israeli citizenship leaves them feeling
not liberated or authentic. Rather than resolve the question of their identity, it only further complicates it. Relieved of its interstitial metaphorical
geography between Jewish Israel and the Occupied Territories, the Israeli
Palestinian village is now a *Palestinian* village. It has been pushed out of
the hallucinatory space of no-man's-land and into the clear cartography
of the new Palestine: "And the territories being handed over to the Palestinians are colored blue. Our village is colored blue. . . . It must be a
mistake. Some idiot graphic artist who always thought that Wadi Ara and
the Triangle are both located on the West Bank" (Kashua 2006, 262). But
it is no mistake. With their unambiguous new identity absurdly established
by the appearance of their village on a color-coded map ("I think we're

Palestinian now," the protagonist says to his wife [266]), all they can ask is, "What do we do now?" (267).

Kashua effectively rewrites the collective Palestinian story centered by the trope of return in his representation of the Israeli Palestinian village. *Dancing Arabs* ends with the protagonist's determination to return: "I go back to Tira more often, in search of an answer, trying to find out what others like me, people with a blue ID card, have decided to do, trying to see if there's any hope left. . . . I've got to go back. Mother says they're liable to load each village onto a different truck, and we'll wind up being taken from Beit Safafa to Jordan" (2004a, 223–24). Kashua's next novel has a different cast of characters but picks up where the first novel leaves off, its protagonist having arrived at the village, ambivalent yet ready to continue his life there. Unlike refugees, Kashua's Israeli Palestinian characters are able to return to the place of their memory, yet they find that the village has changed, responding to and integrating the influences surrounding it. As we have seen, the modest Tira remembered in *Let It Be Morning* has been replaced by an amalgam of religious Islam, imitations of "authentic" Palestinianism and Western cultural signifiers. Straddling past and present, Palestine and Israel, authenticity and artifice, tradition and change, the Israeli Palestinian village exemplifies the Israeli Palestinian's interstitial existence.

Conclusion

Intimately bonded to both the Israeli Jew and the iconic Palestinian, Kashua's protagonists warily and somewhat apologetically inhabit their place. Their Israeli citizenship secures no room for them in the schema of Israeli national identity, which imagines the Israeli presence on the land as the culmination of a Jewish narrative of homecoming after a long exile. Israeli Palestinians obviously cannot lay claim to this commonality and to the exilic past that informs it, and are therefore barred from full participation in Israeli national culture. On the other hand, they cannot fully participate in Palestinian national culture, either, since its central components are memory, yearning, and the dream of return—to the land where Israeli Palestinians still live. On the most fundamental level Israeli

Palestinians can participate neither in the mainstream Israeli narrative of place relations nor in the Palestinian one. In some respects these two narratives are strikingly similar, for instance in the importance they attach to the land, the significance of return, and the experience of exile. Yet the concrete political tension between them hums like an electric fence. When Anton Shammas writes that he hallucinates "in no-man's-land," he is referring specifically to language—to his position as a poet of both Arabic and Hebrew verse—and also nodding to its relationship with place, as we see in his play on the Hebrew *safa* as both language and geographical entity. More broadly, however, he refers to the interstitial existence signified in Kashua's novels by the *mahsom* stage, the penetrable house with its kitschy decorations, and the "inside" village and its ambivalent "authenticity." This in-betweenness, which precludes any possible movement toward one side or the other, strips Kashua's protagonists of a clear identity and of a coherent sense of self. Ultimately, they realize that their return and emplacement, while physically viable, are more impossible than for exiled Palestinians. Whereas the latter remember their home from their place of exile, the former can only hallucinate in no-man's-land.

Sight and the Diaspora Chronotope

Yoel Hoffmann

> There is more to the landscape than that which is visible.
> —DELL UPTON, "Seen, Unseen, and Scene"

The failure of the Zionist narrative to account for the diverse experiences of those it purports to unite can induce terrible anxiety about one's relationship to place. Since the 1980s, Hebrew literature has been preoccupied not only with expressing this distress, as I have explained, but also with responding to it. The first chapter of this book sketches the contours of the antagonistic and domineering Zionist spatial sensibility, as represented in Amos Oz's novels. Oz's characters ultimately come to terms with this sensibility and the angst it generates by restraining urges that threaten their identity. The next two chapters demonstrate the terrifying isolation and the paralysis of in-betweenness, respectively, that result from a spatial anxiety that remains unresolved in the novels of Orly Castel-Bloom and Sayed Kashua. Concerned more with the *acknowledgment* of the ill-fitting hegemonic spatial model their characters contend with than with a resolution to the problem, neither Castel-Bloom nor Kashua offers an alternative to it. The remaining chapters, by contrast, demonstrate two different reactions to this spatial anxiety.

Yoel Hoffmann chronologically belongs to the generation of Amos Oz and A. B. Yehoshua. Born in Hungary in 1937, he arrived in Palestine as an infant. Literarily, however, the differences between him and the members of the State Generation (*dor ha-medina*) to which Oz and Yehoshua belong are vast. Unlike those two authors, who began writing and publishing to great critical and popular acclaim in their mid-twenties, Hoffmann, a professor of Japanese poetry, published his first novel only in 1988, when he was nearly fifty years old. His late bloom as an author, his professional academic training, his considerable knowledge of languages, and his extensive exposure to Buddhism and Japanese culture set him apart from other authors of his generation. His poetic style has been identified as sharing certain traits with the younger authors who began publishing around the same time as him. Considered part of the postmodern wave or "Other Wave" (*Gal aher*), in Avraham Balaban's words (1995), that swept Israeli literature in the 1980s, it is fragmented, sparse, and has been dismissed by frustrated readers as esoteric. Accordingly, Hoffmann's reception among the Israeli reading public has been mixed. Despite his awards and critical acclaim (Rachel Albeck-Gidron is completing a monograph devoted to his work), few people outside the world of academe and literary circles have read Yoel Hoffmann. In a country where authors are well-known and recognizable figures active in public life, Hoffmann is something of an anomaly.

His challenging and seemingly impenetrable style expresses thematic concerns that are not so radical in the larger context of twentieth-century literature from around the world: displacement, immigration, assimilation, and exile. His characters, mostly European Jews, develop complex relations with both Europe and Israel in their experiences of immigration and flight. While some of them survive horrific violence, Hoffmann's often laconic prose focuses the reader's attention less on their sometimes overwhelming victimization and suffering and more on their day-to-day interactions in and with vernacular places, which, despite their ordinariness, contain sparks of spiritual and poetic illumination.

Hoffmann's novella *Sefer yosef* (The book of Joseph) (1988) and novel *Kristus shel dagim* (Christ of fish) (1991) portray two different Europes, the former the Europe in which time and place accord but that is absurd nonetheless; the latter the Europe that no longer exists in Europe but has reemerged in Palestine, a displaced space that enables a sense of home for the characters. Together with *Katschen*, the companion novella of *The Book of Joseph*, these works reclaim the European diaspora without overlooking its horrors. This dynamic suggests that Hoffmann's texts sidestep the ideological questions of place that plague the authors in the preceding sections. Instead, these texts find alternative modes of interaction with vernacular places. They reconfigure the kibbutz as marginal, both geographically and literarily; sitting in "salon spaces" such as cafés and in bourgeois living rooms, their characters rearrange the relationship between space and time to redeem, at least partially, Europe, the place containing memories both bright and dark; and they emancipate the Jewish relationship to place from a particularized territoriality, even within Israel itself, and portray it as a multiplicity that is rich but sometimes tragic. Their experiences of vernacular places are integrated with a temporal component that, along with the collected objects and fragmented diasporic memories that they bring to these places, enables them to inhabit a veritable "diaspora chronotope," even while strolling on the Tel Aviv boardwalk. Hoffmann's defiance of established spatial categories is clear in his unconventional gendering of place, as well. The fragmented and multilayered spatial sensibility with which Hoffmann imbues his characters contributes to an Israeli identity, but one that is not bound by and barely engages with the spatiality of Zionist ideology.

The gaze and the faculty of seeing are commissioned as the central means by which a subject identifies him- or herself in vernacular place, providing a counterpoint to Dolly's visually aided disintegration in *Dolly City*. In *The Book of Joseph*, *Katschen*, and *Christ of Fish*, a central metaphor accounting for the relationship between people and place is that of the image or sight, *mar'eh*. The Hebrew word *mar'eh* has several meanings; the two most relevant to this discussion relate to seeing/sight and prophecy. Hoffmann's protagonists articulate their understanding of place, first and foremost, through visual perception: they see yet are not always seen, they watch formless space, they gaze sorrowfully at mirrors, they see worlds unseen by others. Often, they observe rather than participate in their place, whether Europe or Israel. Ironically, their gaze leads them to a more intimate understanding of the place they inhabit than those who have a more "natural" or native relationship to it. "To see" in the sense of prophesying also plays a role in these characters' perception of place, particularly in *Christ of Fish*, in which common objects become the elements of a veritable prophetic vision that annihilates the conventional link between place and time and proposes a new configuration of these phenomena. In *The Book of Joseph*, too, the "hypersight" of certain characters enables them to see their place more sharply than others.

Gaze theory, as it has been articulated predominantly in psychoanalytic, feminist, and postcolonial studies, also plays a role in this analysis. However, it serves more as a contrast than as a methodology. Jacques Lacan's conception of the gaze developed from his earlier notion of the "mirror stage," when the infant gazing at his or her image in the mirror identifies with the image there, establishing "a relation between the organism and its reality" that is marked by "a primordial Discord," ultimately resulting in a "fragmented body" (1977, 4). The *I*, for Lacan, alienates its self and becomes an other. In later writings, Lacan discusses the gaze in terms of "the division of the subject" (1981, 270). The gaze is a function of the "desire of the Other," revealing a lack and the disparity between illusion and "the Real": "What one looks at is what cannot be seen" (182). Jean-Paul Sartre defines the relationship between self and other in primarily visual terms, asserting that "the Other is on principle the *one who looks at me*" (1956, 256). For Sartre, the Other's gaze evokes shock and shame, "the recognition of the fact that I am indeed that object which the Other is looking at and judging" (261). In turn, he continues, by looking at people, "I measure my power" (266). While Hoffmann's texts demonstrate a clear connection between gazing and subjectivity, they suggest that it is possible to reject the hierarchy of power created by gazer and gazed, through the mutual gaze. That is, where gaze theory holds that the act of gazing can fragment, alienate, or objectify, disempowering the gazed, shaming him and stripping him of subjectivity, Hoffmann's texts suggest that, by looking into someone's eyes, the gazer enables the gazed to reciprocate, thereby ascribing him with subjectivity. Moreover, more often than not, the unreturned gaze in Hoffmann's texts signals the loneliness and isolation of the gazer, who watches because he cannot *be* in the place.

From the first sentences of *Katschen*, which takes place in Israel, it is clear not only that Israel poses no solution or resolution to the crisis of exile that will emerge in *The Book of Joseph*, but even that it deepens it by creating a sense of exile in the place that is supposed to be its antidote. Europe is too deeply embedded in these characters to be erased by the

Hebrew language and Zionist ideals. Despite the dark barbarity that under-lies Hoffmann's Europe in *The Book of Joseph*, his characters in *Katschen* and other works cannot repudiate Europe or forget it. They are inextrica-bly bound to its culture, its languages, its mannerisms, its objects. They therefore engage in a seemingly illogical resistance against the forgetting of Europe in Palestine. The Europe they remember and that they sometimes bizarrely reconstruct in Tel Aviv, Haifa, and Jerusalem has been, in effect, destroyed. Yet, with their feet firmly planted on Mediterranean ground, these characters are able to do what they could not do if they were still living in Austria or Germany: they re-create the Europe of their memories, frequenting Viennese cafés and serving strudel in German drawing rooms.

Beyond the Kibbutz

The metaphorical value of the kibbutz was tremendous in the formation of an Israeli national identity, as discussed in chapter 1. It provided not only an ideal type of Jew, the muscular and taciturn farmer-soldier with a social consciousness, but also an idealized place where the new breed of Jews would thrive. This place was imagined as a native space, and con-structed in opposition to stereotypical notions of Jewish spaces in Europe. Rural and collectivized, the kibbutz offered Jews a new self-conception, far from both the cramped study houses and the bourgeois urban settings of Europe. The kibbutz inhabitants were considered by Israeli society to be the true inheritors of the *halutsim*, or pioneers, and therefore to represent native Israeliness. The kibbutz gained a mythological status, becoming in the popular Israeli imagination a place endowed with transformative pow-ers and the capacity to reshape its people. Despite economic difficulties and various scandals, to this day in Israel the kibbutz and its inhabitants are regarded with reverence and admiration. The kibbutz remains a sym-bol of *erets yisrael ha-ktana*, "The Little Israel" from the bygone heyday of the 1950s and 1960s. Much as the Land of Israel had been replaced by the State of Israel, the Jew by the Israeli, the text by the plough, so had the kib-butz replaced Jerusalem as the center of the new Jewish collective identity.

In his autobiography *Sipur al ahava ve-hoshekh* (A tale of love and dark-ness) (2002), Amos Oz recalls the mythical status ascribed in his Jerusalem childhood to pioneers who established and lived on kibbutzim. In the city considered by Judaism to be the holy center itself, even those people who were opposed to Labor ideology identified with the pioneers and with kibbutzim and admired the "new breed of heroic Jews, . . . a tanned, tough, silent, practical breed of men, totally unlike the Jews of the Diaspora" (2004, 5). Oz recalls looking "over the hills and far away" to the pioneers "beyond our horizon, in Galilee, Sharon, and the Valleys," to define the society that was, to a large degree, still unshaped in practice (2004, 5). Oz himself chose at an early age to construct his life around this ideal, leaving Jerusalem for the fields of Kibbutz Hulda as an adolescent, spending three decades there, and setting many of his stories and novels in kibbutzim. Even Oz, a firm believer in kibbutz ideology, has been aware of its flaws. This has been apparent since his first collection of short stories, *Artsot ha-tan* (Where the jackals howl) and his first novel, *Makom aher* (Elsewhere, perhaps), published in 1965 and 1966, respectively. Yet, regardless of this critical awareness, and despite the fact that he is not a native-born son of the kibbutz, Oz writes about it from a sympathetic perspective.

Other Israeli authors have written stories and novels that take place at least partly in kibbutzim and that illuminate their hypocrisy and ideological failure in a much less flattering light. Eli Amir's well-known novel *Tarnegol kaparot* (Scapegoat) (1983) tells the story of Mizrahi youths who are separated from their families and sent to a kibbutz to be inculcated with Zionist values, only to realize that their culture is being erased and their traditions mocked. Yehoshua Kenaz's *Hitganvut yehidim* (Infiltration) (1986), about a platoon of young men with slight disabilities that have earned them a low army profile, takes place on an army training base in the 1950s. One of the main characters, admired and respected by the others since he hails from a kibbutz and embodies its ideals, is ultimately revealed as deeply troubled beneath his suntanned, idealistic exterior. In such novels, even the most critical ones, there is an acknowledgment of the lure of the Labor ideology that dominates kibbutzim, as well as of the attraction of the various symbols, values, and figures associated with the kibbutz (the Sabra, closeness to the land, anti-bourgeois values, etc.). Central to these plots or subplots dealing with the kibbutz is the struggle to come to terms with its imperfections and injustices, to reconcile the actual with the mythical. A place like any other, with its petty rivalries, narrow-minded prejudices, and even apathy, the kibbutz, they suggest, is nevertheless a model home characterized by social justice, a place evoking admiration and hope. Even those texts that have criticized the kibbutz, in short, have acknowledged it as a place at the center of Israeli identity.

Yoel Hoffmann treats the kibbutz differently in *Katschen*, which takes place in prestate Palestine during the 1940s. Told in third person from the perspective of a small child nicknamed Katschen, whose mother has died and whose father is in a mental institute, the story follows Katschen from home to home and from one de facto foster parent to another. The story's progression on a more or less conventional temporal trajectory sets it apart from some of Hoffmann's subsequent works.

The representation of place, on the other hand, has remained consistent in most of his novels. His characters, often older European immigrants living in Haifa or Tel Aviv, inhabit Israel like permanent visitors. Utterly removed from the ideological and internal political squabbles of the day, which preoccupy characters in other novels and stories set in that period (for example, those of Moshe Shamir and S. Yizhar, who actually wrote in the 1940s and 1950s), their relationship to Israel is characterized by disconnection. These are not the Israeli-born Ashkenazim at the top of Israel's cultural and social hierarchy. These are not pioneers, Labor ideologues, or Zionist revisionists. There is no space for them in the European Israeli narrative of the 1940s and 1950s, except perhaps the terrible category of refugees or Holocaust survivors. Yet the men and women in Hoffmann's novels seem to exist outside the familiar bounds of literature set in Israel. Indeed, they seem distinctly *foreign*, not only because we are constantly reminded that they are speaking languages other than Hebrew but also because of their mannerisms, their cultural references, and myriad other details provided by the author. While such details are often ascribed to European-born *halutsim* and *kibbutznikim* in other novels, they are usually portrayed as part of a Zionized or Israelized identity of the typical first-generation pioneer who reviles his own diasporic past but accepts it as a fundamental part of his identity and the basis for his own place at the top of Israel's ethnic hierarchy. In Hoffmann's novels, this diasporic "foreignness" evokes neither a sense of self-disgust nor ideologically heated self-analysis. Embedded at the core of these characters' identity, their unquestioned "diasporic" traits mark them as strangers in their homeland.

The Austrian boy Katschen is no exception. After bouncing from place to place with his penniless uncle, who must constantly move since he cannot afford to pay rent, Katschen is sent briefly to his aunt's, and from there it is decided that he would be best served at a kibbutz. Shortly after his arrival at the kibbutz, Katschen is told that his uncle has died and his aunt has returned to Vienna. He is left, for all intents and purposes, an orphan. The section of the novella that takes place in the kibbutz actually spans one day. Having quickly realized that the kibbutz is no place for a boy named Katschen, the boy wanders beyond its boundaries.

It is there, beyond the kibbutz itself, that most is revealed about the kibbutz. In the brief time that Katschen spends within the kibbutz, he goes to the school and attends a biology lesson, where the teacher cuts a leaf to discuss photosynthesis. This scene is no longer than one page in the novel, but its reverberations echo throughout it and, arguably, in Hoffmann's other novels. Katschen's "diasporic" persona is articulated deftly through various details. His name is "not a proper name for a kibbutz," since it is not a Hebrew name (Hoffmann 1998b, 128). He is humiliated when he responds "*nein*" when asked if he is familiar with photosynthesis, which he takes to be a German word (129). The other children laugh at his polished shoes and neat clothing. Despite his youth, Katschen understands that there is something different about the kibbutz, that it must be defined according to a particular principle. His childish definition of this principle is astute: "'The work of the people in this place,' thought Katschen, 'is cutting'" (129). This conclusion is based on Katschen's observation in the kibbutz, where he is greeted by the proclamation that his name must be severed and replaced, where he walks into the classroom of a teacher wielding a knife and a cut leaf, and where he sees a woman in a tree with a saw. To the Israeli reader in 1988, Katschen's innocent notion of the kibbutz as a "place that cuts" one's cultural identity to create a homogeneous, unified national identity was already a familiar one, as it had been addressed directly in several novels, such as Amir's *Scapegoat*.

Katschen, however, ventures beyond the kibbutz. Indeed, he leaves all recognizably marked territory altogether. In Amir's novel, the protagonist is caught between the kibbutz and the *ma'abara*, the transit camp, and in Oz's *A Perfect Peace*, Yoni ventures to the desert and to the ruined Arab village of Sheikh Dahr. These places, like the characters who move in them, occupy a clear space within the Israeli national narrative, one with an identifiable cultural currency. The space in which Katschen wanders after leaving the kibbutz, however, is not clearly defined in this way. A collection of ordinary vernacular places, it is significant because of the characters who inhabit it, whom Katschen meets in his wanderings.

This emphasis on the humanity of the characters, rather than on their symbolic or representational capacity, is central in *Katschen*. This is one reason that people's names are so important in this novella as well as in Hoffmann's other works. Of his nine books, four—*Katschen*, *Bernhardt* (1989), *Ma shlomekh dolores?* (How do you do, Dolores?) (1995), and *Efrayim* (2003)—include names in their titles. In *Katschen*, it is Katschen's realization of the kibbutz as a place where things are cut that illuminates the importance of his own name: "Katschen remembered that when Herr Grossman came to the kibbutz they cut off his Herr. 'Soon, when the people here turn to me,' thought Katschen to himself, 'they will cut my name off'" (1998b, 129). The literal knives and saws that Katschen sees are transformed to metaphorical agents of cutting. Yet even before he arrives at this realization, Katschen had internalized and rebelled against the inadequacy of his name in the kibbutz. The rejection of his name is pronounced three times, first by a woman in the kibbutz office, then by Uncle Arthur, who repeats what she said to Herr Grossman, and finally by Herr Grossman, who confirms the unacceptability of the name. Later, when Herr Grossman asks him why he escaped from the kibbutz, Katschen thinks, "He knows that my name is Katschen," and imagines Herr Grossman uttering his name in the kibbutz: "A man in blue clothes waves a knife and says, 'Did you say it? Did you say it?' A woman descends from a ladder, her saw extended before her, saying, 'Did he say it? Did he say it?'" (Hoffmann 1988, 37). For Katschen, the kibbutz, the place itself, is incompatible with his name; since he wants to keep his name, he flees the kibbutz and its nightmarish blades.

Besides the obvious connection between name, identity, and subjectivity, the name in the Zionist-Israeli context contains an additional ideological valence. "The new Hebrew names," notes Oz Almog, "became a Zionist symbol that distinguished between Jews from the Diaspora and Jews from the Land of Israel" (2000, 91):

> The practice of changing an immigrant's name characterizes most (perhaps all) immigrant societies. But in Yishuv and Israeli society, unlike other immigrant societies, this process was imbued with ideological content and was accomplished with the open intervention of the agents of socialization, which testifies to its importance. In schools and immigrant transit camps, teachers and social counselors urged pupils and their parents to Hebraicize both names, but especially family names. The army also mobilized itself enthusiastically for this mission and even appointed a names committee. . . . This cultural campaign was not coercive, but the suggestion to change one's name was nevertheless made aggressively and was supported by ideological and nationalist arguments. (Almog 2000, 94)

That Katschen still answers to his unmistakably diasporic name designates his failure in "closing the door to the Diaspora past" (Almog 2000, 93). In the kibbutz, the bastion of Zionist ideology, this failure prompts immediate corrective action: "Here we'll have to call you by a name that's suitable for a kibbutz," asserts a woman there (Hoffmann 1998b, 127).

Immediately after this veritable burial of Katschen's name, Herr Grossman leads Uncle Arthur and Katschen to the kibbutz school. When, on the way, they pass a cow, "Katschen looked into the cow's eyes and the cow looked into Katschen's eyes" (Hoffmann 1998b, 127). The eyes—not merely the act of looking—are emphasized. The sentence strikes an odd chord not just because of the unnecessary repetition of Katschen's name, but also because of the almost disconcerting symmetry in the sentence structure and in the act it describes. The cow's ability to look into the boy's eyes humanizes it; the reciprocity of the gaze equalizes Katschen and the cow. The next time he passes it, "Katschen looked into the cow's eyes and said, 'Ich bin Katschen!'" (128). Having endured the repeated rejection of his name, Katschen asserts the validity of his diasporic Austrian self by saying his name, aloud and in a German sentence, to the one creature that has *looked into his eyes* and not merely *at* him. Far from the kibbutz grounds after nightfall, Katschen imagines that the cow speaks for his dead mother, Margarethe: "And the cow would look into Katschen's eyes and say, 'There, you have found your way, mein kind, and you need never stray so far again'" (132). Merely looking *at* someone or something does not allow for the possibility of the seen object to return the gaze, yet looking *into* *someone's eyes* implies the expectation of a response, of a returned look. This reciprocity is crucial. Theories of the gaze (*le regard*) from Sartre's to Lacan's, from literature to film, and from feminism to post-colonial studies discuss the gaze as a one-sided, subjugating phenomenon that "others" and objectifies the one who is gazed at. In this scene, however, in which the gaze is emphatically two-sided, each gazing subject, by looking into the other's eyes, enables the other to gaze back and thereby assert subjectivity. By recognizing the other as a legitimate subject in his own right, the gazer can assert his own identity, as Katschen does.

The eye and the act of seeing permeate the novella as a whole. Katschen recalls what his mother had told him about Cyclopes: "He who sees with two eyes," she said, "closes one eye when the sights he sees are painful. If he is also pained by the sights he sees with the eye that remains open—he closes both eyes. But the Cyclops never closes his one and only eye" (Hoffmann 1998b, 120). This explanation, a hyperbolic deviation from the original Greek tale of the Cyclops, suggests a connection between seeing and the pain of consciousness. It also implies that one has a choice to close the eyes and therefore to prevent or avoid pain. The Cyclops, who never closes his eye, differs from the human not only because he has just one eye, but also because he does not (or *cannot*) avoid pain. He must confront this pain, unlike the non-Cyclops, who may choose not to acknowledge painful sights. The Cyclops eye also alludes to the Buddhist and Hindu concept of "third eye" or "inner eye" that symbolizes enlightenment and consciousness.

Katschen closes his eyes, expecting never to see again, "but then, when his eyes were closed, an eye in his forehead opened. The sight he saw with this eye was not clear, but it held a kind of transparency missing from the sights he saw with his two other eyes" (Hoffmann 1998b, 120–21). Since Katschen has a Cyclops eye, he cannot avoid pain even by closing both his regular eyes. He seems doomed to see painful things. Yet when he looks through this eye he is able to see things he cannot see with his regular eyes. This "transparency" implies a link between the pain from which the Cyclops cannot avert his gaze and a truth that is invisible to the human eye. The special eye in his forehead enables Katschen to see things that other people cannot see, or from which others turn away. It also enables him to recognize his own kind. Hoffmann recounts that "Since that day, Katschen knew he was a Cyclops and would look at people to see if they had an eye in their foreheads. . . . Katschen looked at Margarethe, his mother, and saw that she too was a Cyclops but what the eye in her forehead saw pained her and she closed this eye and opened her other two eyes. Katschen understood that Ernst, his father, was also a Cyclops. But Ernst was no more than a Cyclops and could only see through the eye in his forehead" (Hoffmann 1998b, 121). Each of the two types of seeing is valuable in its own way, but the Cyclops eye takes a toll on the one who has it. Katschen's father, who has no other eyes, is institutionalized. Katschen himself recognizes the value of this eye but he is also aware that it can lead to pain and that it provides a somewhat distorted vision of truth. This is clear when, after their reunification toward the end of the story, Katschen walks with his father and asks where he is going, a seemingly innocuous question. Ernst stops and tells Katschen never to ask such a question again, "'Because time . . . is not a line, and place is not a space.' And although Katschen did not know what his father was saying, he understood that from now on both of them would only look through the eye in their foreheads" (151). Looking through one's Cyclops eye reveals a truth that defies convention. Katschen's recognition that he would see only through this eye from now on announces, in effect, his rejection of conventional truths, such as those represented by the kibbutz, where presumably people use their two regular eyes to see. He joins his father at the end of the novella, both of them fugitives from the heights of institutionalized places, the kibbutz as the site of convention and exclusivity, the mental hospital as the place to hide those who deviate from the social norm represented by the kibbutz. Fittingly, the novella ends with Katschen and his father departing from an inn toward an uncertain future.

Keeping in mind the scene in which Katschen and the cow look into each other's eyes, I return to Katschen's arrival at the kibbutz. It is intriguing to compare the reciprocal gaze between Katschen and the cow, on the one hand, and the one-sided encounter he has with the two kibbutz members who greet him upon his arrival. Here, too, the name and the gaze are linked: "Then the woman looked at Katschen and asked, 'And what's your name?'" (Hoffmann 1998b, 127) The scene is repeated almost verbatim when Herr Grossman arrives: "Then he looked at Katschen and said, 'And what's your name?'" (128). Neither the woman nor Herr Grossman looks into Katschen's eyes. Katschen is not described as looking at either of them, much less as looking into their eyes. The one-sidedness of the gaze objectifies Katschen; coupled with their proclamation, which immediately follows, that Katschen is not a name that befits the kibbutz, it establishes a clear hierarchy, whereby Katschen awaits his transformation from ridiculous diaspora bourgeois to salt-of-the-earth Hebrew youth.

Compared to the arrival of Azariah Gitlin at Kibbutz Granot in Amos Oz's *A Perfect Peace,* discussed in the first chapter, Katschen's arrival is relatively benign. Azariah is not led to the kibbutz in daylight or met by well-meaning kibbutz members. He arrives through a muddy side path in the middle of a dark night, soaked from rain, trembling, pathetic, and alone, and meets the blond, burly Etan (a Hebrew word meaning "strong"), who does not hide his amusement at the eccentric stranger. Yet Azariah, a grown man, has come to the kibbutz of his own will. He believes wholeheartedly (if a bit naively) in its ideals and is determined to mold himself accordingly. To this end, he takes on a new persona, complete with a new nickname, the faintly Zorro-like "Zaro," and considers changing his family name, Gitlin, to "a more Hebrew-sounding name, like Gat or Geytal" (Oz 1985, 360). Changing his name would be the final step in erasing the shameful identity that he brings to the kibbutz like a dog with his tail between his legs. For Katschen, changing the name is a veritable mutilation, a cutting off of a past that he does not want to lose or replace—certainly not with a future filled with mockery and exclusion. Indeed, later in the story, "as things and the names of things become one, the fear in Katschen's heart disappeared" (Hoffmann 1998b, 131).

Immediately upon arriving at the conclusion that "the work of the people in this place is cutting," Katschen links this work to his own name, whose lopping off he realizes is inevitable. This ominous thought reminds him of the cow, the audience of his earlier proclamation of (German) self:

"And as Katschen thought of his name, he remembered the cow" (129–30). Katschen searches for the cow but cannot find her in the cattle pen. Hoffmann composes the final sentence of this section, the turning point of the story, in a characteristically efficient and unembellished style: "[Katschen] left the kibbutz and walked into the fields to look for the cow" (130). Thus the "Israeli story," which the reader expects will finally begin in this "Israeli place," the kibbutz, defies expectations, picking up the diasporic thread from Katschen's Europe-steeped Tel Aviv and continuing in the space surrounding the kibbutz. The kibbutz itself is a foreign place, Katschen's time there no more than a brief stop on his way elsewhere.

What is significant about the space beyond the kibbutz is that it is not only outside the kibbutz but outside any other clearly defined space. Katschen does not wander to a village, a city, or any other type of settlement. The space of his adventures remains undefined throughout the novella. Yet it is not uninhabited or empty by any means; he does not experience an uplifting spiritual awakening because of his sudden intimacy with nature, as might be expected. Nor does his closeness to the natural world frighten him back to the embracing arms of the civilization that, in the guise of the kibbutz, has rejected him. This section is devoid of any such Romantic clichés. The setting is symbolically valuable insofar as it demonstrates the harmonious co-existence of people and place. Moreover, it represents everything against which the kibbutz has fenced itself, geographically as well as socially and culturally.

In this liminal space, Katschen encounters two of the quintessential outsiders of Zionist Israeli society: Palestinian Arabs and Mizrahi Jews. Night has already fallen when Katschen meets an old man who questions him in Arabic: "Min inti?" he asks (Who are you?). "Min neyn jit?" (Where are you from?): "But Katschen looked at the old man's face and said nothing. The old man also looked at Katschen's face and remained silent. The old man and Katschen looked at each other for a long time" (Hoffmann 1998b, 132). Again, the reciprocal gaze suggests mutual recognition and acceptance. After the old man has turned to leave, Katschen faints, "floating above the earth," ready to join his mother and uncle in "the sky" (132). When he wakes, he is in the old man's tent. There, the old man feeds him, saying only two words, "kol" (eat) and "nam" (sleep) (133).

The tent and the man are imbued with a strangely comforting familiarity for Katschen, who has never been to this place nor met this stranger: "Suddenly, it seemed to Katschen that he had once been in this place, and had once eaten what he was eating, and the old man had once sat like that and looked at him. 'Never,' thought Katschen, 'will I have to leave this place again'" (133). He is convinced that this place is not only a place where he had been before, but also a place from which he had been exiled. Here, again, Katschen reveals an understanding of place much deeper and more complex than that of other characters. As he had articulated the kibbutz's purpose in terms that are applicable both literally and metaphorically, here he is able to see beyond the superficial differences of physical space to bring together two places that are most likely very different in terms of physical characteristics, culture, and language. The place that Katschen will never have to leave again is home. The old man, despite his different ethnicity, religion, and language, is, for Katschen, "a kind of Uncle Arthur," not only because his gun reminds Katschen of Uncle Arthur's cane, or because he says "komm" (arise), which Katschen mistakes for German (come), but also because he cares for Katschen (134).

Meaning transcends language throughout Katschen's encounter with the old man, who takes care of Katschen's immediate needs and then directs him back to the kibbutz, which, unbeknownst to the old man, is not the place where Katschen feels at home. When the old man departs after taking Katschen to the outskirts of the kibbutz, he asks Katschen "Shu ismak?" (What's your name?) (Hoffmann 1998b, 135). Whereas the man's initial questions in Arabic remain unanswered when the two had met the day before, now, upon their parting, Katschen answers as if their language barrier had melted away. These final words they exchange constitute their first real dialogue, and it is central to the novella as a whole. The old man asks him, in Arabic, what his name is, and Katschen says, "Katschen." The old man responds by offering his own name: "Ana ismi Ahmad" (135). He does not comment on Katschen's name, does not reject it, does not ignore it. Of the people in the story who have asked Katschen his name, he is the first person who accepts it. Moreover, he responds by telling Katschen his own name. Their two names, uttered in the last lines of this section, represent the two poles of otherness in Israeli society, the almost diametrically opposed figure of the Palestinian native, on the one hand, and the diasporic European Jew, on the other. Beyond the simple Arab/Jew dichotomy, then, and more important than the difference that we have been taught to understand in this pair, is an important sameness: the sameness of finding home outside the kibbutz, of having names that are "not proper" for a kibbutz, of mutual, unquestioning acceptance. This latter commonality is crucial since it does not rely on the perception of hegemonic culture to exist. That is, Katschen and Ahmad accept each other because they see each other as human beings, not because they are both at the fringes of Israeli society.

In Katschen's subsequent encounter with the religious Yemenite family, he again manages to transcend linguistic difficulties, deciphering the heavily accented Hebrew and sometimes responding in German. The old Yemenite is a Jew, yet he represents difference from the hegemonic norm as much as do both Ahmad and Katschen: His religious observance and his accent establish him as an other in direct opposition to the secular European kibbutznik. When he first sees Katschen, the younger Yemenite notes his ethnic difference immediately, calling, "A child of the Ashkenaz! A child of the Ashkenaz!" (Hoffmann 1998b, 137). Upon entering their home, Katschen notices a picture of a horse and rider in a desert landscape, and is reminded of Aunt Oppenheim's picture of a horse-drawn cart in a European forest. Yet, despite these commonalities, differences abound. The Yemenite family's arrival in Israel "on eagles' wings" is unlike the arrival of Katschen's family, which we understand to have been just beyond the jaws of Nazi wolves (138). Moreover, when the older Yemenite reads the story of Creation to Katschen, Katschen's questions and comments convince him that Katschen is Christian—that he is not only ethnically different but also fundamentally and radically other.

Hoffmann's portrayal of these two figures, the old Palestinian man and the old Yemenite man, defies facile dichotomies. Without idealizing their relationship, it establishes the humanity of both the diasporic Jew and the native Palestinian Arab and endows both with an independent identity. Yet, despite Katschen's fervent hope that he will never "have to leave this place again," Ahmad, presumably all too aware of the impossibility of their continued relations, leaves him on a hilltop overlooking the kibbutz (Hoffmann 1998b, 133). While Katschen's encounter with the religious Yemenite family illustrates certain similarities (their accents and their memories of diaspora), it also emphasizes the differences—different accents, different diasporas, different experiences. The fact that they are Jews is not enough to re-create the kind of intimacy and warmth that Katschen feels when he is with Ahmad.

The kibbutz, as the representation of the center of Zionist space, is marginalized in *Katschen*. We have seen that, unlike other critics of the Zionist ideology at the center of the kibbutz, Hoffmann is more concerned with what happens beyond its bounds than within it. Outside the kibbutz, those in the shadows of Israeli society emerge, and their commonalities with Katschen establish him as part of a collective that is an alternative to the Zionist collective. Yet it also clearly marks his difference from the various characters that he encounters. Though being European warrants Katschen's inclusion within the hegemonic group in Israel, this inclusion is superficial at best, as his experience does not align with the established racial hierarchy. Moreover, this young boy consciously and deliberately defies the kibbutz's attempt of imposed homogeneity, whether it is expressed through the rejection of his name or the ridiculing of his dress and speech.

The Diaspora Chronotope: "Salon Spaces" and Fragments of Europe

Katschen's experience of Israel is informed not only by the kibbutz and the space beyond it, but also by the Europe that his elders have re-created in Israel. Central to the creation of European space in Israel are those types of vernacular places that informed the characters' quotidian life in Europe, notably the café and the *salon*, or bourgeois living room. Both these types of spaces, and the activities set in them, were derided by the anti-urban, anti-intellectual, and anti-bourgeois Zionism of the pre- and early years of statehood as symbolizing the antithesis of that ideology. Almog writes that

> [t]he people of the kibbutzim and moshavim considered urban leisure practices (cinema, clubs, coffee houses)—in fact city life in general—not

only contemptible bourgeois activities but also expressions of vapid addiction to the capitalist vanity fair and sacrifices to the bourgeois Moloch. . . . Spending time in a coffee house and, even more so, in the cinema was for the youth movements—especially at the beginning of the 1950s—a sign of going bad and of abandoning one's values. It was associated with egocentric hedonism (the opposite of self-sacrifice or *hagshama*), anti-asceticism, courtship culture, capitalist economy, and submitting to foreign culture (which contradicted the ethos of supporting local production). . . .

The rejection of the city and its culture was also expressed in the adjective "salon": in "salon society" couples did "salon dances." (2000, 214–15, 216)

The hostility to bourgeois social norms was understood and articulated in explicitly spatial terms. Almog cites the observation of the sociologist Yochanan Peres that "there was a diametric opposition 'between adherence to the ideological movement centered on the country's open spaces, fields, and developing areas, and the clique shutting itself up between the four walls of its salon'" (Almog 2000, 216). This remark expresses succinctly the spatial dichotomies that aligned with two antithetical mentalities in early Israel: that of the native Hebrew or Sabra, which was open, developing, rural, and organic, and that of the diasporic Jew, which was closed off, decadent, urban, and artificial. Just as the Sabra, the Hebrew, or the "New Jew" defined himself in direct opposition to the Diaspora Jew linguistically, culturally, and physically, he did so spatially as well. Thus the dichotomies of urban/rural, artificial/natural, and closed/open can be understood as examples of a broader oppositional identity, which also included the dyads ornamented/unadorned, weak/strong, and Yiddish/Hebrew.

In the Israel of both *Katschen* and *Christ of Fish*, "salon" spaces are at the center of the characters' experience. Filled with "bourgeois" objects that evoke another place and time, these spaces represent a passive but powerful resistance to the ideological assimilation that Zionism sought. It is the objects within a particular space that define it. Ben-Gurion's humble apartment, as described by Barbara Mann, stood as the epitome of the self-sacrificing collectivist ethos that derided luxury and comfort.

Comparing a photograph of his simple, austere kitchen, typical of others of its period, to an image of a plush European 1910 Tel Aviv living room, she observes, "we notice not only the difference, crudely put, between bourgeois luxury and socialist spartanism; Ben-Gurion's kitchen seems more an extension of the public sphere and of the nascent national culture that valued self-sacrifice and a sense of collective purpose" (Mann 2006, 160). The apartments of Hoffmann's characters, on the other hand, are filled with decorative material objects. These fragments and the bourgeois spaces with which they are associated function in the two texts as traces of Europe. Like the ruins of a destroyed civilization,[1] these fragments reconfigure the relationship between redemption and place: Whereas the Zionist narrative envisions redemption as arrival-in-place, Hoffmann's novel imagines it in the preservation of the diasporic world through the collection of fragments, suggesting that redemptive possibility resides in the interaction between place and time.

Hoffmann's European immigrants are not the typical immigrant protagonists represented, for instance, in the novels of Meir Shalev or Amos Oz. Hoffmann's Europeans find themselves in Israel not out of choice or ideological conviction, but out of necessity or chance. Even when other authors do portray a situation that brings non-Zionist Jews to Israel out of necessity, this situation in and of itself, and the problems it creates

---

1. Walter Benjamin writes about ruins in the context of allegory. In *The Origin of German Tragic Drama*, he argues: "Allegories are, in the realm of thoughts, what ruins are in the realm of things" (1977, 178). He characterizes the appearance of the ruin, or the fragment, in baroque literature as "the exuberant subjection of antique elements in a structure which, without uniting them in a single whole, would, in destruction, still be superior to the harmonies of antiquity" (178). Noting his "invocation of the fragments and ruins of allegories to critique the wholeness of the symbol," Susan A. Handelman argues that "Benjamin's problem was how to open the material world to redemption without invoking either a crude Marxism or a transcendental theology" (1991, 257). I adopt Benjamin's concept of the ruin to analyze Hoffmann's representation of fragments of the destroyed Jewish European civilization, which in their survival and accumulation (to use another Benjaminian concept) redeem the European past without idealizing it or succumbing to an illusory memory of wholeness.

upon their arrival in and acclimation to Israel, often becomes a central tension of the text and a driving force behind the plot. In Hoffmann's novels, the main tension experienced by characters in Israel is not the tension of *olim hadashim*, the ideologically loaded term for immigrants to Israel, but rather of immigrants, *mehagrim*, in a more general sense. Even in *Katschen*, which is concerned with the specifics of the Israeli situation as we have seen above, the text engages as much with the typical difficulties of immigrant experiences as it does with the particular tensions engendered by the institutionalized ideology of Zionism and the characters' apathy and even antipathy toward it. This leads to a central distinction between Zionist Ashkenazim and Hoffmann's "other Europeans": instead of undergoing *'aliya*, which includes the concept of *shlilat ha-galut* or "negation of the diaspora" in an effort to create a new Hebrew or Israeli culture, the characters in these novels reconcile the culture of the place left behind with the new place. Their ambivalent relationship to Israel is typical of immigrants confused in the face of a new culture. Thus Hoffmann not only acknowledges the diversity of European Jews' experience in Israel, he also counters the assumption of the uniqueness of the Jewish-Israeli case. Why, after all, are these people different from others fleeing persecution, injustice, or genocide? Like other immigrants, these characters attempt to maintain some of the cultural practices and habits that they brought with them from their home-place, even if it has rejected them; they feel most comfortable speaking their mother tongue; they decorate their homes according to the aesthetic of their original place. They inhabit geographical space in the Middle East, but, as evidenced by the fragmentation that is so prominent in their lives, their hearts and minds are entrenched firmly *be-sof ma'arav*, at the end of the West, to invert Yehuda Halevi's famous poem.[2]

2. Yehuda Ha-Levi (c. 1080–1141), a Spanish Jewish philosopher and poet perhaps best known for his philosophical treatise, *sefer ha-kuzari*, which defends Judaism against non-Jewish philosophies, wrote one of the most oft-quoted poems of the medieval era, "*Libi ba-mizrah*" ["My heart is in the east"]. Its famous first line reads: "My heart is in the East and I, at the end of the West."

This kind of fragmentation is an integral characteristic of Hoffmann's writing. It reflects his rejection of conventional notions of narrative and experiential totality or unity. Walter Benjamin's notions of the fragment and the aura further illuminate Hoffmann's use of fragmentation, suggesting a rejection not only of totalizing narratives but also of conventional understandings of place. The fragment, which alludes to the past, necessarily includes a temporal component. In bringing together the spatial and the temporal, the fragment is at the center of the text's chronotope, to use Bakhtin's term for the literary representation of time-space.[3]

For Benjamin, fragments are related to allegory, which functions against "the will to symbolic totality" (Benjamin 1977, 186, 187). Fragments or traces of the past are not intended to re-create "things as they were," but "to renew the old world" (60). Taken out of its original context, the fragment is linked to the threatened world of the past; indeed, it is this world's coded image. Like the ruin, each fragment contains the whole within it, emphasizing an absent totality and evoking a sense of a past time. It is important to note that the fragment does not strive to "connect" to other fragments and thereby to re-create a whole, but rather *refers* to a lost place and time. Emphasizing the central role of the fragment in Benjamin's thinking about redemption,[4] Randall Van Schepen asserts that "the . . . fragment gives a glimpse of redemptive potential" (2007). As Richard Wolin has written of Benjamin's redemptive aesthetic, "origin is still the goal, . . . not as a fixed image of the past that must be recovered in toto,

---

3. Bakhtin defines the chronotope as "the intrinsic connectedness of temporal and spatial relationships that are artistically expressed in literature" (1981, 84). He elaborates on this concept in chapter 4, "Forms of Time and of the Chronotope in the Novel."

4. It is worthy of note that, owing to Gershom Scholem's influence on his thought, Benjamin's ideas regarding the role of the fragment in redemption are often interpreted in light of the kabbalistic notion of *tikkun*. According to kabbalistic doctrine, vessels of divine light were shattered in the process of the creation of the world. "The goal of humanity in the kabbalistic view," writes Handelman, "is to redeem the sparks of holiness still attached to these vessels as they fell and became embedded into the material world, to repair and redeem (*tikkun*) the world by restoring the sparks to their source and so bring about the final redemption" (1991, 42).

but rather as the fulfillment of a potentiality which lies dormant in origin" (1982, 38). Hoffmann's characters redeem the diaspora not by yearning for a sentimentalized European past but rather by evoking the lost European world to create a diaspora chronotope in Israel.

Benjamin's characterization of the aura, a phenomenon he attributes to original works of art, is significant for understanding the chronotopic workings of Hoffmann's *Christ of Fish:* Experiencing the aura reverses the flow of time, thereby situating the subject within the place where it originated—in this case, Europe. The aura clings to its object unchangingly, resisting the linear progression of time by pulling it backward, indeed reversing it in Benjamin's words, through its association with a particular place. We encounter this reversal several times in Hoffmann's text, often in conjunction with a character's experience with a work of art: "Shockingly [Mr. Moskowitz's] hair began to grow inward into his body," relates the narrator. "This was the external sign of the breakdown in the directions of time. His hair returned as if to that other time that Casals had seen with blind eyes when he was ninety-six and playing Bach's Suite in C Minor, almost with no body" (1999, 194). In another instance the narrator recalls a scene from Chaplin's film *Limelight:* "I think of the horse harnessed to the carriage that carried Claire Bloom and Charles Chaplin in Hollywood, in 1950. The horse is dead. But it has acquired an *aura*[5] (in the opposite direction to the arrow of time) and now, over and over again, countless times, harnessed to a two-dimensional carriage, it carries the dancer Terry to Calvero, the old clown, in the London of 1920" (Hoffmann 1991, 44). This scene, in particular, relates directly to Benjamin's ideas about the aura almost antithetically: Here, the film (a means of mechanical reproduction) creates the horse's aura by reversing time and thus allowing its continual, eternal reproduction. That is, the reproduction does not stifle the aura or bring about its "withering," but rather allows its aura to emerge and the audience to accept that the horse in 1950 Hollywood is actually in 1920 London. The last lines of the novel relate Magda's experience of this reversal of time and also assert the continuity between

5. Transcribed in Latin letters.

worlds (in this case between life and death) despite the disruption in the flow of time: "And she knew (oh, she knew!) that this world continues into the next unchanged. And there is no division. And only the directions are reversed" (Hoffmann 1999, 233). It is the aura, the *"Hier und Jetzt,"* that allows an object to transcend its material function and to acquire a redemptive value that displaces it from linear time and from *pastness* and allows it into eternal *presence.*

This is also the point where place and time intersect, enacting the emergence of a diaspora chronotope, which depends not only on a faithful reproduction of the fragmented European experience of these Jews, as expressed linguistically and stylistically by Hoffmann, but mostly on the concrete objects they use to transform their small, ever-foreign Israeli space into a familiar European one. Indeed, the diaspora chronotope depends on their collection of distinctively European objects, relics from their past that reflect and maintain their internalized diasporic orientation. The Europe of their homes and speech, which no longer exists in the place they left behind, emerges in their new place, disrupting nationalist conceptions of unity and establishing spaces and identities that are at odds with the Zionist ideals of their time.

The fragment functions on several different levels in this novel, most obviously in the structure. The text is constructed as a series of textual snapshots of Aunt Magda and other immigrants. As in several other books by Hoffmann, the sections are numbered in lieu of page numbers. Each textual fragment, in effect, enacts a structural mimicking of the episode itself, in its brevity and its fleetingness, and in its resistance against the urge to forge connections and lines where they do not necessarily exist. Moreover, it echoes something of the disconnectedness of the immigrant herself, whose experience is marked by instability and disjuncture.

Other representations of fragmentation contribute more directly to the notion of the fragment as a trace of a lost world. For instance, Hoffmann's Hebrew is punctuated by words and phrases in their original German, Hungarian, Romanian, French, Yiddish, and more. Multilingualism has been represented in canonical Israeli texts, usually demonstrating intergenerational differences and the transformation of Israel from a nation of immigrants to one of natives, and ultimately supporting the notion of a teleological national story. Hoffmann's text resists the notion of a total-izing experiential and literary narrative. Also striking is Hoffmann's occa-sional use of distinctively European turns of phrase in Hebrew, typical of older immigrants from Europe, such as the bilingual mixture "*tmunat fotograf*" (literally "photographic picture") for photograph (rather than the Hebrew *tsilum*) (1991, 54).

In *Katschen*, Hoffmann demonstrates the tensions that accompany lan-guage choices, particularly Yiddish, for these immigrants. Yiddish has faced accusations of exclusivity (as a European Jewish language that is therefore identified with the upper echelons of Israeli society) as well as of not being a "real" language but rather a "miserable, stunted [jargon]," "the stealthy speech of prisoners," as Herzl called it (1917, 38) not worthy of the Hebrew glory of Zionism.[6] Through Aunt Oppenheim, the language hierarchy amongst European Jews, today usually lumped together as sharing a com-mon culture, becomes very clear: just as she only nods to people wearing faded shirts but stretches out her hand to be kissed to those wearing suits (Hoffmann 1998b, 105), her eyes soften when Herr Schneider addresses her in German and harden again when he switches to Yiddish (Hoffmann 1998b, 123). Yiddish was certainly derided by Zionists in Israel as a diaspora tongue, yet (like Herzl) she rejects it not for Hebrew but rather for German. Utterly uninterested in assimilation to the cultural norms of the place she inhabits, where Hebrew is the language of choice, she transfers the lin-guistic hierarchy of Europe to Israel. Each linguistic fragment in the text expresses an experience of Israel through one of various diasporic prisms.

6. Writing in 1896, Herzl does not, in "The Jewish State," reject Yiddish in favor of Hebrew as the language of the future state: "We cannot converse with one another in Hebrew. Who amongst us has a sufficient acquaintance with Hebrew to ask for a railway-ticket in that language?" (38). Instead, he proposes a "federation of tongues" similar to Switzerland's: "Every man can preserve the language in which his thoughts are at home," and, over the course of time, "the language which proves itself to be of greatest utility for general intercourse will be adopted without compulsion as our national tongue" (38). His objection to Yiddish does not pit it in an ideological war against Hebrew, which he did not consider a viable possibility for a national language, and therefore does not anticipate the heated "language wars" of the prestate period.

Another, fascinating, type of fragmentation in these texts is expressed through synecdoche. "How the folds of her flesh passed from September into October!" exclaims the narrator of *Christ of Fish* (Hoffmann 1999, 77). Along the same lines, he imagines that in the days preceding the Messiah's arrival, "Parts of bodies that got separated will return to one another" (127). But Hoffmann also uses synecdoche to describe the relationship between people and place, creating characters who are, quite literally, composed of pieces of their original place. For example, the narrator asserts that "the cornfields of Romania sprouted from [Mr. Moskowitz's] nostrils," and relates how, during the High Holidays, Mr. Moskowitz "held the story of the Creation of the World tight against the nipples he had brought with him from Romania" (72, 78). The nostrils and the nipples constitute bodily fragments that are separate from the rest of the body but that represent it; at the same time, they are an integral part of the place these people have left.

The fragment in these novels is most striking as a concrete object with the ability to shape or create a space. It is in this context that I wish to examine the power of objects and their contribution to a diaspora chronotope. Detailed descriptions of material objects abound in Hoffmann's sparse texts. They evoke distinctly European spaces within Israel, the café and the bourgeois living room, or more generally, those "salon spaces" that run counter to the most valorized Zionist spatial and social practices. By creating, maintaining, and inhabiting such spaces, Hoffmann's characters find a home that is independent of hegemonic ideals.

When objects are removed from their original spatial and temporal context, they disrupt and even render impossible the concept of linear historical time. At the beginning of the novel, the narrator relates that, despite the deaths of her husband and brother, Aunt Magda's "passion for all kinds of *hafatsim*," objects, remained intact (Hoffmann 1991, 16). The source of her passion is not a shallow materialism but a desire to salvage and reconstruct a sense of home. The bourgeois *hafatsim* that fill her home and that the narrator collects in the text are traces of the European culture she has lost. The sheer number of such objects is only emphasized by the author's decision to list them in detail, providing a veritable catalogue of European *things*. In one such breathless inventory, we are told that "she had a special recipe [*retsept*] for apple cake and a glass mouse and an alarm clock that played a Viennese waltz at the appointed time, and she had a cherry-wood jewelry box and an inlaid ivory salt shaker and a picture of a wagon done in embroidery and she had porcelain dolls (a shepherd and a baby and Italian noblemen) and silver dishes and colored postcards. And she had flowerpots" (Hoffmann 1999, 35). It is not only from the objects themselves, but also from the literary choices made by the author and narrator that Europe emerges. The word *retsept*, for instance, is a Hebraization of the German word *rezept* (originally from Latin: *recipe*), and is precisely the kind of word that fervent Hebraicist Zionists were trying to edge out of the new Israeli Hebrew lexicon in favor of purely Hebrew equivalents such as *matkon*.

Throughout the text, the narrator enumerates and catalogs such distinctly European objects, some of which he mentions repeatedly: a harpsichord, a corselet, strudel, a new kidskin purse with Gothic initials inscribed on the clasp, a silver fox fur collar, a pearl necklace. In *Katschen,* too, such European objects abound. Frau Kurtz's apartment contains a piano with a bust of Beethoven (Hoffmann 1998b, 156). Aunt Oppenheim has a grandfather clock, an embroidered picture of a palace and horse-drawn carriage surrounded by fir trees (110), china cups (100), and a green crocodile handbag (104). The elaborately decorative nature of most of these objects, as opposed to the almost ascetic aesthetic ideal promoted by Zionism, is another factor that links them to a bourgeois sensibility. Baubles, jewel boxes, and porcelain dolls have no use in a society that values labor and closeness to the land above all, and are considered corrupting and threatening to these values. Certain objects that might have had some use in the European climate (cultural and otherwise), like furs, become utterly useless in Israel, but remain status symbols, another bourgeois concept that, in Israel, reeked of diaspora. The spaces filled by these objects, small urban apartments, became havens of the familiar within the harsh, exilic landscape and cityscape of 1950s Israel. In these spaces, the characters listen to records on the phonograph and wax philosophical about the universality of music and its contrast to the narrowness of Zionism. They shut themselves away from the persistent sun and the intrusive dust,[7] they drink tea from delicate china cups, and they have discussions about a variety of subjects, but, significantly, never about Israeli politics.

The "courtship culture" that Almog notes was reviled by Zionist youth is glorified by Aunt Oppenheim, who yearns for a man in a horse-drawn carriage to bring her flowers, as depicted on an embroidery, no less. Katschen, excited by the scenario, promises her that when he grows up he will be the knight who brings her flowers. In the meantime, Aunt Oppenheim must make do with the embroidery that adorns her wall. Thus private spaces are informed by artifacts that, perhaps unintentionally, are much more than merely decorative: they signal the characters' detachment from Zionist values.

The diaspora chronotope is enacted not only within the characters' homes. Certain public spaces are mobilized for this purpose as well. "In Vienna," Katschen recounts, "Aunt Oppenheim had sung in the opera house but in Palestine she sat in the coffeehouse on the seashore and ate cream cakes" (Hoffmann 1998b, 98). The coffeehouse may be a poor substitute for the opera, yet both places represent the height of decadent bourgeois culture in the context of 1950s Israel. Aunt Oppenheim's café is a mainstay of her Israeli existence. Less a participant in this, the culture of her adopted homeland, than she was in the place from which she fled, Aunt Magda attempts to re-create her glorious Vienna by painting her face and sitting in a café (Hoffmann 1999, 104). There, "red tablecloths fluttered in the wind. . . . A man dressed in white clothes bowed and said, 'Guten Morgen, Frau Oppenheim'" (105). The café, at which she is clearly a regular, constitutes her home away from home in more ways than one. Not only does it provide a public space for social interaction, but it allows

7. In his autobiography, for example, Oz relates his Polish grandmother's assertion, upon her arrival in Jerusalem in 1933, that "'the Levant is full of germs'" (2004, 32). Describing her obsessive, relentless drive to disinfect every crevice of her apartment and her body, Oz offers "a peephole that may afford us a glimpse of the effect of the sights of the Orient, its colors and smells, on my grandmother and perhaps on other immigrants and refugees who like her came from gloomy shtetls in Eastern Europe and were so disturbed by the pervasive sensuality of the Levant that they resolved to defend themselves from its menace *by constructing their own ghetto*" (Oz 2004, 33; my emphasis).

Aunt Oppenheim to escape Israel and inhabit, if only for an afternoon, the Vienna of her memories, with its particular aesthetic, language, and rules of etiquette.[8] The tablecloths, the bowing, uniform-clad waiter, and his German greeting collaborate in an astonishing re-creation of what might well be a lakeside European café in the summer.

It is worth noting that the existence of bourgeois public spaces is testament to the fact that there was a demand for them. Aunt Oppenheim is not sitting in the café alone, after all. Yet Hebrew literature has portrayed the café experience in a manner that aligns itself with the moralizing condemnation of such spaces. Two examples from the period in which Hoffmann's text takes place are Aharon Megged's *Ha-hai 'al ha-met* (The living on the dead) (1965), in which the protagonist's evenings in pubs and cafés are in constant tension with the open spaces frequented by the Zionist hero whose biography he writes; and Moshe Shamir's famous *Be-moh yadav: pirkei elik* (With his own hands) (1951), the novel about his brother Elik, a martyred Zionist hero who spent his days not in a café like his bourgeois brother but in an open agricultural field or battleground. Today, the café is firmly established at the foundation of Israel's westernized leisure culture. In the decade after statehood, however, such spaces threatened the spartan ethos at the very heart of Zionist ideology.

Whereas they have no special significance in their original European context, in Israel the objects surrounding Aunts Magda and Oppenheim represent a fading culture. This repositioning constitutes not only a nostalgic memorializing of this culture, but actually an insistence on its continued life despite its seeming disappearance. The ending of *Christ of Fish* illuminates, once again, the significance of seeing in Hoffmann's representation of place. Here, however, seeing transcends sensory experience, and refers to a more spiritual, prophetic one. In the final weeks of her life, Aunt Magda "saw a great vision and everything was in it. She saw . . . the soul of her brooches. And of her porcelain cups. And of her iron. And her purse"

---

8. Aunt Oppenheim is the only one of the characters who surpasses the act of redemption and actually reinstates herself in the diaspora, returning to Vienna after Katschen is installed in the kibbutz.

(Hoffmann 1999, 233). The anthropomorphizing of these objects and their centrality in Magda's vision of "everything" demonstrate their presence despite their rootedness in the past, disrupting the flow of time and thereby reconfiguring place chronotopically: "And only the directions are reversed," concludes Magda (233). In Aunt Oppenheim's case the reversal is literal, for she ultimately returns to Vienna, enacting the ultimate rejection of Zionism and of the concept of *shlilat ha-galut*.

The collection of the European fragments in these novels suggests that the experience of diaspora may be redeemed. There is something worth salvaging even from that darkest place and time, since the place whence it issued never constituted a whole or a totality. The object, therefore, suggests not a re-creation of "things as they were," which for Jewish emigrants from Europe is inconceivable, but rather a renewal of a Europe that existed only potentially. This is a marked departure from other representations of European immigrants to prestate Palestine or Israel, which tend to be preoccupied by the tension between yearning for the past place and longing to be a part of the present place. In Shulamith Hareven's novel about prestate Jerusalem, *Ir yamim rabim* (City of many days) (1972), for example, the ridiculous but endearing German Jew Dr. Barzel exemplifies this tension, literally re-creating his beloved Germany by shipping his entire apartment in a crate to Palestine, while at the same time trying to strike roots in Palestine by planting a cedar tree in his yard. "Sometimes, on late afternoons," the narrator relates, "when the heat had died down, the air was full of the fragrance of flowers, and the next-door neighbors could be heard conversing softly in German on the other side of the fence, he wasn't sure whether he was here or there. He played his violin for hours on end, . . . consumed by longing" (1977, 41).

The act of collecting, like the traces or fragments themselves, is not just part of the process of remembering a culture but of assuring its continuation. While *Christ of Fish* is concerned with death (both of the individual and of an entire culture), it ultimately affirms this continuity and rejects the supposed nullity of death, as is clearly indicated at the end of the novel. The Europe known by Hoffmann's characters in both *Christ of Fish* and *Katschen* is preserved by the fragments that represent it and their "eternalizing" aura. Thus Hoffmann's Europe continues to exist within the

Israeli cities inhabited by his characters, not only in their language and memory, but also in their living rooms, on their shelves, in their handbags, and on their walls.

This interpretation charges physical objects with the responsibility of something that is more tangible than memory, with all the ambiguity, ambivalence, and amorphousness that inform it. Having departed the hostile diaspora for the place that is supposed to function as their true homeland, these characters adapt by salvaging fragments of their familiar world and integrating the experience of diaspora within vernacular places in Israel. This notion suggests a configuration of space that is altogether different from those we have encountered in the preceding chapters: Instead of the linear, teleological, place-based notion of arrival, Hoffmann suggests a back-and-forth, constantly moving *chronotope*, in which place is actually defined by time and not only by space. Redemption through arrival is replaced by redemption through preservation or re-creation of exile. Instead of place, Hoffmann's characters inhabit and identify with place-time.

The Jew's Landscapes

The notion of inhabiting place chronotopically gives way to even more abstract ways of experiencing place in Hoffmann's works. In this respect, the physicality of the eyes that is crucial in *Katschen* plays an important role in *The Book of Joseph* as well. As Katschen can use his Cyclops eye to see things that others cannot, Joseph understands that the Jew in Europe has visual access to multiple places, but that he sees these places differently than Christian Europeans see them.[9] Ironically, this plurality of landscapes is possible because he senses the limitations of the Jew's claim

---

9. It is worth noting that one of the most striking characteristics of Hoffmann's writing is his intimate relationship with Christianity. Arguably, the many allusions to Christianity and to Christian motifs and symbols in Hoffmann's works constitute part of his characters' closeness to European culture. For more on Christian motifs in Hoffmann's work, see Stahl 2008.

to place in Europe. In what is perhaps the most revelatory passage on place in this novella, Joseph remembers riding the train before his Bar Mitzvah with his father, Reb Chaim, to see the Rabbi of Kishinev: "And on the train he looked at the face of an old Russian woman and saw that the fields outside were passing by inside her eyes. At first he did not know where those same images[10] went to from there, but when he looked at the face of another Russian, he saw they were inside his eyes. . . . [And] Joseph saw that the rooster looks at one place and then at another, but it does not look at the space between places. . . . It was then that Joseph saw that in Reb Chaim's eyes, too, there was an image, but this image had no form at all" (Hoffmann 1988, 99). From the perspective of Joseph, the child, the ordinary phenomenon of the reflection of the vernacular Russian countryside in the eyes of the Russian passengers is transformed into an extraordinarily precocious observation, encompassing his adult experience of place and of the way political, ethical, and historical forces have shaped this experience. Like Katschen, Joseph literalizes that which his eyes see—in this instance, the fields in the Russians' eyes are not merely reflections of the fields outside, but the fields themselves, which seem inherent in these Russians' effortless gaze. The rooster, on the other hand, looks at places (places do not pass through its eyes), but it is not interested in the space between them. Its glance is firmly rooted in one defined place, then another, in a series of abrupt metaphorical hops. This is another example of Hoffmann's uncanny descriptive methodology, which couches the familiar and the common in such concrete and literal terms that they suddenly become strange and foreign.

Whether it is in a form that is continuous or choppy, the Russian passengers and the rooster both see formed, well-defined place. This is what sets them apart from Reb Chaim, whose eyes take in a formless image. Reb

---

10. Hoffmann uses the word *mar'eh* repeatedly in this and several other passages. The English translation, which uses different words for *mar'eh*, does not maintain this consistency: It is translated as "landscape," "form," and "images." I have chosen to use the word "image" for *mar'eh* throughout since it retains the visual element of the original Hebrew and does not add layers of meaning not present in the original.

Chaim sees *only* the space that is between places, the utterly abstract and undefined territory that is outside the well-bounded fields and other places that are an inherent part of the experience of the Russians, the space that the rooster impatiently dismisses in its search for fixed points.

This phenomenon, in which visual perception is used to distinguish between different beings' relationship to place and space, parallels the Cyclops vision postulated by Katschen: Certain people can see only from their two regular eyes; others can see only from their Cyclops eye; and still others can see from both. In this case, the metaphor of the Jew's exile is literalized: only the Jew's eyes contain a formless image, while his fellow passengers see places that are formed.

Significantly, the Jew *has* an image. He is not left placeless. Whether that landscape is interpreted as the dream of Zion, the Land of Israel itself, or a different experience of the same fields that pass through the Russians' eyes is left up to the reader. What is clear is that the Russians' interaction with place is one that occurs without any effort on their part, even in their utmost passivity, almost in spite of themselves. It becomes a part of their eyes. Reb Chaim's landscape is a part of his eyes, and presumably of his being, as well. Yet, again, their spatial image is a field, whereas his might be an idea, a dream, or a space between places.

That this scene emerges in Joseph's childhood memory is consistent with the pattern established in *Katschen*, whereby the boy understands the world around him in a far more nuanced way than the adults who surround him because he is the one able to see rather than merely to *look at* things. The sense of sight seems to dull with adulthood in Hoffmann's literary world, except in adults whose mental illness preserves the unabashed open-eyed stare that enables them to see things that are invisible to others. It is the young Joseph who makes these astute observations on the train, which seem as naïve and innocent as Katschen's pronouncement that the kibbutz is "a place where things are cut," but which are, in the end, as sophisticated and chilling in their depth of understanding.

Just prior to this scene, Yingele, Joseph's son, considers a statement made by Pomerantz, the watchmaker: "The world of images . . . is insubstantial and nothing but the reflection of another world which contains no images at all" (Hoffmann 1988, 96). The world that seems to be the concrete, the substantial, the *real* is revealed as nothing more than a mere *reflection* of the real. The fields that pass through the Russians' eyes are reflections not in the sense that they mirror the fields outside, but rather in that those fields out-side are themselves mere reflections of a formless reality. That which seems to be the most indisputably substantial is actually least substantial, and that which seems to contain nothing of substance is the *real*. The "world of images" subject to the senses is a surface world that most people inhabit, never even sensing the existence of another world. This understanding of images evokes Plato's famous notion that reality exists not in the sensed material world but in the *intelligible* world, which is made up of essential Forms (εἶδος [*eidos*]).[11] Hoffmann's characters, whose experience is typified by change and uncertainty, find a stable reality in the world of Forms.[12] True to Plato's theory, the phenomena that constitute their world are intelligible, not tangible. They are also, significantly, aspatial, outside of place. In keeping with this notion, Pomerantz asserts that the objects we consider real are illusory, a deceptive and imperfect reflection of immutable reality.

Miriam, who was adopted by Pomerantz and his wife after having been abandoned in her cradle on the Alexanderplatz, is one of the characters who can see what others do not. Hoffmann writes that "Pomerantz wishes to understand the purpose of things, while Miriam sees their form. . . . Sometimes it seems to Pomerantz that Miriam sees straight to the heart of the matter, and does not need the steps of reason" (Hoffmann 1998b, 68). Joseph, who himself is inclined to describe things more lyrically than the eminently reasonable Pomerantz, observes that "in most people . . . lives the soul of a dog that looks through the holes of its eyes in submission and only wishes to please its master; but in Miriam's body lives the soul of a cat that contracts its pupils, removes the picture of the world and remains sealed like a mountain" (69). Indeed, Joseph, unlike Pomerantz, is

11. Plato does not systematically articulate his theory of Forms in one particular text; for more on Forms, see Hamilton and Cairns 1961, especially "Phaedo," pp. 40–98; and Bloom 1991.

12. "Image," in the Platonic context, should be distinguished from "Form." For Plato, an image is a mere copy of a real object or Form.

not frightened by Miriam's special way of looking at things. "Joseph understands that she dwells in both worlds at the same time. . . . Though she knows nothing, her eyes take in everything" (70, 71). Thus, again, seeing and place are brought together. Her ability to comprehend phenomena that seem incomprehensible is described in terms of "seeing" again and again, thus encompassing the hypersight of the Cyclops eye, as well as the prophetic implications that accompany it. It is a capacity, rather than an ordered ascension from ignorance to knowledge; it implies a concrete act, rather than an abstract development.

Miriam's ability to see things is what enables her to inhabit "both worlds at once," as Joseph admiringly observes. "Both worlds" refers to the world that is visible to everyone as well as the world that is visible only to a few. It is important to note that Hoffmann never attributes Miriam's double-sight to a clichéd, mysterious feminine intuition. Her ability "to see to the heart of things" is valued, not disparaged, because of its independence from reason, an inferior faculty. Indeed, the text suggests that reason can cloud people's vision, disabling them by keeping them from seeing or inhabiting any world but their own.

Perhaps the most poignant example of the multiple worlds inhabited by Jews, however, is that object that literally reflects and multiplies objects, the mirror. In order to be more like the other children "with straw-colored hair and pale eyes," Yingele decides to abandon the black-eyed self he sees peering at him from the mirror: "When he sees his image in the mirror, he wants to be separated from it" (Hoffmann 1998b, 58). This interaction with his reflected self constitutes a very different experience than the one Lacan describes in his famous essay on the "mirror phase" in human development. In Lacan's formulation, it is an infant who encounters his reflection in the mirror, and who is simultaneously attracted to and threatened by its (illusory) wholeness and unity, which he then tries to emulate. This is how the infant, according to Lacan, passes from the imaginary to the symbolic order and develops an ego (1977). Katschen's experience with the mirror is different. As he is no longer an infant, he has already departed from the imaginary order by the time he experiments with the mirror. Rather than attempting to become like the image he sees there, he recognizes that image as an obstacle to becoming who he wants to be and attempts to abandon it, only to discover that he cannot do so. Unlike the infant in Lacan's mirror scenario, Katschen yearns to escape his reflection because he is already sufficiently familiar with the symbolic order to understand that his "black-eyed self" is somehow inferior—in other words, to recognize himself as other. Rather than idealizing the image *in* the mirror, Katschen idealizes the images *beyond* the mirror.

Moreover, the mirror is seen here as the agent of two separate worlds (the Jewish and the non-Jewish), as the site of their intersection, where the images pass from one to the other. After several unsuccessful attempts to leave his image behind, Yingele realizes the impossibility of his endeavor: "I cannot be other than I am, Yingele thinks, and is filled with sadness" (Hoffmann 1998b, 58). His recognition of the existence of another world (even if he cannot enter it), his attempt to find that other place, sets him apart from those he tries to resemble, who cannot fathom another possibility of being.

Katschen also experiences enlightenment while looking at the mirror. At first somewhat frightened by the sight of his own image leaving the mirror, he consoles himself with the understanding that that particular mirror is not "the real mirror": "The mirror in the wardrobe was framed on all sides and images entered it and left it, while the real mirror covered the whole world and there was nothing which it did not double. . . . Eventually, Katschen decided that the mirror was crystal clear and that even its reflections were real things" (Hoffmann 1998b, 101–2). Katschen thus resolves the mystery of the mirror in a manner that allows him to reconcile the formless upper world where his deceased mother dwells with the lower world of images which he inhabits: If the mirror is transparent then there is no hierarchy of the real established between these worlds. There is no original and no copy. Rather, they become equally possible and equally real, and one can move between them effortlessly. This interpretation, which allows Katschen to accept his mother's absence, is a compromise based on an impossibility. A mirror, after all, cannot be crystal clear, because it becomes a window and not a mirror at all. Katschen himself realizes, to an extent, his own self-deception when he waits for his reflection to answer one of Aunt Oppenheim's questions and it remains silent (102).

Katschen's interaction with the mirror and with his own reflection precedes Yingele's more sophisticated understanding of his place within the worlds. It is in itself an example not only of the intersection of these two characters' worlds, but also of the way that each boy reflects the other. Indeed, *Katschen* and *The Book of Joseph* reflect each other on a broader scale. The line that divides them represents the mirror separating the upper from the lower worlds, life from death, Israel from Europe, after the Holocaust from before the Holocaust—yet it does not divide these binary pairs to position one half on one side of the line and the other half on the other side. Instead, the line is a porous one, through which the images can move back and forth. In contrast to the seemingly impregnable boundaries in Oz's novels and the constantly shifting demarcations in Kashua's, this line *encourages* crossing. Katschen's understanding of the mirror as crystal clear makes sense in this context. This exchange is what makes the two worlds imagined in these texts, which on the surface are different in so many ways, ultimately so similar. It is also this fluidity and porousness that makes formed images so useless and irrelevant. This concept is central in the Jewish characters' self-perception in these texts.

This is confirmed by the description of Siegfried Stopf, the German youth whose life runs parallel to Joseph and Yingele's in the text, and whose violence ultimately ends their lives. He embodies the horror that awaits Europe's Jews. Herr Still, the tobacconist, recognizes the violence in Siegfried: "he saw what he saw and his heart filled with dread" (Hoffmann 1998b, 74). The Austrian Herr Still realizes that the harbinger of the impending disaster is a Basilisk, who "kills with a glance" (76). According to lore, the Basilisk's gaze is, indeed, lethal. Yet, as the text relates, "The Basilisk will die if it looks at its own reflection in the mirror" (77). Presumably, the deadliness of its glance does not spare even the Basilisk itself, which falls prey to its own hideous gaze. Yet this particular Basilisk defies the lore. It *feeds* on narcissistic self-absorption, imbibes the hate reflected by the mirror: "But alas! The Basilisk is in love with its face. It is pulling a comb through its hair" (77). The latter sentence reminds the reader that this monster is no fantastical creature but actually Siegfried Stopf and his comrades, who, far from shrinking back at the image of themselves enacting violence, only puff up with self-admiration. Thus, after crushing Yingele's skull and Joseph's chest, Siegfried proudly congratulates himself on his skill with a club (79). When Siegfried looks in the mirror, he does not seek to escape himself like Yingele, but is satisfied with what he is, and with the familiar world of images that he inhabits. Siegfried Stopf exemplifies the kind of person who inhabits unquestioningly this illusory world. Here the issue of names is instructive once more. Whereas, in *Katschen*, the name signifies an endangered identity, we are told in this text that "all his life Siegfried Stopf never doubted that he was Siegfried Stopf. Whenever he heard his name he always answered without hesitation, 'Yah'" (74). This unquestioning, unhesitating certainty about one's own identity is related directly to the sureness experienced by those who inhabit and can only see the material world. It is a constricted oneness, an inability to imagine anything beyond the narrow confines of one's own small experience. By contrast, those who are able to see and move about in the world of Forms can imagine a world beyond the one at their fingertips.

The multiple names of many of the Jewish characters, who must inhabit two worlds simultaneously in more than one sense, provide an example of this kind of multiplicity, of a Jewish world and a goyish world, an eternal world of forms, and a changing substantive world. Joseph was Yosl in his childhood. Gurnisht was Shimele Kleyn, then Sandor Kis. Elizabeth's father, Fred Goldstone, was Froyke Goldsteyn, and Herr Cohn's ancestors were Cohen. Each of these shifts represents the capacity (and the necessity) to transcend the world in which one's name is everything—yet, at the same time, the original Yiddish name, the one that had to be discarded, is the one most closely related to the characters' conception of home. The other, assumed, names take on the characteristics of a mask, lending the displaced life itself an air of performance.

For children, however, there is a slightly different pattern. Yingele, which means "dear child" in Yiddish, replaces Yingele's real name, which is never revealed in the text. Yingele is called so in memory of his murdered mother, who called him not by his birth name but by this term of endearment. Katschen, too, is called Katschen, "kitten" in Yiddish, because of his mother's decision (Hoffmann 1998b, 111).[13] The children are thus allowed

---

13. The fondness for Yiddish children's nicknames was not uncommon even among Zionist Europeans and is represented in much Hebrew literature set in the prestate and

to retain a connection between their name and their self, while resisting the transformation of that name into one that would erase their history. Upon their displacement and throughout their wanderings, their name functions as the constant signifier of their identity. The tragedy of the victims of Siegfried Stopf is that he inhabits a singular world that leaves no room for another.

The Book of Joseph ends with an Alexanderplatz that has been eerily emptied of its Jews. The only witness to this sudden transformation is a drunkard. What initially seems no more than a hazy memory takes shape, in his mind's eye, as poetry. As in *Katschen*, those people who have been relegated to the fringes of society because of their mental or psychological health, or because of their inability to conform to certain social expectations, are those who see with the Cyclops eye. Hence, the drunkard's long, lyrical vision of all the figures who used to populate the Alexanderplatz and who are now dead functions as a moving elegy. It pieces together seemingly unrelated fragments of quotidian life on the Alexanderplatz to create a brilliant mosaic of a world that has disappeared entirely almost overnight. This vision is revealed only to the drunkard, who seems to be the only one able to see the emptiness of the place and to sense the loss, presumably because of his Cyclops eye. For one moment, he is able to resurrect the forms of those who have been forced violently into a literal formlessness (Hoffmann 1998b, 80–90).

Woman as Place, Place as Woman

While Miriam's ability to see and inhabit multiple worlds is not linked to her gender, other place-related concepts are attributed specifically to

---

early statehood periods. In his novel *Shel mi ata yeled* [Whose little boy are you?] (1970) Hanoch Bartov's character Nachman, son of Polish immigrants to Palestine, is called both *ketzele* (dear kitten) and *yingele* (dear boy), even though his father insists that the family speak only Hebrew. See, for example, Bartov 1978, 11. In Meir Shalev's *Ke-yamim ahadim* [As a few days; titled in English both Loves of Judith and Four meals] (1994), the main character's mother calls him Zayde, Yiddish for grandfather, to outsmart the Angel of Death.

women in these texts. One consistent metaphor relates women, and specifically sexual intercourse with them, to sacred space. Inverting the conventional association present in all three monotheistic religions between extramarital sex and defilement, Hoffmann portrays the red-light district as a portal to the sacred, as opposed to the rest of the city, which languishes in ordinary profanity. The prostitutes on Auguststrasse "entice [men] with words. . . . And to Joseph's ears the voices sound, at times, like a melody of prayer" (Hoffmann 1998b, 49). When Joseph resists them and takes a different route to Alexanderplatz to avoid them, "there is nothing special to be seen, and all is profane" (49). On another occasion, he returns to Auguststrasse and, expressing his desire inwardly through biblical allusion, "he went with a woman and knew her" (50). After this sexual encounter, he returns to Alexanderplatz and "saw that all the other streets were full of sights, and all was holy" (50). It is the physicality of the sexual act that is holy; thus, an anonymous prostitute evokes the sacred from the most seemingly ordinary place. Later, Joseph describes Miriam's body as a "shrine," which he yearns to enter (71). The prostitute's body makes the ordinary world a sacred space; Miriam's body is *itself* the sacred space, the act of intercourse an act of worship. After the war, Gurnisht mourns Yingele and Joseph by reciting Kaddish while having intercourse with a German woman (93). Sex between Jews and Christian Germans had been, of course, forbidden by the Nuremberg Laws[14] since 1935, and this act in the wake of the Holocaust seems blasphemous. Yet Gurnisht is able to sanctify the memory of his friends precisely by confronting this taboo. The woman's body enables men to experience the sacred, either functioning as the sacred place itself, or transforming the external place into a holy one. Moreover, Joseph even goes so far as to envision the woman's body as the site of homecoming: "He pictures to himself how he will caress Miriam's breasts until her nipples harden. Ten thousand years of exile, Joseph thinks, and at their end, redemption" (74). This thought intensifies an idea that

---

14. Section 1.1 of the Nuremberg Laws forbade marriage between Jews and Christian Germans, while section 2.1 stated that "extramarital intercourse between Jews and subjects of the state of German or related blood is forbidden."

emerged previously in *Katschen* when the boy meets a prostitute in a police station. She tells him that "a little dwarf" lives between his legs: "At night he wakes up, stands up straight, and goes off to look for another house. . . . What you lack you can always get from me" (143). This prostitute embod-ies, for Katschen, not pleasure or sin but the promise of a home he lacks.

The connection between women and place in this novella is not lim-ited to this physical interpretation. The womb as a metaphor for a safe haven or even a home plays an important role in *The Book of Joseph*. At night, Yingele and Joseph cuddle together in bed, pulling the blanket over their heads to create a dark cave where they hide from an imaginary wolf. Yingele delights at this game, "and he too imagines himself a baby in his mother's womb" (Hoffmann 1998b, 38). In this scene, the dead mother's womb is directly linked with the warmth and security of being ensconced in one's home. The scene is distressingly ironic, not only because of the missing mother but also because the reader knows what fate awaits the Jews in their German home. Nevertheless, the moment is one of the few in the story that articulates a real sense of home, and it does so by literal-izing the isolated nourishment of a womb in Joseph and Yingele's game under the covers.

Later in the novel, when the narrative breaks suddenly into a poem, the first line describes Yingele as "a kind of holy / Child who does not need / A womb. . . . A child / Who was created from the seed of man with-out a woman's womb" (Hoffmann 1998b, 73). Thus Hoffmann inverts the story of the Immaculate Conception, in which Jesus needed a womb but not "the seed of man." Yingele does not need a womb because wombs are interchangeable. Indeed, "The seed / Which Joseph planted inside Chaya-Leah emerges / From the body of Miriam,"[15] demonstrating the extent to which the womb is unnecessary (73). If one considers the home/womb equivalence suggested earlier, then it is possible to extend the metaphor: Just as Yingele does not need a womb and can move from one to another,

15. Mary is a variation of the Hebrew Miriam; that Miriam and Joseph are imagined as Yingele's parents suggests an identification between Yingele and Jesus, confirmed by Hoffmann's reconfiguration of the Immaculate Conception.

so the Jew does not need a conventional home and can move from one place to another. Indeed, Joseph imagines himself as a seahorse, one of the few male creatures to carry and give birth to its young: "Now the egg in his pocket of life. His blood vessels embrace his fetus-son" (76). This is Joseph's solution to the problem that worries him earlier in the story, when he considers marrying Herr Cohn's daughter, a bourgeois German Jew, for Yingele's sake: "Joseph saw how Yingele looked at other children and thought about their mothers. . . . I have not yet brought my son, whom I saved from murderers, to a safe haven" (43). Joseph convinces himself to make the acquaintance of Herr Cohn's daughter, who, as a potential mother, represents the possibility of a safe haven. Thus the symbolic value of the woman's body shifts from holiness to security. Yet after he meets her and determines that Yingele and he are better off without her, he envisions himself as the seahorse charged with the responsibility of creating a defeminized "womb" or "safe haven" for his only son. This section, preceding as it does the arrival of the Basilisk in the streets of Berlin, proves woefully naive. As Berlin explodes into shards of cold glass, Joseph and Yingele are violently cut off from the place-womb, whose poison they mistook for nourishment.

Conclusion

Rather than attempting to forge for themselves an identity within Zionist spatial configurations, Hoffmann's characters find acceptance beyond established boundaries. In their experience of vernacular salon spaces, they embrace the bourgeois diaspora aesthetic and thereby redeem their European history. Their preservation of worlds of fragments and their recognition of spatial multiplicity constitute a resistance to nationalist claims of wholeness. Finally, they defy the masculine dominance of place not by assigning to women puritanical and virginal sacredness, but by ascribing to their sexuality the power to sanctify rather than defile ordinary places. Subject to a hypersight akin to the one that afflicts Orly Castel-Bloom's Dolly, Hoffmann's characters are able to see place differently than others. Even when they perceive this hypersight as threatening to their own well-being, they understand that, like the Cyclops who can never shut his one eye, they are destined to see clearly. Gazing at the other, looking in the mirror, seeing worlds that are invisible to others, having prophetic visions: *ha-mar'eh* shapes these people's interactions with vernacular places. More broadly, their hypersight establishes them as observers of mainstream culture, both in Europe and in Israel. In opposition to the action-centered ideology of the Sabra, for Hoffmann's characters, it is seeing that enables them to maintain their own identity in a place that is at once their home and their site of exile, fragmented and plural, familiar yet foreign, Israel but distinctly European. In representing such sights, Hoffmann restores visibility to those people who have been rendered invisible.

In a typically precocious moment in *Katschen*, the boy thinks to himself, "'All I ever do . . . is come and go, and come and go.' But as he was mulling this over he was uncertain again whether it was he who came and went, or other people came and went while he stayed in the same place" (Hoffmann 1998b, 143). Despite his tender age, Katschen is able to draw a sophisticated distinction between literal and metaphorical movement. Notwithstanding his constant geographical shuffling in Israel, Katschen's sense of his place, as demonstrated by his loyalty to his name and to his diasporic European identity, remains stable.

5

Toward a Subversive Spatiality

Ronit Matalon

> Being free has several levels of meaning. Fundamental is the ability
> to transcend the present condition, and this transcendence is most
> simply manifest as the elementary power to move. In the act of mov-
> ing, space and its attributes are directly experienced.
> —YI-FU TUAN, *Space and Place: The Perspective
> of Experience*

The crisis of subjectivity discussed in chapters 2 and 3 can evoke a relationship with space that is firmly grounded in memories of the pre-Israeli
European past. The defiantly historical spatial relation present in Hoffmann's works, despite its quiet resistance to the Zionist denigration of
diaspora and exaltation of the nation, is markedly apolitical. Ronit Matalon's oeuvre offers another alternative to Zionist spatial practices. For her,
the pre-Israeli past figures prominently as well, though it is not Europe
but the Arab world that her characters remember. Moreover, her texts
confront the political implications of their reconfigured spatial relations.

In both of Matalon's first two novels, *Ze im ha-panim eleynu* (The one
facing us) (1995) and *Sara, Sara* (Bliss in the English translation) (2000),
space is highly politicized. Two clearly demarcated types of place stand
in tension with one another: the "native place," a usually squalid place
that an indigenous group has been compelled to inhabit by law or by
circumstance; and the "exploitative place" that benefits, directly or indirectly, from their situation. The tension between these places results from
something more complex than antithesis (native/nonnative), but, as we
shall see, their relationship makes it difficult to conceive of one without

invoking the other. In each novel, a privileged character transgresses boundaries by visiting the "native place." This place, she discovers, empowers its exploited inhabitants and disempowers her, reconfiguring the power relationship that exists in the "exploitative place" and serving as a site of subversion. This shift, like the empowerment itself, manifests itself in the acts of seeing and not-seeing. In *The One Facing Us*, Esther, who lives in her uncle's luxurious villa, visits an African shantytown, where she feels eyes following her every move, and where she looks directly in the eyes of a black servant for the first time. In *Bliss*, Sara, a leftist Jewish-Israeli activist from a wealthy family, visits Gaza often to document the Intifada, but instead photographs people sleeping, incapable of allowing their gaze to penetrate that of her camera's lens. I bring these two examples together to demonstrate the power exerted by vernacular place in these novels and the crucial role of vision in establishing this power. Without the protagonists' transgression of spatial boundaries, however, the eye is impotent. Movement, in Matalon's novels, is the place where seeing and blindness organize and dismantle relationships of power.

Matalon's representation of the airport, the house, the terrace, and the African shantytown demonstrate the significance of movement and vision in her conception of vernacular places. In this, as in previous chapters, the gaze constitutes one of the most important means of the characters' relations to place. Movement through and between places in Matalon's novels blurs the line between observer and observed, enabling the gaze to rearrange spatial configurations and thereby to undermine normative power relations.

The choice to analyze *The One Facing Us* may seem incongruous, since most of it takes place outside Israel and is concerned with spaces inhabited and experienced by non-Israelis speaking languages other than Hebrew. In fact, however, this feature enriches our understanding of the relation between place and identity: the displacement of the Hebrew-speaking Israeli Jew and her encounter with diverse ethno-spatial configurations allow her to reconsider assumptions implicit in her understanding of herself and of others. Thus Matalon's Egyptian-Jewish Israeli protagonist finds herself interpreting her family history and her own complex, unfixed identity through her sometimes disorienting experience of African places.

By tracing a spatial consciousness not bound by national boundaries and their attendant ideological loyalties but instead primarily defined by processes of movement and vision, Matalon subverts conventional modes of Israeli identity.

Born in Israel in 1959 to Egyptian-Jewish parents, Ronit Matalon is herself a Mizrahi Jew. Mizrahim, literally "Orientals," designates the Jews who immigrated to Israel from Arab lands. Primarily an ethnic designation, *mizrahiyut* (the state or condition of being Mizrahi) connotes a particular experience within the Israeli context that was sometimes the only commonality binding the diverse people grouped in this category. The Israeli vernacular places most commonly associated with *mizrahiyut* are the development towns and the tents and tin shacks of *ma'abarot* (immigrant transit camps); both are linked, by definition, to immigration. Development towns were planned, as we saw in chapter 1, to settle large numbers of new immigrants; many immigrants spent months to years in *ma'abarot*, waiting to be settled. Even upon their settlement around Israel, Mizrahim struggled because of the institutionalized and non-institutionalized efforts to expunge the Arab components of their identity and to transform them into native, Hebrew-speaking, Western-oriented Israelis. The rift that has developed in Israel between Mizrahim and European Jews, Ashkenazim, continues to shape identity discourse there today. Mizrahi activists such as the poet and scholar Sami Shalom Chetrit and others insist not only that Israeli history must be rewritten to account for the marginalized narratives of Mizrahim but also that prejudice continues to taint inter-Jewish relations in Israel. Some scholars, such as Ella Shohat, have suggested that the Mizrahim in Israel have more in common with Palestinian Arabs than with Ashkenazi Jews, and urge them to develop a joint agenda.[1] The very notion of Mizrahi identity is problematic, since it lumps together people whose histories, backgrounds, and geographical origins are diverse, and in doing so erases important cultural nuances. Yet it is useful insofar as it

---

1. In her essay "The Invention of the Mizrahim," for instance, Shohat proposes a discipline of Mizrahi studies existing alongside and in relation to Palestinian studies. See Shohat 1999.

acknowledges the common experience of immigration to, arrival in, and, most importantly, acclimatization in Israel.

Matalon, a first-generation Israeli, grew up in a liminal category between native and immigrant. The resistance to singularity that she developed has left its mark on her fiction as well as on her journalism, including her reporting on the first Intifada from Gaza and the West Bank for the prestigious Israeli daily newspaper *Haaretz*. Simultaneously passionate and bleak, humane and hard, her authorial voice is devoid of cliché and sentimentality. Her fascination with memory and representation emerges in her fiction not only thematically, but also in the style and construction of the text itself, which refuses to conform to a linear conception of space and time but rather flits back and forth dizzyingly between continents and decades. An intensely cerebral author, Matalon is intimately familiar with postcolonial and race theory, with photography and literary criticism, with Orientalism and the discourse of exile. The infusion of her prose with the language of theory is as common as is its injection with French and Arabic words and phrases. Deeply reflective and exceedingly self-aware, Matalon creates plots that transcend their immediate situations to move toward a broader understanding of phenomena like racism, hypocrisy, violence, and love. The places Matalon represents in her novels, more than mere settings, exemplify her notion of "place as process" and of her association of place with movement. For Matalon, as for Hoffmann, the place of the Jew (and of the immigrant in general, for that matter) is the space between places, the movement from one place to another. Arrival denotes stagnation, decay, even death, a notion that presents a direct challenge to the Zionist narrative of homecoming.

Recent scholarship in Jewish Studies has contested even more radically the teleological nature of Zionism and its valorization of arrival and denigration of exile.[2] Yet this viewpoint is far from mainstream among Israeli Jews and in Israeli Jewish literature. Even for left-leaning authors such as Amos Oz and A. B. Yehoshua, Zionism and arrival at the Jewish national home constitute the legitimate goal of collective Jewish existence.

---

2. See, for instance, Boyarin and Boyarin 2002. Also see Steiner 1985.

Matalon is therefore something of an anomaly in this regard. Her conception of place includes a reconfiguration of home that is no less than radical
in the Israeli context and indeed in any nationalist context. To begin with,
her novels suggest that the experience of immigration is not, as the Zionist
conception of 'aliya would have it, an ascent from a lesser to a higher state
or a means to the end of a decisive home. Rather, they posit, immigration
is a permanent condition, a state of mind so intimately intertwined with
one's own personal temperament that it is not clear which informs which
(Matalon 2001, 43). The constantly changing home in which Matalon's
family lived can be understood in terms of a perpetual immigration, a state
which her brother wanted dearly to escape: "In [my brother's] dream house,
he claimed, the furniture would be nailed to the floor, glued with cement
and mortar" (43). Nailed down, immobile, permanently unmoving: that is
the home that Matalon's characters cannot inhabit, just as they cannot
inhabit one country, or one language, but many.

It is important to emphasize at the onset that this impossibility of
rootedness does not constitute a rejection of the concept of home or a
valorization of homelessness. Matalon's characters yearn for a home but
they do not equate it with roots. Esther's mother Inès, in *The One Facing
Us*, exemplifies this seeming contradiction of the rejection of rootedness
and the desire for home. Despite the fact that "she was constantly pulling
up and planting, moving things from place to place," when she and her
husband had lived in the *ma'abara*, she "hung bright curtains, arranged
flowerpots, sewed her own lampshades. . . . 'It may be a tent,'" she tells her
astonished husband, "'but for the moment it's our home'" (1998b, 144, 171).
Without sentimentality, she cuts down the cypress tree that was "practically a monument" in front of her house because its roots were growing
into the septic system. "How could you have done that? . . . How could
you have cut it down?" asks her sister. "With an ax," she responds matter
of factly (140). Not only does a home not need roots to be a home, but
roots can *encumber* a home. Her indifference to roots is not just literal.
Exasperated by her niece's persistent questions about her family history,
she responds, "Roots, roots, roots. A person doesn't need roots, Zuza. A
person needs a home" (278). This dismissal of roots signals a rejection of
the conventional understanding of a person's relationship to her home,

not a rejection of the concept of home itself. Matalon's most recent novel, *Kol tsa'adeynu* (The sound of our steps) (2008), set in a transit camp in the 1950s and 1960s, confirms the importance of home in its extended reflection on the tenuous line between having a home and longing for one.

Movement and Place: Rootless Homes

"How do you tell the story of immigration from its inside, not from outside, not in the language of the rooted Israeli?" (Matalon 2001, 47). This question, which appears in Matalon's collection of essays, *Kroh u-khtov* (Reading and writing), propels her first two novels, *The One Facing Us* and *Bliss*. By asking it, Matalon brings our attention to a dialectics of inside/outside that differs profoundly from the one espoused by Zionism and represented by authors like Amos Oz, for whom the one "inside" always speaks the language of the rooted Israeli. In this formulation, the immigrant to Israel, formerly an exile, replaces the exile as the antithesis of the native. The immigrant becomes the one against whom the existence of the native is defined. However, whereas the native/exile opposition hinges on the *place* one inhabits (Israel or diaspora), the native/immigrant opposition defines identity according to one's *movement* in space. In her essay, Matalon proposes that this movement itself constitutes the immigrant's place, in radical opposition to the rooted stasis of the native: "I prefer . . . the home that is a process," she asserts (2001, 49). This scarlet thread that subtly reworks nativeness as stasis and exile as movement weaves through all her novels.

Identifying herself as someone who is not an immigrant but who is familiar with the story of immigration through her parents' experience, Matalon articulates a space for narration between these two identities of native and immigrant: "I am the daughter of immigrants but not an immigrant myself, that is—I'm already someone who functions from the strength of a sense of place and a sense of Hebrew. . . . From this place, of a certain ownership of language and place, there comes into existence the territory of literature, the ability to narrate, and in Hebrew. Literature, especially prose, needs a home. The home, the sense of place and language, perhaps make possible the protest against the one place, and the appeal of Hebrew as the one language of the society of immigrants" (2001, 48). Without denying the importance of a sense of home and the strength that comes from "a certain ownership of language and place," Matalon here refutes the notion that having a home necessitates the denial or forgetting of other places. Rather, she suggests that it is the home itself that enables a rejection of the *singularity* of place at the heart of the Israeli Zionist idea. Thanks to her own "certain ownership of language and place," she can traverse "the territory of literature" and narrate the experiences of a "society of immigrants." This conception of the home not as an end in and of itself but rather as a *means*, the point from which one can reject the dominant oneness of "the rooted Israeli," allows Matalon to tell the story of immigration from the inside.

Matalon's first novel has been described and discussed as a "roots saga" (Abramovitch 2001), yet a few critics have made the important point that the novel, while dealing with the fate of a fragmented Egyptian-Jewish family from the early twentieth century to the present, defies such conventional notions of identity.[3] It's about place—or, more accurately, about places. Homi Bhabha's remark about Frantz Fanon applies to Matalon: She, too, is too aware of the "fetishism of identities . . . to recommend that 'roots' be struck in the celebratory romance of the past or by homogenizing the history of the present" (Bhabha 1994, 9). For the characters in her novels, experience and life have been shaped by the places they have inhabited, including the Egypt of King Farouk and then Nasser, Zionist Israel, postcolonial Africa, and provincial France. This plurality of places is about anything *but* roots; it is about the kind of flexibility that is, by definition,

---

3. Hanan Hever writes that "Ronit Matalon has created in the novel a literary construction unprecedented in Israeli literature, which confronts the obsession of identities that has accompanied Israeli literature for many years, in an attempt to salvage the treatment of the dynamics of identity from the question of ethnic, national, sexual, gender, and social emplacement, and toward a deep understanding" (Hever 2000). For elaborations on Matalon's unconventional treatment of identity, see Hever 2007, 329–43; Hochberg 2007, 44–72; Rattok 2000; Kalderon 1995.

opposed to the image of the root, which is associated with stability and a static existence. The experiences of Matalon's characters rather evoke Deleuze and Guattari's rhizome (1987) in their interconnected, nonhierarchical multiplicity. This multiplicity, which is so conducive to the characters' movement, shapes profoundly their experience of home.

Sara Ahmed argues that home *always* includes the notion of movement: "There is already strangeness and movement within the home itself. . . . ['Homes'] always involve encounters between those who stay, those who arrive and those who leave" (1999, 340). She argues against "identifying home with the stasis of being" (340). Situating herself against this conventional equivalence of home and stasis, she articulates a conception of home as an *agent* of movement. Matalon's novels take this concept one step further, suggesting that the flutter of constant movement becomes home. It is the place of literature, the site of memory, the space of constantly propagating desire. When one attempts to achieve finality, to aspire to "the stasis of being," the home is transformed into a site of imprisonment. The Algerian-French Jewish feminist Hélène Cixous writes about her similar fascination with movement and her disdain for the finality of arrival symbolized by Zionism: "The chance of my genealogy and history arranged things in such a way that I would *stay passing;* in an originary way for me I am always passing by, in *passance.* . . . I have always rejoiced at having been spared all 'arrival.' I want *arrivance,* movement, unfinishing in my life" (1998, 169–70). Having attested in no uncertain terms that Israel is a "society of immigrants," Matalon suggests that movement and "unfinishing" is a defining component of the Israeli experience.

Airplane/Airport: Movement as "The Right Place"

In *Reading and Writing,* Matalon relates the telephone conversation she had with her uncle after her father's death. Upon learning of his passing, Uncle Bernard surprises her with his strange first question: "Where?" (2001, 41). He and his wife are interested in the locale of his death, he explains to his niece, because of their own qualms about the permanence of place that death brings, a permanence that does not correspond to their experience of place in life. He explains: "We told ourselves that when we die, we want to die together, inside an airplane, in the air. That's actually the place where we were the most in our lives, the airplane. That's the right place for us" (41). Intrigued by this concept of "the right place," Matalon considers how it might have shaped the immigrant identity of her parents and their generation, people who left Cairo in the middle of the twentieth century and dispersed around the world. "Was there a right place?" she wonders (42). It goes without question for Matalon that her family's experience as immigrants affects their relations with place. Uncertain whether this experience allows for a conception of "the right place," with its singular noun and its definite article, she is somewhat surprised by her uncle's assertion that there *is* a "right place" for him. Yet ultimately, instead of denying the impulse for or the existence of "the right place" for people who do not or cannot settle down in one place, she draws altogether new boundaries for the concept: "I would like to embrace here this choice that Uncle Bernard made: the airplane. The movement itself, from one point to another point, as the 'right place.' The place that isn't really a place, but a means of identity exchange, the almost sole constant component of which is movement" (42).

Yi-Fu Tuan has written that "place is a pause in movement," distinguishing it from space, which allows movement (1977, 138). The concept of pause confirms the importance of movement, for, unlike the act of striking root, pausing is temporary, always looking ahead to the inevitable continuation of movement through space. The importance Tuan attributes to movement echoes Levinas, for whom "the chosen home is the very opposite of a root. It indicates a disengagement, a wandering [*errance*] which has made it possible" (1979, 172).

The ever-growing significance of movement in thinking about place has shifted beyond the somewhat abstract conception of "wandering" to a political and technological discourse. John Di Stefano writes explicitly that "in the context of transnationalism the new paradigm for home is the routine and habitual practice of mobility itself" (2002, 41). He argues that "transit itself might be thought of as a new way of belonging within the interstices of displacement—a type of porous home-space that can be occupied regularly, but that can never be inhabited in the traditional sense"[4] (41–44). Similarly, Leonard Lutwack suggests that "the house is no longer a significant place in the writing of our time. . . . A moving place—automobile, van, spacecraft—may be the nest for people of the twentieth and twenty-first centuries" (1984, 37). In this vein, "the right place" for Matalon is not a geographical location at all but a *process,* a movement both literal (between nations and continents) and metaphorical (between identities). Neither Israel nor Egypt alone can respond to her characters' need for "the right place," but the movement between and within them does. Matalon's representations of vernacular place in these terms reflect that "an increased proportion of humanity lives, at least part of the time, outside territory," in what Marc Augé calls "non-places" (1995, 112). The airplane is an exemplary "non-place," not only because it brings people from one place to another on endlessly recurring and intersecting flight paths, but also because while aloft it is in a borderless, liminal space that is quite literally above the territorial squabbles preoccupying the people below. On an airplane, one is indeed "outside territory." Leah Goldberg, in her poem "'Al 'atsmi" (About myself), provides a lyrical expression of this experience: "There was snow in one land / and thistle in another / and a star in an airplane's window / at night / above many lands" (1964, 75). The airplane hovers between snow and thistle, forest and desert, Europe and Israel, but the star in its window departicularizes the poet's place, enabling her to transcend the specifics of territory to recognize "many lands."

4. Di Stefano reminds us, however, that this idea "should not be confused or conflated with a means of transcending nationalism in search of some abstract emptiness of non-allegiance. Rather, we might envision a sense of belonging as a type of multiple rootedness" (2002, 44, n. 12). While Matalon's conception of place clearly *does* transcend nationalism, it certainly does not do so "in search of some abstract emptiness of non-allegiance," as each "pause in movement" acquires some value of having been, even fleetingly, a place or even a home. Arguably, the notion of "multiple rootedness" may be applicable to Matalon's characters, though the rhizome, as mentioned earlier, describes their situation more accurately. Careful, like Matalon, not to romanticize this perspective of place and its implications on identity, Di Stefano reminds us that "mobility may be chosen or forced" (2002, 44).

The airport, being the "home" of the airplane, is related to its special spatiality. Its geographical isolation is one of its distinguishing features. The fact that it is often positioned at the outskirts of cities to minimize noise and to ensure enough space for takeoffs and landings sets it apart from other types of places, particularly from those that serve similar purposes of transportation, such as train or bus stations, which are usually located in the center of cities and tend to be much more easily accessible than airports. "The difference between being in an airplane and being in a subway or on a train," writes Rico Lie, "is a difference of an 'in-daily-life' experience versus an 'out-of-daily-life' experience" (2003, 141). The airport, unlike other modes of transit, can be the point of departure for faraway places, crossing oceans and continents in mere hours. For these reasons, waiting to board a plane in an airport terminal is not the same as waiting to board a bus. Partly because of its relative isolation, the sensation of being *already elsewhere* is implicit in the airport. As the place where people converge for the sole purpose of boarding planes, the airport symbolizes the phenomenon of movement. Certainly, being grounded, it cannot transcend borders in the same way that the airplane does in flight. Nevertheless, despite its location within the territory of a particular city and country, the airport is a unique type of place. Duty-free shops, for example, remind the international traveler that, once inside the international terminal, she might as well be aloft, in that she is not obliged to pay taxes to any particular country. The duty-free space is accessible only to departing passengers: "As soon as his airport or identity card has been checked, the passenger for the next flight, freed from the weight of his luggage and everyday responsibilities, rushes into the 'duty-free' space; not so much, perhaps, in order to buy at the best prices as to experience the reality of his momentary availability, his unchallengeable position as a passenger in the process of departing" (Augé 1995, 101). This as-of-yet unrealized departure, the sensation of being "on one's way," the *process*, supersedes the destination. Sara Ahmed expands on this idea. She writes of

the in-between space, the interval, of the airport. Such a space is comforting, not because one has arrived, but because one has the security of a destination. A destination which quite literally becomes the somewhere of home. Home is here, not a particular place that one simply inhabits, but more than one place: there are too many homes to allow place to secure the roots or routes of one's destination. It is not simply that the subject does not belong anywhere. The journey between homes provides the subject with the contours of a space of belonging, but a space which expresses the very logic of an interval, the passing through of the subject between apparently fixed moments of departure and arrival. (1999, 330)

Similarly, Di Stefano writes that "the transitory nature of the space of the airport—defined by its comings and goings—[suggests] simultaneously a home-space and a place-of-disappearance. Disappearance here does not mean vanishing, but rather a refusal to appear definitively and singularly" (2002, 41). The two important characteristics of the airport are its representation of process and movement, on the one hand, and its resistance to singularity, on the other.

At the same time that the airport promises movement, it is also a site where people are stuck in a state of seemingly interminable waiting, on the *verge* of movement yet hovering in immobility. The spidery flight paths that crisscross back and forth across the globe, symbolizing perpetual movement, seem to contradict the strange suspension of time and place in airports, providing an apt milieu for characters typified by the tension between movement and stasis. Matalon's representation of this tension in her fiction reflects her refusal to idealize or sentimentalize not only the rootedness that is foreign to her characters, but also its alternative. Discussing Jacqueline Kahanoff, the intellectual exemplar of *levantiniyut*[5] whose work she quotes generously in *The One Facing Us*, Matalon writes that "Kahanoff's generation, the 'Levantine' generation, stood at the intersection of European culture and Eastern culture (*tarbut ha-mizrah*), took the best of both the cultures and paid a price of double loyalty and confusion" (2001, 36). The price of this double loyalty, as it is

5. For more on Levantines and *levantiniyut* (Levantinism), see Hochberg 2004, 219–43; and chapter 2 ("The Legacy of Levantinism: Against National Normality") in Hochberg 2007, 44–72.

represented in Matalon's novels, is the other face of its reward, a suspension in unceasing movement.

It is no coincidence that Matalon's first two novels begin in airports, and that her second novel, *Bliss*, contains an airport scene that is repeated with slight changes no less than five times in the novel. The airport occupies the center of the characters' symbolic landscape. In *The One Facing Us*, Esther, an Israeli teenager, is sent to Africa to stay with her uncle and his wife for several months. She spends her time there imaginatively piecing together her family's history through old photographs. Shifting back and forth between the novel's present in Cameroon and various past time lines in Israel and Cairo, the narrative itself mimics the constant movement of Esther's relatives. In the words of the Egyptian-born Jewish intellectual André Aciman, such characters are "always from elsewhere, and from elsewhere before that" (2000, 109). Those Levantines in *The One Facing Us* who moved from Egypt to France, or to sub-Saharan Africa, or to an Israeli kibbutz, came, before Egypt, from places like Aleppo, Italy, and Lebanon. In the context of their multiple migrations, they find the notion of roots ridiculous and the concept of national identity simplistic. Esther's narration of their movements forms the foundation of the novel.

Early in the novel, hours after Esther's arrival in Cameroon, she relates the story of her Uncle Sicourelle and his "many moves across the African continent": "For thirty years he lived a life apart, roaming Africa like a tyrant" (Matalon 1998b, 13, 14). Esther recognizes this geographic restlessness as a hereditary trait that had marked the generation before her uncle and father: "Always just one step ahead of a legion of irate landlords who demanded the cost of repairs, they moved twenty times or more— from neighborhood to neighborhood or within the same neighborhood in Cairo, from one side of the street to the other, from an apartment that faced the yard to one that faced the street" (21). This passage echoes Matalon's observations about her own family's moves in *Reading and Writing*:

> I grew up in a family in which people moved all the time: from country to country, from city to city, from apartment to apartment, from room to room, from language to language, from one family situation to another. Everything, all the time, stood at the pinnacle of some *process*: if they

didn't literally move from an apartment, or a city, or a country, they would talk ceaselessly about moving. If they didn't talk about moving, they'd move inside the house—they demolished walls, built corridors, tossed furniture, turned the house on its head at least once a year, no matter in what season. The movement, the enthusiastic kick in life's behind, did not necessitate as might be imagined an effort or mental enlistment. To the contrary, it was stability that was conceived of as an impossible effort. (2001, 42)

It is the process, the movement itself, and not the place, that is the object of these people's desires. They move not in order to arrive but in order *not* to arrive, to avoid standing still. This dynamic legacy leaves its mark not only on Esther's uncle but also on his brother, Esther's father. Even as a child, the impulse to wander gripped him: "From the age of twelve he wandered, quick-witted and plucky, savvy about people and life, finding other homes" (Matalon 1998b, 176–77). The constant search for "other homes" proves to have been formative, becoming his defining trait as an adult. "He hated the specifics of place and portrait," she recalls. "In Israel, he was constrained to only one place and one portrait. But not in Cairo. In Cairo there were a thousand possible places. He never missed Cairo, though; he just kept inventing new places, preserving his illusion that there would always be a thousand places for him to go, a thousand shimmering possibilities of place" (30). Lest the reader mistakenly sense a slip into sentimentality, Esther quickly explains that even the one place that contained "a thousand possible places" does not become a site of longing for her father. Always "away on one of his trips, . . . vanished to some European capital and then to Africa" (65), he simply resorts to his imagination when these places cannot replicate the multiplicity of Cairo.

Other characters in the novel share this resistance to rootedness and the appetite for movement. Jacqueline Kahanoff also moved back and forth, among France, Israel, and the U.S. As for Esther's father, the lack of specifics, of "a real sense of space and time," was central to her conception of the Levantine experience (Matalon 1998b, 126). Marcelle, Esther's aunt, lives with her husband, Henri, in France. A free spirit who had, with her cat, "crossed half the world," Marcelle "doesn't sit still for a minute—not for a minute, like a yo-yo" (140, 147). Madly traversing the French provinces with her husband in pursuit of electronic gadgets, "she and Henri would travel about for hours, to far-flung suburbs, coal-blackened slums, and remote villages where cows chewed their cud in vast green pastures" (149). Henri, a Holocaust survivor, contacts possible relations in every country he visits, eagerly charts their locations, and "imagines them engaged in a global conversation that went on over his head" (149). His alternative genealogy is based on an imaginary cartography that itself becomes a home.

Yet Matalon does not idealize these characters' situations. Just as significant as their movement in this novel is the periodic sensation of stillness that invades them, in spite of—and arguably even as a *result* of—their constant movement. Aciman writes of people who are "in permanent transience" (Matalon's "permanent immigrants" [1998a, 170]) that, "in this jittery state of transience, they are thoroughly stationary," (1990, 13) an idea expressed throughout *The One Facing Us.* Contemplating a photo from Cairo in 1945, Esther notes that her uncle, who was to spend a good part of his life wandering from one African nation to another, "seems frozen even before the camera froze him" (Matalon 1998b, 270). Ironically, the flexibility of rootlessness can bring with it an immobility that allows neither the stability of roots nor the freedom of wandering. "The Levantine aristocracy was so scared of doing the wrong thing," Esther relates of her family in Egypt, "that it did nothing at all, frozen in a strange, worldly death of stultifying inner contradictions" (175). These contradictions were the consequence of simultaneous identification and disidentification with both the East and the West, colonized and colonizer, as attested by the section from Jacqueline Kahanoff's *The Sun Rises in the East* quoted in *The One Facing Us:* "What were we supposed to be when we grew up," she writes of her childhood as a Jew in Egypt, "if we could be neither Europeans nor natives? . . . [We] were ashamed of the poverty of what we called 'the Arab masses,' ashamed, too, of the advantages a Western education had given us over them" (181–83). The liminal intercultural space they inhabit affords them the freedom to wander but also traps them in perpetual movement, which itself becomes a kind of stasis.

The contradiction of simultaneous movement and stasis is confirmed by a key scene in *The One Facing Us,* in which the narrator analyzes the painting from which the novel takes its title. She describes the man standing by the pool in the painting as being "one with the place. It is impossible to distinguish between the two": "At one with the place, the man standing out of the water is, at the same time, out of place. The water and the figures who seem to be splashing in the water, *who seem to be able to move*—what does he feel toward them? *He cannot move*, blocked as he is by the light, detached by his shadow, *standing in place as if blinded*. He is trying to take the form of a man, to be a man, but instead he is a situation. Situated in this pool scene, he himself is the pool scene: *not a person but a place*" (Matalon 1998b, 230, emphasis mine). The tension between movement and stasis is unambiguous here, and it parallels the tension between being *in* place and simultaneously *out* of it. The divergent forces pull apart the man in question until he is no longer quite a man. His inability to move robs him of his humanity and relegates him to the status of *being* place instead of *being in* place. Moreover, this passage forges an explicit link between blindness and stasis and therefore also between seeing and movement (which is in turn linked to humanity), an idea that will be addressed in the second part of this chapter.

The black Africans in Cameroon, like the Jews in this novel, move constantly. Natives of a country that has the dubious distinction of having been colonized by three European countries, Germany, Britain, and France, they have experienced their share of revolutions, upheavals, and movement among various layers of society in their employment in urban centers and as domestic servants. Yet in Matalon's novel they, too, are ultimately paralyzed because of their position both in and out of place, unable to move past the bequest of colonialism, finding themselves, after independence, in a place very similar to the one that was colonized. As Ambe J. Njoh has shown, the reality of land policy in Cameroon has contributed greatly to this stagnation, or even regression: "The land policy arena in Cameroon, as in most other African countries, has witnessed a lot more continuity than change. For one thing, the indigenous authorities decided in favour of inheriting colonial land policies rather than crafting new ones. For another thing, almost all land reform measures that have been adopted in the country have originated in erstwhile colonial nations" (2000, 255). No longer shackled by colonial rule but not yet liberated from its legacy, these people engage in movement that does not constitute freedom but only desperately chases it.

Bliss shifts settings every few chapters, moving between Israel, where Ofra has grown up and lives, and France, where her extended family lives. Her friend Sara travels between Israel and Gaza because of her job as a photojournalist, because of her political activism, and also because of her inner restlessness: "She'd wander from room to room like a Fury. . . . She was always moving, rustling with every breeze," recalls Ofra (Matalon 2003, 70, 63). Yet the stagnation of stillness in this novel affects Sara, and, by extension, the Israeli Left. Since Sara's obsession with political activism and with her Arab-Israeli lover Marwan stem from her desire to maintain her own moral purity, all her attempts to *do* something ultimately fail, "binding her like ribbons tied around a gift" (189). When Sara finds herself in the middle of an angry demonstration in Jabalia, she lets herself be swept along, suddenly passive as a rag doll, unable to participate and act: "I froze. I couldn't move. I wrapped the camera inside my coat so it wouldn't break and let the crowd carry me along. I did nothing, just let the movement of the people running, throwing stones, fleeing the tear gas, carry me along" (66). For all her dynamic activism, at the moment of truth she freezes, like the sleeping subjects of her Gaza photos, while the Palestinians around her flow like a raging river. The oppressed Palestinians, so dynamic in this scene, are trapped between the dream of return and the actuality of homelessness in refugee camps and around the world. Arab-Israelis like Marwan are positioned in an even more complex situation: the hyphen between "Arab" and "Israeli" denotes the movement between two cultures, yet it also symbolizes the incompleteness of these people's relationship to both "Arab" and "Israeli." Like the man standing by the pool, Marwan is simultaneously in and out of place, moving between Israeli and Palestinian people and places yet standing still between them, unable to participate in their integration.

Bliss, like *The One Facing Us*, begins literally in an airport: Sara and Ofra are waiting for Ofra's flight to France, where she will attend the funeral service for her cousin who has just died of AIDS. This encounter, their first one in over a year, launches the narrative of their love and parting, which centers on Sara but is actually more about her observer and closest friend, the narrator Ofra. She brings us back to the airport four more times, imagining four alternate scenarios that continue the opening scene in the cafeteria and in which Sara and Ofra part at the escalator leading to the departure lounge. Matalon retains and rearranges several minor details, alerting the reader that this is actually the same scene, reimagined and rewritten four times: a group of Hadassah women who spill first Sara's and then Ofra's cups of coffee; the vending machine from which Sara buys candy, first for Ofra and then for Mims, her son; a group of Italian pilgrims; an irate security officer; a misplaced boarding pass. Moreover, each version is completely self-contained, with the same beginning (sitting together at the airport cafeteria) and the same end (the separation at the escalator).

The first version of this picks up where the opening scene leaves off, at the cafeteria, and continues to the escalator leading up to the departures lounge, where Sara and Ofra must separate. Their conversation is tender and they part with a hug. In the next version of the scene, they speak of Marwan instead of about their own relationship. A tense Ofra walks to the escalator, forgoing any embrace or goodbye, and Sara is left at the bottom of the escalator desperately calling Ofra's name. In the third version, they speak of Sara's photographs of sleeping people in Gaza. They embrace this time, but their parting is melancholy: "You left ages ago," Sara says (Matalon 2003, 223). In the fourth and final version, when Sara leaves Ofra to search for the lost boarding pass in the cafeteria, Ofra finds it in her pocket and ascends the escalator, hearing Sara's desperate cry a few moments later. The mechanics of the scenes are, for the most part, the same: the airport cafeteria setting, the crowds, the sensation of waiting, the inevitable parting. What changes from scene to scene is the nature of their conversation and of their parting. Moreover, the subject of their conversation becomes less personal and increasingly political with each alternative scenario, from their own relationship, to Sara's affair with Marwan, to the photos of the sleepers in Gaza.

The airport becomes, quite literally, the place of literature, as it provides the setting for the different versions of Ofra's memory and narration of their story. As in *The One Facing Us*, several timelines intersect in this novel. The opening airport scene constitutes a point between the novel's past and its present. It is the point from which Ofra reflects on the past, on her highly complicated friendship with Sara, on its abrupt end and the year that had passed between then and the trip to the airport. It is also the point just before Ofra's departure for France, and her immersion in the equally complex relations she has with the relatives she will meet there. The parts of the novel that take place in France are interspersed with those episodes that Ofra remembers and narrates from the vantage point of the airport cafeteria, where she has time to kill. The question of which version is real never arises in the novel, because it is not important. The cyclical repetition of the airport scene not only allows Matalon to destroy hierarchies of fiction and "fact" but also suggests that Ofra's departure, like the process of her remembering, is *perpetual*. We meet Ofra in France and read of her past with Sara, but her perpetually present departure becomes a dominant trope of the novel.

Sara's periodic responses to the narration alert the reader that these thoughts and memories are not confined to the page but that Sara is *listening* to the same stories the reader reads. For instance, the first version of the departure scene is preceded by a brief anecdote that leads Ofra to see Sara as invulnerable for the first time; that realization gradually parted her from Sara, she recalls, "like a letter of dismissal" (Matalon 2003, 170). After the section break that immediately follows this assertion, Sara responds, "No one dismissed anyone, Ofri" (170). Her use of the verb form of the noun that Ofra uses in her seemingly internal narration (*hoda'at piturim; piter,* Matalon 2000, 207) demonstrates that the narration is not as internal as the reader may suppose; indeed, it shows that the narration is actually oral, and that it takes place in the airport cafeteria. The next version is immediately preceded by Sara and Marwan's separation, and Marwan's insistence that his relationship with Sara may be over but his relationship with her son is not; accordingly, at the airport the first thing Sara says is that "He [Marwan] wanted to spend one day a week with Mims" (2003, 215). The dialogue in each of these scenes follows an event or a memory to which it is related. What seems to be an intimate internal procedure of Ofra's remembering turns out to be her narration of the stories that belong to both her and Sara. The airport constitutes a neutral setting, a "non-place" where the accumulated observations of a longtime friendship find expression. Presumably, the sensation of being *already elsewhere* that accompanies the experience of waiting at the airport gives Ofra license to express the sentiments she had kept to herself.

In the final airport scene, as Ofra impatiently waits for the time to pass, Sara proclaims, "I like airports. . . . I'd be willing to live here for a year or so" (Matalon 2003, 248). The comment is strange because, on the one hand, the airport is likely attractive to her precisely because of the sensation it imparts of being already elsewhere; on the other hand, to *live* in an airport violates the functional relationship between the person and the place. Since what makes the airport exciting is the prospect of departing, to live at an airport either destroys that process, substituting stillness for mobility, or preserves it by privileging the anticipation of departure over departure itself. One can interpret Sara's desire to perpetually inhabit an in-between place either as missing the metaphorical significance of the airport entirely or as literalizing it to an absurd extreme.

Airports and airplanes play a role in the lives of other characters, as well. Michel, the cousin whose funeral Ofra is flying to, was an Air France flight attendant, and many of the people attending his funeral are also stewards and stewardesses in uniform. Henri, Michel's father, was the manager of Lufthansa's Paris branch. Ofra's mother, who at the time of Michel's death is on a Golden Age tour of Scandinavia, must be located and flown to France for the funeral but gets lost along the way, presumably in the air "somewhere between Oslo and Paris. They couldn't locate her on any flight" (Matalon 2003, 16). All of Ofra's relatives are connected in some way to the world that Matalon imagines, in *Reading and Writing*, as "the right place" for the immigrant, the world of the airplane, the world of ceaseless movement.

Gil Hochberg argues that the desire for a home in *The One Facing Us* can exist independently of the need to belong and for nationalism. "[Home] is configured in Matalon's novel," she writes, "as nothing more (or less) than the need for a point of reference or 'a place in the world'" (2007, 60). Yet she attributes the characters' movement to their impossible desire for a specifically national home: "The gap between the desire for home and the inability to attach to a homeland is emphasized by the novel's frantic movement, back and forth, through many different, failing attempts to follow the promoted Zionist narrative of arriving at the promised land" (59). This analysis suggests that movement is nothing more than a symptom of these characters' ever-thwarted desire to find a home in Israel. While this is true for some of the characters, it does not account for the constant movement of those who reject the Zionist dream outright, like Uncle Sicourelle. As we have seen, these people move not only in a desperate search of "a point of reference," but also "in a certain happiness" (Matalon 2001, 47). Movement helps them escape the oppressive oneness prescribed by the Zionist narrative as well as by the very concept of home as *locale*. Therefore it is not only the conflation of "home" with "nation" that repels them, but also the very notion of home as *any* singularity, as any rooted, static place. As is clear from the central role of the airport and airplane as metaphors and as actual settings in these novels, "frantic movement" comes to constitute the characters' home in and of itself, the state that is most familiar and in which they feel most comfortable. Arguably, for Matalon the seemingly benign "desire for home" that is place-based, even outside the nationalist context, is on some level equated with "the forcing of place" (47).

At the end of her essay in *Reading and Writing*, Matalon answers the question with which she begins: "In order to tell the immigration story from within it I had to do two things: to break the one language—Hebrew, and to break the one place—Israel" (2001, 47). She uses her own "certain ownership of language and place" to promote the validity of fragmented, unemplaced identity, characterized by a plurality of places and tongues. By doing so, she rescues her characters from "the forcing of place. Once again, everyone could move, and not in sorrow, but also in a certain happiness: there isn't one place, there is a wandering between places, that same airplane of Uncle Bernard" (47). The metaphors of airport and airplane extend beyond the locale in which these characters find themselves to the people themselves, as Matalon imagines "the Jew as a citizen of the world—the total immigrant, he who not only flies in an airplane but is himself a kind of airplane" (48).

Sight and Site

Movement in and between places both depends on and enacts one's ability to see. "The One Facing Us" cannot move because he is blinded, suggesting a fundamental relationship between seeing and place. The link between Uncle Sicourelle and the anonymous "One Facing Us" therefore demonstrates that the uncle's ambiguous identity—between colonizer and impartial outsider, between European and Arab—is shaped by the attentiveness of his gaze. Bill Ashcroft, in *Post-colonial Transformation*, discusses this connection in terms of Martin Jay's "ocularcentrism." He argues that the representation of colonized place is always visual and therefore limiting: "The European dominance of space is also a matter of the dominance of vision over other ways of experiencing [space]" (2001, 128). The way colonized peoples experience space differs substantially from the way the West has represented it in its quest for "the creation of an 'objective universe' through vision" (136). He points out that the ocularcentric relationship with place characteristic of colonialism has been so efficiently and relentlessly imposed that it continues to influence postcolonial understandings of place. In his discussion of the imperial gaze, he analyzes the historical processes that forged the link between vision and place: cartography, perspective, surveillance, the discipline of geography, and language. Tracing these processes, he concludes that the imagination, appropriation, measurement, and mythologizing of place occurs, first and foremost, via the eye. Similarly, Tuan asserts that "the organization of human space is uniquely dependent on sight," also citing cartography as an example of the link between place, sight, and power (1977, 16, 178). This link is crucial for understanding the subversive relationship between sight and site in Matalon's texts, particularly *The One Facing Us*. As in prior chapters, we shall find that the sharp vision that inevitably accompanies movement can at times be excessive and painful. Sara Ahmed discusses this link between movement and vision, arguing that the "questioning of boundaries, and the movement across borders, leads to an expansion of vision, *an ability to see more*. Such a narrative clearly demonstrates how some movement across spaces becomes a mechanism for the reproduction of social privileges, the granting to some subjects the ability to see and to move beyond the confined spaces of a given 'home'" (Ahmed 1999, 337). Uncle Sicourelle provides a literal example of the power exerted by seeing when one day, "dropping his gaze to the floor, forgetting his protective instincts," he is almost murdered by a worker, for whom the dropped gaze signals vulnerability (Matalon 1998b, 240). Yet the "ability to see more" does not necessarily pave the road to privilege, as we will see in the following examples, and as we have seen in previous chapters. Dolly's hypersight in Orly Castel-Bloom's *Dolly City* constitutes the physical manifestation of her madness; in Yoel Hoffmann's novella, the value of the Cyclops eye, which leads Katschen and his father to flee their respective borders, is ambiguous at best. As seeing is not always a privilege, so is movement not always a choice. Arguably, the refugees and political exiles who have been forced from their homes may prefer being at home to seeing more clearly. Moreover, those who do not or cannot move sometimes have the most powerful gaze.

As a girl, Esther sees for her blind grandmother, Nona Fortuna: "I was her eyes,"[6] she recalls (Matalon 1998b, 64). Nona Fortuna listens intently to her young granddaughter's descriptions of photographs, resisting "the greatest temptation, the one she can never yield to, the one without substitute: to see" (112). Yet she considers her blindness a merely physical limitation: "'I see far from the eye . . .' was how she accounted for her knowledge, even before her blindness" (238). The ability to "see far from the eye" establishes Nona Fortuna against the grain of ocularcentrism by suggesting a different way of experiencing space. Accordingly, she remains unmoved by her son Moise's attempts to explain the significance of a Jewish state. In Israel, "she hated everything in sight. Jews and Arabs, Ashkenazis and Sephardis, the religious and the secular, the wealthy and the poor . . . cruel and ridiculous in their endless war over a piece of land she didn't consider

---

6. This statement literalizes an Arabic metaphorical pronouncement of endearment, *'ayuni*, my eyes. Though the term varies from one country or region to another, the eyes and sight in Arabic symbolize what is most precious, and thus loved ones are often addressed or referred to by terms related to seeing or to eyes.

'worth spit'" (225). Her blindness does not impede her ability to see—and to hate "everything in sight."

The most explicit example of ocularcentrism appears at the end of *The One Facing Us*. Dr. Cohen, a guest at the Sicourelles' Christmas and farewell dinner for Esther, relates an experience he had in Malawi, where he worked with an Israeli ophthalmologist to perform cataract surgery on two hundred blind Malawian children. After the operations, "the children were able to see. And then something really strange happened— . . . When the operations were over, the children didn't want to see. . . . As soon as they'd regained their sight, they began to go at their eyes with glass, nails, sticks—anything to make themselves blind again" (Matalon 1998b, 295–96). Clearly, for these children, seeing proved to be more of a curse than a privilege, something that astounds the uncle's guests. Dr. Cohen relates this bizarre story after multiple interruptions by Uncle Sicourelle, who seems strangely intent on derailing the narration. A few lines later, the novel concludes with Uncle Sicourelle's fierce cry, "*À nous les Orientaux!* To us sons of the East!" (296). This assertion of his collective identity seems to come from nowhere but in fact is consistent with the uncle's behavior. In the context of his disdainful disapproval of Esther's friend Jean-Luc's exploitative engineering project, of his own determined demolition of the colonial house he bought from a man he refers to as "that German," and, most importantly, of his own distaste for and refusal to identify with Europeans in Africa, it is clear that, rather than simply asserting who he *is*, he asserts *who he is not:* a European colonialist. It is not only Dr. Cohen's story that evokes his reaction, but also his guests' reactions to it. The complexity of his identity is expressed in one of the narrator's analyses of a photograph of him, which she weaves into a commentary on his difficult position in Africa: "In Africa he had no family or social network to protect him, to soften the blows, to absorb the errors and the personal failures; his keen eye and swift powers of judgment were not a luxury but his means of survival. He had no choice but to look the world in the eye. And he did. He would fix his stare on the camera that sought to expose him, exposing the camera in turn, an eye for an eye. . . . With chilling calm he's nailed his prey, holding it in his unflinching gaze" (226–27). The uncle's ability to see, which, as expected, is related to his constant movement, is not a privilege but a necessity in the place he has chosen to occupy. In a startling reversal of roles, the uncle's eye captures that of the camera, overturning the surveying gaze, as we shall see the black Africans do when Esther enters their space. His desperate cry is a feeble attempt to overcome the ambiguity of his identity: neither colonizer nor colonized, neither European nor African. Despite this ambivalence, his pronouncement girds itself against those contradictions that *do* point to imperialist elements of his behavior: his grand house, his wealth and servants, his terrace and other modes of surveillance, including his imprisonment of his niece, and, when she leaves, of his stepson Erouan's little boy. Torn between these neocolonialist tendencies and symbols, on the one hand, and his inability to align himself with Europe—indeed, his *fear* of Europe—on the other, he dissociates himself from those doctors who help African children "to see," announcing his Eastern identity and implicitly rejecting Western ocularcentrism.

All this is not to deny the empowering potential of the gaze. At times, the gaze is what makes movement possible. In both novels, the heroine is the observer and recorder of events, but she is by no means passive. To the contrary, her gaze imbues her with the power to instigate movement. In *The One Facing Us*, Esther not only observes the people and events surrounding her in Cameroon, but also chronicles her family's history by looking through old photographs, recording her thoughts and observations in a diary, breathing life into a narrative encompassing three continents. Ofra, the narrator of *Bliss*, is riveted by Sara's constant motion. Sara is the professional photographer, but Ofra's eye is steadier, more patient, more sharply focused than Sara's: "You're my biographer, Ofri," says Sara (Matalon 2003, 33). From her school days, Ofra established herself as an observer, the still one: "I never moved from the desk, not once from the beginning of the day until the end. . . . I hated every movement; I despised its complacency and confidence. Most of the time I observed. I put all of myself into my gaze and imagined two spouts of hot lava gushing from my eyes, pouring over the tumult and wiping it all out" (133). She dreams of imposing stillness, yet she is the one who sets the story in motion with the impassioned violence of her gaze. Like Esther, she writes the story, imbues it with the movement of time and with the cinematic reel of memory, stretching from their childhood to their repeatedly imagined separation at the airport. These characters, who either resist or are denied movement, can enact it through the power of their gaze.

Eye and Lens: The Space of the Photograph

In both novels, photography constitutes one manifestation of the gaze, producing an alternative space that is related to but distinct from the physical space it represents. *The One Facing Us* opens not with one who faces, but with one who turns his back, "the back in white": the uncle, who himself is compared to a camera because of his "unwavering gaze," exercises the "dominion" of the colonial (Matalon 1998b, 3, 4). The narrator analyzes the photographs printed at the beginning of every chapter. Sara in *Bliss* is herself a professional photographer and has drawers full of her photographs at home.

Roland Barthes writes that "the Photograph is violent: not because it shows violent things, but because on each occasion *it fills the sight by force*, and because in it nothing can be refused or transformed" (1981, 91). The one who looks at the photographs risks this forced filling of her sight, while the one who is the subject of the photograph risks objectification: "Photography transformed subject into object," asserts Barthes (13). Yet its potential for violence can also empower the photograph. Barthes writes of two themes in photography, *studium* and *punctum*. *Studium*, "a kind of general, enthusiastic commitment," an "average affect, almost from a certain training," is disturbed by *punctum*, something that "shoots out of [the photograph] like an arrow, and pierces me" (26). The *punctum* is a "wound," a "prick," a "sting," a "cut," "an accident which pricks me (but also bruises me)" (27). The diction Barthes employs to discuss the *punctum*, that which makes a photograph striking, speaks to the sometimes painful relationship between the viewer and the photo.

The concept of a violent and violating eye is central in these novels. Photography amplifies and concretizes the metaphor of the powerful eye, the eye that hunts, traps,[7] or penetrates. "A photograph," says the narrator

---

7. The Hebrew equivalent to the English phrase "caught one's eye," *lakhad et ha-'ayin,* is literally translated as "trapped one's eye."

at the beginning of *The One Facing Us*, "offers evidence of what is remembered, but it also intimates what might have been" (Matalon 1998b, 4). That is, the space of the photograph blurs the boundary between what happened and what *might* have happened. In its capacity to resist a singular narrative, the photograph has the potential to become a space of subversion; both the interpreter and the subject of the photos can participate in this subversion. In *The One Facing Us*, Esther's musings on certain photos convey the irrelevance of place. Her father is sprawled on a bed in one photo she examines: "Father sits in a room, the time and place unknown: it could be any time within a twenty-year period, any of twenty different places or circumstances. . . . [There] is nothing to indicate the place" (29–30). The seemingly trivial detail of what type of floor is in the photo—for Esther, its *punctum*—provides the only clue about whether or not Father is in Israel. By invoking the association of Israel with tile floors rather than, for instance, with an ideologically laden element of the Israeli landscape, Esther reflects Father's own indifference to the idea of Israel as the realization of a dream. Thus a photo of a man sprawled on a bed may be read as a political statement. "Ultimately," writes Barthes, "Photography is subversive not when it frightens, repels, or even stigmatizes, but when it is *pensive*, when it thinks" (1981, 38).

The power of the photographer is even more explicit. As the one who creates the photo through a "super-gaze," she can presumably manipulate her subject, something that makes Sara in *Bliss* a somewhat reluctant photographer. She rejects the methodology of portraiture even though she is fascinated by portraits. Ofra notes that Sara "disdained the notion of 'capturing' subjects of their momentary suspension of consciousness during which the photographer captures someone who is not watching. She belittled the opposite effect as well: cooperation between photographer and subject, when the subject would turn himself into a third entity, material" (Matalon 2003, 64). Sara hides her most poignant photographs in drawers because they are too "intimate" to exhibit; she spends time in Gaza to document the Intifada and Israeli atrocities, but in the middle of the chaos all she can do is put her camera away, actualizing the metaphor of her own "blindness toward her position [*mikuma*], and toward its moral price" to use Hanan Hever's words (2000, 362). The camera's lens empowers her, but, though she intends to harness this power in the service of political ideals, and though she is committed to humanism and the rights of the Palestinians, she cannot disengage from the capacity of the camera's eye to invade and penetrate. Ultimately she fails to relinquish her power as photographer to the subjects of her photos by never allowing them the opportunity to *gaze back* at the camera.[8]

Matalon's integration into her writing of photographs, actual or described, and of the theory of photography, has been discussed by several scholars. Nissim Kalderon has noted the connection between the physical location of a character within the square of a photo—a location that is actually a frozen motion—and the situation of the Levantine, hovering between the East and Europe. Hanan Hever and Lily Rattok both emphasize the concealment inherent in the photograph, arguing that it is a misleading and flawed form of representation (Rattok 1997, Hever 2007). But Hever finds in this flaw a redeeming quality: since photos suggest a lack, they provide a starting point for the story. Similarly, Rattok points out that photos are meaningless without an interpreting narrator, suggesting that the media of text and photo, each of which "strips" its object in its own way, can complement each other in a project of representation. Both Hever and Rattok link the photo to violence, but in significantly different ways. While for Hever it is the dissonance between truth and its representation

---

8. It is telling to consider the sleeping Gazan subjects of Sara's photographs in light of a scene at the end of *The One Facing Us* in which Zuza, the pseudo-intellectual who is writing a book on "roots," asserts that "In order to really see a photograph you have to avert your eyes or simply shut them" (Matalon 1998b, 268). This line is from Barthes's *Camera Lucida:* "Ultimately—or at the limit—in order to see a photograph well, it is best to look away or close your eyes" (1981, 53). Clearly, Zuza does not understand the sentiment behind it, which Barthes explains thus: "(shutting your eyes is to make the image speak in silence). The photograph touches me if I withdraw it from its usual blah-blah: 'Technique,' 'Reality,' 'Reportage,' 'Art,' etc.: to say nothing, to shut my eyes, to allow the detail to rise of its own accord into affective consciousness" (55). This is an idea that Matalon incorporates into the structure of *The One Facing Us* by including captions of supposedly "missing" photographs, which the narrator then proceeds to analyze.

that is, in itself and by definition, violent, for Rattok it is the gaze implicit in the eye of the camera that creates violence.

In an article on wartime identity-card portraits of Algerian women by the French photographer Marc Garanger, Karina Eileraas opens with a quotation of Edward Said that applies precisely to Sara's dilemma as a photographer: "The act of representing others almost always involves violence to the subject of representation" (2003, 807). Drawing on the ideas of Barthes and Jacques Lacan, she writes of misrecognition as "a disavowal of a socially sanctioned identity, or a strategic dis-identification," a concept that "allows for the possibility that a photographer may be disarmed by unintended elements of his or her own images" (811–12). The word "disarm" is particularly fitting when we consider the camera as enacting violence on its subjects, even when their eyes are closed to it in the intimate and private act of sleep. Garanger, a French army photographer from 1960 to 1962, became a critic of French colonial policy in Algeria, dedicating his two years in Algeria to "memorialize colonial injustice" through his identity card portraits of Algerian women. Eileraas notes that, "although photography constituted Garanger's official duty relevant to the French nation, it also offered a tool with which to record his opposition to colonial practice. . . . Driven by this spirit of revolt, Garanger exploited photography's capacity to shape the national imaginary. He tried to create images that would question the authoring (and authorizing) functions of the colonial gaze. . . . Garanger opens up a space for dis-identification with the racial and sexual politics embedded in colonial imagery" (814).

Like Garanger, Sara intends to use her camera to record injustice and register her own opposition to the occupation. In Garanger's portraits, however, "women were expected to meet the camera's eye" since their portraits were intended for purposes of identification (Eileraas 2003, 816). This requirement unwittingly empowers these women who, having been forcibly unveiled for the camera, "most strikingly communicate resistance with their eyes and facial expressions. . . . [They] also communicate an explosive mix of indifference, curiosity, indictment, and hostility with their eyes" (817). After his time in Algeria, Garanger arranged for his photographs to be exhibited in France "to spark public debate about French military practices in Algeria" (827). The searing gazes of the women in his photographs would shake the most stoic viewer. In Sara's photographs, people in Gaza never confront the camera's gaze head-on, because she photographs them asleep, inert. Unlike Garanger, she fails to realize her potential as a critic of the occupation through her camera. She does not give her subjects the opportunity to resist or return its violent gaze, and therefore her camera does not disrupt the power relations that she attempts to protest. Her refusal to exhibit them makes them even more useless as spaces of subversion.

The Tyranny of the Neocolonial House

The house is intimate and private, the space of individual memory, history, and identity. Yet its geographical and political context, its style and architecture, and the story behind its construction and habitation all situate the house at the center of a broader discourse. Before confronting these issues, however, it is necessary to distinguish the specific *house* from the more abstract *home*. Shelley Mallett writes that "most authors uncritically conflate house and home" and that, even while attempting to examine the relationship between them (which in itself implies that they are separate entities or ideas), their research relies on this conflation (2004, 66). On the other hand, she points out, "it is generally recognized that the relationships between the terms house and home must be established in varying cultural and historical contexts" (68). A wide range of spaces can serve as home, from concrete topoi like huts, tents, apartments, and houses to increasingly conceptual spaces of cities, nations, or even continents, which may be considered large-scale "imagined" homes, to borrow Benedict Anderson's term (1983). The literature on home in various fields ranging from anthropology to philosophy is dizzying.[9] For the purpose of this analysis, we can distinguish the concepts of house and home thus: At the most basic level, houses are vernacular physical structures generally intended to become homes, but a house in and of itself is not a home; it is

9. For a multidisciplinary literature review on the concept of home, see Mallett. For specifically postcolonial perspectives of home, see, for example, Bhabha 1992 and Ahmed 1999.

lived experience, "the various modes through which a person knows and constructs a reality," that enables it to transcend its own physicality and to become "an intimate place," a home (Tuan 1977, 8, 144).

For Gaston Bachelard, the house not only shelters intimate lived experiences, such as dreaming, but also helps shape the distinction between one's individual identity and the world outside. He argues that "the house is one of the greatest powers of integration for the thoughts, memories, and dreams of mankind" (1969, 6). For Bachelard, the house is the ultimate home. But not all scholars regard house or home in such positive terms. Mary Douglas refers to "the tyranny of the home" as one of its most fundamental characteristics, offering a counterpoint to the "homely home"[10] in the writings of Bachelard, Yi-Fu Tuan, and other humanistic geographers. She writes that "[home] starts by bringing some space under control" (1991, 289). This ominous observation attributes agency to home. "This is how the home works. Even its most altruistic and successful versions exert a tyrannous control over mind and body," Douglas asserts (303).

Certain broadly conceptualized notions of "home" in Matalon's novels arguably have tyrannical tendencies, particularly Zionist Israel, with its demands of assimilation to European Jewish culture and its cultural, political, and military campaigns against Arabs. Yet the "tyranny of the home" also finds expression in the context that Douglas herself discusses it: the house. In *The One Facing Us*, houses, whether large or small, luxurious or shabby, are often "extremely coercive" (1991, 306), literally restricting or limiting the movement of those whom they seem to shelter.

"Unhomely" houses abound in both novels. In *Bliss*, every house that receives the narrator's attention is described negatively. Ofra's family's house in Plessis Belleville is "slightly lopsided, crooked, like a face being twisted by the hand of a thug" (Matalon 2003, 13). Udi, Sara's husband,

---

10. For more on the "homely" and the "unhomely" sensations evoked by different homes, see Blunt and Dowling 2006. Blunt and Dowling link these sensations to experiences of belonging and alienation. Homi Bhabha uses the term "unhomely" in "The World and the Home" to discuss home in the contexts of displacement and migration (1992).

grew up in a loveless house: "His parents' bungalow in Tzahala was cold, with the chill of spaces deliberately filled to conceal the emptiness that nevertheless persists" (85). After Sara gives birth, Ofra recalls, "a weight hung in the air, permeating the apartment—a vague sense of catastrophe" (90). These houses not only demonstrate something about the relations of those who inhabit them, but also exert a force—violent, melancholy, or ominous—on the characters themselves.

The most tyrannical house in these novels is Uncle Sicourelle's luxurious house in Douala in *The One Facing Us*, which, by exposing the ambivalent identity of its owner, becomes a veritable prison. The pathetic huts outside the airport, "strange, flimsy structures, shacks or makeshift houses," strike a marked contrast to the uncle's ostentatious house (Matalon 1998b, 9). Lined in dark wood, flanked by white marble columns, and lit by numerous chandeliers, this aristocratic villa seems to defy its surrounding landscape, declaring itself European. This contradiction echoes that of M. Sicourelle himself, whose "consuming fear of Europe" together with his fluency in Arabic-peppered French and his marriage of convenience to a French woman are in keeping with the "inner contradictions" of his Levantine sensibility (239, 175). The uncle has taken great care in making this house his own:

> Uncle Sicourelle bought the house in 1967 from a German leather merchant who moved to the Ivory Coast. He took pains to wipe out all traces of "that German." The old garden was dug up and a new one planted in its place; the bathrooms, the tiles, the wooden beams on the high ceilings, the fireplaces in every room, the goldfish pond in the rear with its cupid shooting water arrows—everything was destroyed and rebuilt. . . . This was the first house he had bought since leaving Cairo, after staying in a succession of rented homes, friends' apartments, huts and hovels in the factories or mines where he'd worked—any place to lay his head. (Matalon 1998b, 49)

By demolishing and rebuilding the house from scratch, Uncle Sicourelle attempts to distinguish himself from "that German" and the colonialism he represents. This dissociation is a survival tactic that has served him well, and that establishes him as independent of the bloody politics that determine the fate of those around him, identifying with neither the colonizers nor the postcolonial "experts" who come to Africa to develop and invest: "He has held on in Africa for thirty years partly because he minds his own business and respects the social barriers; he is able to fade into the landscape or the human throng" (Matalon 1998b, 190). Yet, while he is technically neither a colonizer nor colonized himself, as a Jew in Egypt and a "white" man who has become wealthy in Africa, the uncle carries within himself elements of both experiences, an ambivalence that is reflected by his fancy villa even after his determined renovation.

It is not inconceivable that another reason the uncle disdains "that German" and determines to rid the house of his lingering presence is that in 1967 the Holocaust is still a fresh wound.[11] The year is also significant because it marks the war that would transform the Israelis indefinitely into occupiers. As the house in Cameroon is the first one the uncle has bought since his departure from Egypt, the fact that he finally decided to do so in 1967 symbolizes the finality of his determined rejection of the Zionist dream.

"A house," writes Bachelard, "constitutes a body of images that give mankind proofs or illusions of stability" (1969, 17). Such "illusions of

---

11. Although the Holocaust was primarily a tragedy suffered by European Jews, Nazi rhetoric, of course, did not distinguish between Jews from different parts of the world, a fact that was not lost on those Jews who were fortunate enough to live outside Europe. Though they might not have been touched personally by those events, Jews the world over sympathized with European Jews and recognized that these events were relevant to them quite simply because of the fact of their Jewishness. In *The One Facing Us*, Esther's mother, Inès, attributes the childlessness of Rabbi Levin and his wife to "the war in Europe" (Matalon 1998b, 211). Nevertheless, Matalon does not miss her chance to remind her readers that, despite the Israeli determination to inculcate every Israeli Jew, regardless of origin, with a deep personal identification with the Holocaust in order to create a legitimate stake for the existence of a Jewish state and to claim the homogeneity of worldwide Jewry, *not* all Jews experienced the Holocaust. At the end of *The One Facing Us*, Esther's father explodes when a private detective he has hired to find his sister assumes that he lost her to the Holocaust: "No Holocaust, no camp, Mr. Armando, understand? Egypt, you know what is Egypt? Good life, good people, good country, no Holocaust" (252).

stability" are especially frail in the uncle's house. Always on the verge of some dramatic upheaval, Cameroon might well spew him out from one day to the next. He is well aware of the fragility of his life there: "Uncle Sicourelle . . . fusses over the volatile household whose sole purpose is to divert him, to lock him in the moment and keep him from thinking of his uncertain existence, of his dispensable and all too prominent presence at the factory, a lone white man among 160 blacks" (Matalon 1998b, 232). After he is stabbed, he retreats to the safety and comfort of his home to recover, and spends a week "padding about the house like an animal" (279). The irony is that it is precisely the wealth and privilege trumpeted by his villa that leads to his attempted assassination; the place he regards as his haven is the place that makes him vulnerable. His sensation of being caged even in his purported sanctuary is magnified by his intuitive and weary understanding that this is not an isolated incident but rather part of a pattern of which he and his wife are all too aware: "[Marie-Ange] persuades Uncle Sicourelle to invest outside the country, save something for a rainy day. Who knows? Within twenty-four hours they could find themselves under a bridge with nothing but the shirts on their backs" (189). The specter of homelessness, however, does not frighten Uncle Sicourelle as it does his wife, the daughter of rooted Breton farmers. He jokingly replies, "What bridge, what are you talking about, Marie? . . . There are no bridges around here" (190). Bridges, signifying a means of transit across a barrier, presumably do not threaten the formerly nomadic uncle. Refusing to attach himself to one or another side in the political struggles and violence he has witnessed, he simply goes with the flow, allowing the current of the place to carry him where it will.

Yet his house, ostentatious and luxurious, is one of the primary markers of his participation in the legacy of colonialism—more so, even, than the somewhat ambiguous whiteness of his skin. Particularly since his house and wealth are managed by black servants upon whom he depends (he himself cannot even write), Uncle Sicourelle is not as detached as he may feel from the postcolonial enterprise he so disdains. Sara Mills discusses the porous borders of the British colonial house in India, owing to the constant coming and going of servants and the need for colonial performance: "Because of the performativity of colonial subjectivity, and the necessity to enact these relations of power at all times, partly because of their precariousness, the private sphere—the bungalow—was not the space of haven from the rigours of the public sphere [Butler 1990]. Private life was lived as if always in public, as if colonial superiority had to be on constant display" (2006, 114). A space conventionally associated with intimacy and private life thus became the space of formality and pub- lic life. Esther encounters this porousness of private domestic space and the performativity of colonial domestic existence during her first dinner in Douala, when she complains, "I can't get used to the 'boy' standing behind me. I feel like he's looking into my mouth. It's very tiring to eat politely all the time" (Matalon 1998b, 43). The constant presence of the servants symbolizes the house's preservation of colonial socio-spatial rela- tions. Significantly, it is the pretended invisibility of the servants, coupled with their disconcerting ability *to see*, that requires the performance of politeness and that Esther finds so disorienting, particularly after another guest assures her that she, too, will acquire the "white gaze," the ability to look *through* the servants.

After his attempted murder, Uncle Sicourelle is not the only caged animal in the Douala house. As the novel progresses, it becomes clear that he intends to keep Esther there for as long as possible, preventing her departure by withholding her passport. His sentimental urge for the close- ness of *"quelqu'un de la famille"* confirms the tyrannical bent suggested by the neocolonial element of his house (Matalon 1998b, 14). For two hun- dred days, Esther spears mango leaves from the Sicourelles's swimming pool, writes in her journal, and generally languishes in *ennui*. Her move- ment is restricted within the house and beyond it. She is not allowed to walk to town, she is advised against sitting in the kitchen with Julien, a servant, and she feels compelled to lie when she wants to wander in the city center. As lavish as her surroundings are, and although she wants for nothing there, the uncle's house feels increasingly suffocating: "life in the house had become more and more like a nightmare" (280). She writes her grandmother and mother, begging them to liberate her. When her Aunt Marcelle comes to visit, Esther's appeal to her makes her sound more like the victim of a kidnapping than a niece visiting her uncle: "He's put my passport in Richard's safe; he won't let me go. . . . Tell him to let me go. I've been here long enough. Tell him to let me leave" (167). Marcelle, however, cannot help her. "You're telling me I'm a prisoner," Esther observes (168).

The uncle's imprisonment of his niece, followed at the end of the novel with his decision to replace her with his step-grandson, is one of the ways he attempts to implement in his unstable home an "illusion of stability" but that actually is a manifestation of his own unwitting neocolonialist tendencies. These tendencies are reflected by his house, which seduced him with promises of safety but in which he is ultimately besieged. By demolishing and renovating the house, he attempts to purify it from its corrupt association with colonialism and to dissociate himself from Europeans. Yet his maintenance of the trappings of colonialism, particularly the spatial and visual relations between the family and the servants, signifies his neocolonial attitude. In effect, the house becomes the agent of neocolonialism, not only passively allowing for the continuation of these relations but actually enacting them, as we shall see in the next section.

The Eye of the Terrace

In addition to the visual relations between master and servant, two of the house's architectural elements confirm its role in assigning the uncle's identity: the gate and the terrace. The magnificent gate at the entrance to the Uncle's house, described as "large," "heavy," and "tall," is not intended only to keep people out but also to keep them in (Matalon 1998b, 49, 106, 195). This gate and the ones at the entrance to the other "huge villas" in the neighborhood conspire with the "vast spaces between them" to transform the houses into luxurious islands (40). These walls do not contribute to what Bachelard calls the "imagination of repose," in which mountains and shrubs cozily embrace and protect a homely home (1969, 39). This is a poetics of incarceration. The trope of home as prison is recurrent in Matalon's fiction.

The vernacular space of the house comes to symbolize not only Uncle Sicourelle's ambivalent identity but also the way seeing can alter relations of power. While the uncle's house complicates his neocolonial identity by reflecting the tension between his simultaneous resistance to and adoption of this identity, the terrace implicates him unambiguously in neocolonial behavior. The terrace, the most striking element of the Sicourelle house, is a component of a distinctly nonindigenous, colonial architecture.[12] Jane Guyer writes that open verandas were characteristic of "the real colonial architecture" in Africa (2002, xv). Mills notes that the British bungalows in colonial India "were always surrounded by a veranda, a very open sort of private space" in which colonials received traders and friends (2006, 119). The architectural features of the veranda and terrace also offered an opportunity to survey one's estate and those employed on it. Bill Ashcroft writes:

> One of the most powerful strategies of imperial dominance is that of surveillance, or observation: because it implies a viewer with an elevated vantage point, it suggests the power to process and understand that which is seen, and it objectifies, and interpellates, the colonized subject in a way that fixes its identity in relation to the surveyor. . . . [The imperial gaze] defines the identity of the subject, objectifies it within the identifying system of power relations and confirms its subalterneity and powerlessness. . . . For the observer, sight confers power; for the observed, visibility is powerlessness. (2001, 141)

Michel Foucault's discussion of prisons undergirds this analysis. The prisons Foucault describes are centered by a Panopticon, which

---

12. The Hebrew word Matalon uses for this site in the novel is *mirpeset*, which can be translated as balcony (as in chapter 2), veranda or terrace, as I have chosen to do here. Since Matalon translates the word to the French *terrasse* rather than *balcon*, which are roughly equivalent to the English terrace and balcony, I have chosen to retain the meaning conveyed by her French. It is important to note, too, that the architectural structure as it is described in this novel differs substantially from Orly Castel-Bloom's balcony. This terrace is much larger; it is attached to a private house rather than to an apartment; the main structure to which it is attached is enclosed by a large gate, and it therefore provides a much more isolated "private-public" space than Castel-Bloom's balcony, which is a standard fixture of urban Israeli apartments. Perhaps most importantly, its postcolonial African context distinguishes it in terms of social and ideological resonance from Castel-Bloom's Israeli balcony.

arranges spatial unities that make it possible to see constantly and to recognize immediately. . . . The major effect of the Panopticon: to induce in
the inmate a state of conscious and permanent visibility that assures the
automatic functioning of power. So to arrange things that the surveillance is permanent in its effects, even if it is discontinuous in its action;
that the perfection of power should tend to render its actual exercise
unnecessary; that this architectural apparatus should be a machine for
creating and sustaining a power relation independent of the person who
exercises it; in short, that the inmates should be caught up in a power
situation of which they are themselves the bearers. (1995, 200–201)

Similarly, the surveillance vantage point in the colonial or neocolonial
context establishes and maintains power relations whereby the one who
watches dominates the one who is watched (though, as we have seen,
these relations may be undermined). The terrace in *The One Facing Us*,
literally elevated and distinct from the rest of the house, gives concrete
expression to these gaze-centered relations of power and serves as a potent
panoptic symbol.

The first thing Esther notices upon her arrival at the house, the terrace
opens an early chapter: "A colonnade of towering white pillars set at evenly
spaced intervals easily supports a huge white structure that stretches the
length of the façade high above the dense green of the garden, about half
a kilometer from the front gate. The niece looks at it through the windshield. . . . 'What is that white thing over there?' she asks. 'La terrasse,'
Madame Sicourelle explains curtly" (Matalon 1998b, 37). This description
emphasizes the terrace's sheer size, as well as its gleaming whiteness, urging
the reader to imagine "towering white pillars," "a huge white structure," and
a "white thing over there." Before Esther even knows what the terrace is,
she is aware of its whiteness and identifies it by this trait alone: "that white
thing." The color white and the descriptors of power, size, and distance are
paired together repeatedly, suggesting a link between the whiteness of the
terrace and its other traits. When considered in light of its panoptic function, the terrace can be understood as an agent of neocolonialism.

"*La terrasse*" is one of the French words that, when spoken, is consistently rendered in French and not in Hebrew (except in Esther's

journal, where she uses the Hebrew word *mirpeset*[13]). Matalon's polyglossia[14] enables her to "break" the concept of one language so crucial to the "rooted" Zionist narrative: Despite the Hebrew text, the reader is to understand that the characters are speaking French in the novel's present, and Arabic and Hebrew in Esther's memories. Arabic and French words peppered throughout the Hebrew text signal to the reader which language is being spoken. Therefore, the choice to render a word in French or Arabic is the choice of the author or perhaps of the narrator, not of the characters. By choosing to use the French word for terrace rather than Hebrew in her narrative, she distinguishes it from other parts of the house, which are called by their Hebrew names. This choice also suggests that the characters feel a sense of intimacy with the terrace that calls for an avoidance of the filter of translation. Finally, it isolates the terrace as a distinctly European feature.

In addition to its linguistic isolation from the rest of the house, the terrace is isolated in terms of its history and its startling whiteness. Esther notes that her uncle destroyed and rebuilt the house, but

> he didn't touch the terrace. It was the terrace that he had seen first from the large gate, sparkling from cleanliness and whiteness, concealing something from him. . . . He photographed the renovated house from every angle, drawing black arrows on the pictures: "the back," "the pool," "the window of the study by the pool," "the bathroom," "another bathroom," "the entrance," "the kitchen," "the kitchen seen from the garden," "the living room." Then, a white spot, blurry in the bright light, like a puddle of spilled milk, with a bit of black frame and barely discernable pale trees: "*la terrasse.*" (Matalon 1995, 57)

13. See note 12 on Matalon's use of *mirpeset*.

14. Bakhtin writes: "The speech diversity within language thus has primary importance for the novel. But this speech diversity achieves its full creative consciousness only under conditions of an active polyglossia. Two myths perish simultaneously: the myth of a language that presumes to be the only language, and the myth of a language that presumes to be completely unified" (1981, 68).

The sole remnant of the demolition of the German owner's original house, the terrace caught Uncle Sicourelle's eye as it catches Esther's eye on her arrival at the house. Its whiteness, mentioned twice in this passage, out-shines every other part of the house and exerts a magnetic pull on people's vision, asserting the significance of the visual and establishing the terrace as the site of panoptic relations. As the only surviving part of the origi-nal house, the "sparkling" terrace is an outpost of purity in an otherwise defiled place, and a constant physical reminder of the colonial past from which the uncle tries to dissociate himself.

The terrace as panopticon finds its way into Esther's subconscious, appearing as the centerpiece of a strange dream she has, captioned "*La Terrasse*. Madame Sicourelle and the Niece, Douala, 1978":

> In her dream the niece sees a dizzying vista. But the watchful eye cannot be hers; it is omniscient, too calmly surveying the entire landscape; the eye slides over the terrain as the edges of a shawl drape over an object without changing its form. . . . In the distance, at the garden's edge, is something blinding, stunning, white as a ship just christened: *la terrasse*.
>
> The terrace is like an island unto itself, snobbishly turning its back on the house behind it, the thing that gives it meaning: long, white, a waist-high railing embracing the three open sides. . . . The terrace has a human face, but without eyes, lips, nose; all the human details are erased yet its expression is still clear beneath a thick impasto. (Matalon 1998b, 100–101)

The passage is narrated from Esther's perspective; she immediately dissoci-ates herself from the omniscient gaze to which she is privy in her dream. The eye passes over the brown hill facing the terrace, gliding over the hill and its surroundings, implicating the terrace itself as the controlling ele-ment of this all-seeing gaze. The terrace's dazzling whiteness, through its capacity to blind even this omniscient eye, represents the core of its pan-optic power. Esther's dream posits the terrace as the featureless face of colo-nialism, white, imposing, haughty, all-seeing, all-appropriating, refusing to acknowledge the worth of "the thing that gives it meaning." Though it is the niece who sees the "dizzying vista," the dream establishes a clear dis-tinction between her eyes and the all-knowing, all-seeing "watchful eye."

The omniscient eye, the dream suggests, belongs to the terrace, which not only sees everything, but also *blinds* all who look at it.

Similarly, the "white gaze" surveys yet is supposed to be itself impervious and hermetic, unseeable, even blinding, discouraging a returned gaze. Ironically, while the claim to power of the "white gaze" is based on its omniscient vision and its capacity for surveillance, in practice it effects blindness. When Esther feels uncomfortable on her first night in Africa because of the servant standing behind her, her friend Jean-Luc reassures her: "You'll acquire the white people's gaze. You'll simply look past him" (Matalon 1998b, 44). She is taken aback, yet months later Jean-Luc's prediction is realized: "I ignored Julien, looking right through him as if he were air, just like Madame does" (204). By adopting the "white gaze," Esther establishes herself, finally, as white, by turning her unseeing gaze on the servant and thus robbing him of subjectivity.

Ashcroft writes that "the desire for a literal position of visual command is metaphoric of the 'panoptic' operation of the imperial gaze in which the observed find themselves constituted" (2001, 142). The terrace, which provides this position of visual command and thus enables the imperial gaze, is revealed as a direct manifestation of colonialism, spreading across private grounds from one villa to the next: "She turns her gaze to the side, to the edge of the long terrace that stretched into the darkness, as if infinite, indefinable, into the crowded garden and beyond, passing the large entry gate, silently spreading across the street, to the house there, also white with an awesome terrace of its own, a terrace and a terrace. . . . She trembles a bit" (Matalon 1995, 57). The threatening metaphor comes to life in Esther's imagination, replicating itself like a virus, creeping silently over its dominion.

The African Shantytown: The Returned Gaze and the Reclamation of Place

The terrace, an architectural fragment that signifies the perpetuation of the imperial gaze or the "white gaze," is located in a wealthy white neighborhood in Douala. The heart of the uncle's house, it depends on servants for upkeep and maintenance at the same time as it represents the vantage point from which they can be surveyed. We have seen that the panoptically inclined architectural and social constructions (elevated terrace, servants standing by the table at mealtimes) can have the unwitting effect of turning visual relations (and therefore relations of power) on their head. Now moving into a "native space," we shall examine the effect place has on the relationship between the gazer and the gazed and the implications this effect has for the characters' identities.

In a rebellious gesture against her overly protective uncle, Esther enlists a friend to drive her to their servant Julien's home, located in a black shantytown.[15] Reminiscent of the depressing shacks Esther sees outside the Douala airport, the shantytown constitutes an "unsightly attempt at a miserable, dubious urbanity," marked deeply by poverty and a disconcerting unhomeliness (Matalon 1998b, 9). The shantytown is a distinct vernacular spatial type. Akin L. Mabogunje, in his overview of urban planning in postcolonial Africa, notes its important role: "Indeed, after independence . . . the mass of poor rural migrants seeking wage labor in the cities had to create other sorts of productive relations in order to

---

15. The term "shantytown" is controversial. In a report of the seventy-third Wenner-Gren symposium entitled "Shantytowns in Developing Nations" which was held in July 1977, Peter Lloyd cautiously begins by asserting that "In its diversity and complexity, the shantytown is difficult to define" (1979, 114). He proposes several characteristics of the shantytown: "It is a settlement peopled by immigrants to the city in recent decades and . . . housing in it is constructed not by public or commercial bodies but by the migrants themselves, either for their own use or for letting. . . . For some the term 'shantytown' is contentious; it obscures the possibilities seized by many individuals for improving their houses. 'Squatter settlement' emphasizes illegality, yet this may not be the most important factor in the development of the settlement. 'Spontaneous settlement' excludes the notion of poverty. . . . Many shantytown residents engage in informal sector activities because of the insufficiency of stable wage employment in the formal sector; others are in irregular and poorly paid wage employment. . . . Shantytowns are, universally, the product of rural-urban migration" (114–16). In a scathing response to this report, Anthony and Elizabeth Leeds "reject out of hand the term 'shantytown' as a generic designation. . . . The obscurantism of the term . . . is both scientifically and politically irresponsible" (1979, 461). Matalon's narrator calls it "ehad ha-reva'im ha-ele shel ha-shehorim," "one of those black quarters," (1995, 213–14), denoting the place's specific racial designation. I use the term "shantytown" that is used in the novel's English translation.

survive there" (1990, 123). African migration to urban centers led to the development of shantytowns, since laborers from rural areas could earn higher wages in cities but could not afford to live in them. The instability of such communities, which were for the most part illegal and therefore forever at risk of demolition, was not only a product of urbanization but also a direct legacy of colonial housing standards: "as elsewhere in the developing world, the relationship between the high cost of building materials and the colonially derived standards and criteria for determining officially approved housing were critical factors constraining the development of adequate housing facilities for the urban poor whose shelters were frequently destroyed by official demolition" (131–32). While the inhabitants of shantytowns were often marginal economically, they were *not* socially or even geographically marginal. Peter C. Lloyd dismisses the concept of the "cultural marginality" of shantytown dwellers: "the shantytown dweller accepts the dominant values of the society. . . . Yet in another sense the poor are 'marginalised' by the dominant economic processes" (1979, 116). The anxieties and desires of the inhabitants of the shantytown do not differ substantially from those of their society. In spite of their easy access to the city and suburban white neighborhoods where they are employed because of their proximity to urban centers, however, they inhabit a liminal space: Geographically they are positioned between the native village and the urban and suburban settings of their white employers; metaphorically, they hover between autonomy and dependence.

Stepping outside Matalon's narrative for a moment and considering the African shantytown in the broader Israeli cultural context within which the author and the narrator are situated, the reader may recognize that the shantytown's definitive racial constitution is not limited to Africa, but can be found in various Israeli places, such as the slums of south Tel Aviv and the geographically and culturally marginal development towns, both of which are predominantly Mizrahi,[16] or the Palestinian refugee camps in the Occupied Territories. Though fundamentally different from

---

16. For more on Mizrahi Jews, see Shohat 1999 and Chetrit 2004.

one another, these spaces are all associated with an oppressed racial or ethnic category. More importantly, this association has a basis in fact—that is, these places developed or were designed to accommodate specific racial or ethnic groups. I am not proposing that Matalon intends to evoke these ethnically charged Israeli places in her portrayal of the shantytown and of the overwrought scene set there. Rather, I suggest that the shantytown, which does not exist as such in Israel and may seem irrelevant in the Israeli context, resonates there more deeply than may be apparent.

Esther's entry into Julien's world constitutes her first real encounter with black Africa on its own terms, of black Africans in their own place, ravaged by historical circumstance and by the whites they still serve in spacious villas. Jean-Luc winds the car through narrow, filthy alleys and lanes, stopping near Julien's house and waiting for Esther as she goes in, penetrating a space in which she is utterly alien. It is a sorry scene: "The room was almost completely dark, although the floor was lit by some light that came in through the broken blinds. I saw a body lying on a mattress, someone sleeping. . . . It was so stifling I could hardly breathe," she recalls (Matalon 1998b, 199). Julien excuses himself to bring her a drink, "vanishing into a dark hole—the kitchen, I guess" (200). She cannot fall asleep that night for thinking of "the tin-shack alleys" and Julien's "stinking, stifling room" (202). Uncomfortable with the stark unhomeliness of the home she had entered, she tries to remind herself of her own dismal situation, but the pathos of her luxurious prison diminishes somewhat in comparison to Julien's. "I tried to cry," she says, "to force myself to think really sad thoughts about being trapped here, a prisoner, watching my life waste away before my eyes, not knowing when or how I would ever get home" (202). Esther's visit to Julien disrupts her genuine despair and her self-pity, alerting her to the complex situation of the people for whom this place is the only home. In the context of her awakening, Julien's shack becomes a metonymy of the postcolonial nation, nominally independent but still chained to the colonial legacy through poverty, suffering, and segregation. Yet, as we shall see, Julien's house and the shantytown where it is located, despite their atmosphere of imprisonment, actually function as sites of resistance and subversion.

When Esther enters the African space, the city and especially the shantytown, the gazing eye turns upon her in a startling reversal of the usual racially determined power relations. Having sneaked out to the town center alone, she strolls through the streets and immediately becomes aware of the eyes upon her: "I noticed that people were watching me. They have this way of watching you without you noticing them, as if they can make themselves disappear. It's unsettling" (Matalon 1998b, 95). It is not just their gaze, but also their ability to render themselves invisible that Esther finds so disconcerting. Later, she sits at a café and notices a youth watching her. "I stared at the boy; . . . I wanted to see what he would do" (96). The waiter tries to convince her that she would be more comfortable in the air-conditioned interior, but she refuses to go inside: "I wanted to keep my eyes on the boy" (96). This staring contest demonstrates the power implicit in watching: by staring at her, the youth gives her the impression that he intends to do something; by staying outside and staring back at him, Esther conveys that she is not intimidated by his threatening gaze, quite literally refusing to cede her territory, the café terrace.

The city, full of watchful eyes, is a racially mixed space. In the shantytown, which is entirely native, the gaze acquires cannibalistic powers: "Meanwhile, I hadn't noticed that we'd come to one of those black shantytowns. . . . Everyone was staring at us, practically devouring us with their eyes. . . . I didn't like the way people stared at us and I tried not to stare back" (Matalon 1998b, 198). The interplay between watcher and watched changes from one scene to the next. Whereas Esther tries not to return the stares when confronted by the collective gaze of the shantytown dwellers, when she enters Julien's house she makes a conscious effort to look directly into his eyes, to assert her dissociation from the unseeing "white gaze" to this servant she has befriended. She is shocked to find not gratefulness but seething hate in response to this gesture: "I stared right into his face, something I had never dared do. His eyes were black and his pupils dilated; they looked full of hatred. I'll never forget those eyes and their dark, blank, hateful stare. No one has ever looked at me like that before" (200). Back in the car, Julien's gaze continues to sear: "I leaned back and covered my eyes" (200). The aggressive gaze does not invade Esther's space. Her decisions and actions expose her to it: she chooses to come into Julien's town and his house, and she chooses to look into his eyes. Esther renders herself vulnerable to this gaze by violating the socio-geographical code that discourages the trespassing, by the body and the gaze, of designated racialized spaces. By looking at Esther, an act that is inconceivable in a "white" space, Julien and his neighbors assert their own subjectivity to someone who, to them, symbolizes its denial.

It is important to note that the Africans' use of the eye in this black space does not enact the same type of violence as constant surveillance—colonial and postcolonial alike—enacted upon them on the one hand in the form of constant observation, and on the other in the form of the "white gaze," a pretense of their invisibility in white eyes. The panoptic surveillance of servants and other black Africans is not so much a looking *at* as a looking *through*. When Julien gazes at Esther, he gazes directly into her eyes and he *sees* her. The subversiveness of this act, therefore, does not constitute a rejection of the power of the gaze, but neither is it a simple reversal or inversion. It acknowledges its power and reconfigures it to disrupt white authority. Homi Bhabha writes about the gaze in the context of colonial mimicry, "this process by which the look of surveillance returns as the disciplining gaze of the disciplined, where the observer becomes the observed and 'partial' representation rearticulates the whole notion of *identity* and alienates it from essence" (1994, 127). Of course, the situation in Matalon's novel, which constitutes a *double* mimicry, is even more complex than the classic example of colonial mimicry, in which Anglicized Indians are "*emphatically* not . . . English" (125). The mimicked here, the one who gazes, is himself gazed upon—he is himself a sort of "mimic man," "almost but not quite" a European colonialist (129), a man always in-between: in Egypt, not quite European but not really "Arab" because of his Jewishness, and in Africa, not an ex-colonial European but never an "African" because of his whiteness. Though he is unwilling to reside in the colonial house, he insists on keeping intact its great gazing eye.

For black Africans, the subversive gaze works only in certain places, for instance beyond the neocolonial villa with its protective gate and massive white terrace-eye. It would be inaccurate to conclude that the black Africans here appropriate European ocularcentrism, however; their gaze is directed not *at* the place, but *from* it. This subtle reconfiguring of the sight/

site link in the shantytown and other native spaces can lay the ground-work for a reclamation of place. "The most subtly transformative way [of dealing with boundaries] lies in the mode of their habitation" (Ashcroft 2001, 181)—that is, the way that oppressed people choose to inhabit their place can determine, at least to some extent, its valence. Comparing the borders of African nations to the borders of Hausa compounds, Ashcroft notes that "whether they exist as signs of entrapment or empowerment depends upon the will and determination of the inhabitants, and the dis-course within which they are located" (181). Choosing to look back at the perceived oppressor, denying her any identity besides whiteness, overturns conventional racial configurations in a manner that most painfully impli-cates Esther in upholding those configurations. The shantytown, too, can be read as a site that imprisons or one that empowers. Julien's defiant gaze positions him squarely in the latter category.

Conclusion

Both of Matalon's first two novels take place at least partly outside Israel and, more significantly, in multiple locations. This authorial choice for multiplic-ity confirms the idea of place on which she elaborates in *Reading and Writ-ing*. Not only do her characters move from place to place, but the reader, too, must do the same, breathlessly bounding from one continent to another, from one language to another, from the past to the present. These fragments constitute the breakdown of the illusory unity of national and historical narrative. The "territory of literature" that Matalon constructs allows these fragments to collide uninhibited, like the loose ends of memory itself. For the people who inhabit this territory, movement may mean freedom, or it may paradoxically bring about imprisonment. However it constitutes itself in each character's experience, movement (or the denial thereof) becomes in and of itself a *place*. By thus offering alternative conceptions of place itself, Matalon allows her characters not only "to see more" but also to see *differently*. In her novels, it is seeing that disrupts power relations established in and by places. Rearranging the hierarchy of the gaze upsets conventional ways of experiencing place, disorienting and reorienting the seer and the seen and continually remolding the contours of their identities.

Conclusion

In Eran Riklis's film *Ets limon* (Lemon tree, 2008), loosely based on a true story, a lemon grove that has been in a Palestinian woman's family for half a century becomes one of the film's protagonists. Salma Zidane, a lonely widow, earns a meager living from the lemons. Her bond to the trees is first and foremost emotional: they evoke the memory of her father, they rustle outside her window at night, they depend on her care for their survival as she depends on them for hers. When the Israeli defense minister moves into a fancy house adjacent to the grove, it is determined that the thick trees pose a security risk because they could hide terrorists, and Salma is served with a letter informing her of their imminent uprooting. A fence is erected around the grove and a watchtower constructed within it. She is not allowed to enter. As she battles the Israelis in court, we see the trees lose their luster and fullness, the browning lemons drop heavily, the parched earth harden. The high metal fence that separates her from her beloved trees also separates her from her neighbors, a none-too-subtle allusion to the controversial separation barrier that casts its shadow over the entire film. Ultimately, the case is argued in the Israeli Supreme Court, whose judges arrive at a compromise: the trees shall be substantially trimmed for visibility. The film's last shot pans over the now naked grove, a graveyard of tiny, fruitless tree skeletons, dwarfed by the giant separation wall now erected between them and the defense minister's house.

The grove's unfortunate position on the Green Line seals its fate. Yet it has been situated there for fifty years, with nary a problem. The film's innovation, in terms of its spatial representations, lies not in this clash between political and vernacular place (the Green Line and the lemon grove) but in the imagined transformation of this quintessential vernacular place into a threatening political place. The haunting image of the forcibly stunted trees and the long take of the monstrous separation barrier towering above them convey this transformation forcefully. The grove has become indisputably a political place—both in its capacity to harbor terrorists and in its new role as a buffer zone between the defense minister and enemy territory—but we are left wondering if it ever had a chance to escape its fate, considering its location. The politicization of its vernacular spatiality was latent, the film suggests, bubbling just beneath the tranquil surface.

The "unbridgeable gap between the Place and our place," in Yigal Schwartz's words, reflects one of the fundamental tensions of Zionist ideology, which insists on the "normalcy" of Israel as a secular nation at the same time that it bases this nationhood on Jewish cultural bonds and a purported common Jewish historical narrative (2007, 11). Focusing on this irreconcilable clash between Place and place, however, relegates the spatial to abstraction. In a nation as diverse as Israel and as densely packed with "spatial stories," to use Certeau's terminology, the dream of Zion and the discordant reality of Israel do not by any means exhaust the possibilities of place experienced by people every day (1984, 115).

Vernacular places, which occupy a prominent position in contemporary Israeli literature, tell us a great deal about how people conceive of their relation to Israel and to the nationalist ideology that continues to predominate there. Examining representations of vernacular places—the unremarkable places where people eat and sleep, work and relax, where they live their lives from day to day—acknowledges the importance of quotidian experience and thereby humanizes these characters who can so easily be subjected to pure political abstraction and transformed into lifeless symbols and slogans. The disproportionate academic and popular emphasis on Israel's political landscape risks reifying the Israeli experience of place and losing the multifaceted nuance that characterizes this experience on a daily basis. A denial of the ideological resonance of these places, however, results in a crucial blind spot in the examination of Israeli identity. The way people inhabit, move through, construct, and, significantly, *regard* vernacular places reveals the complexity of their understanding of themselves; it also illuminates their role in the larger ideological construct that assigns them to simplistic categories based on ethnicity, religion, or devotion to nationalist ideas.

In my final chapter, I argue that spatial hierarchies determining identity can be disrupted and reorganized through vision and movement. This challenges our basic understanding of space and place. Such a concept of vernacular empowers people not through the abstract and impersonal accumulation or conquest of territory but rather through their experience of and in place and space. People's relationship to place is not only subject to standard social and economic formulas. It is also defined by their interactions *with* and *within* the place, dealings that reconfigure hierarchies of identity and, ultimately, the foundation of the ideology dependent on them, such as nationalism or colonialism.

This notion of the way place shapes identity and ideology constitutes a substantial shift from the literature examined at the beginning of this study. Amos Oz, a moderate Zionist acutely aware of the power of place, demonstrates in his novels the link between place and ideology, which confirms, forces, and even establishes the identity of the characters according to the needs of this ideology. The struggle between the wilderness and its representatives, on the one hand, and "civilization," on the other, characterizes the spatial tension that afflicts Oz's characters. The drive for a utopian Zionist spatiality conflicts with their individual psychological and emotional needs; however, in causing them to transgress literal and metaphorical boundaries in a futile attempt to free themselves, it entangles them ever more intricately. Place, in Oz's novels, serves ideology and compels the characters to inhabit identities that they try unsuccessfully to resist. Despite their discontent with the proscribed identity that forces them to serve place to the detriment of their personal needs, Oz's protagonists occupy the highest rungs of the Israeli social ladder. They attempt to rebel and to reclaim individual identity not because they reject the Zionist ideology that valorizes them but because they resent the fact that their entire identity is determined by and subject to it.

The vernacular places in Orly Castel-Bloom's novels are not only powerful; they are downright sinister. These places purport to exist for the social, biological, and psychological well-being of the individual. Never announcing themselves as overtly ideological, they nevertheless play important roles in serving and maintaining important Zionist ideals, particularly the centrality of the Israeli collective. Castel-Bloom's characters, women well aware of their position as ill-fitting cogs in this ideological machine, find themselves fragmented and alienated. The balcony, the hospital, the cemetery, and the city, places intended to combat the individual's isolation by creating a sense of community, only intensify the characters' instability and aloneness and drive them to psychological despair. These places, in the service of hegemonic ideology, cast the characters out of familiar categories of identity, depriving them of even the most fundamental sense of self.

This instability reaches a feverish pitch in Sayed Kashua's novels, in which vernacular place is explicitly and insistently political. For his protagonists, the identity of in-betweenness established by their existence between "Israeli" and "Palestinian" is experienced regularly in the places of their quotidian experience. These places, including the roadblock, the house, and the village, are represented in Kashua's novels as the mutilated reflections of Israeli-Palestinian identity, mirroring the paralyzing in-betweenness that characterizes the position of the Israeli Palestinian in Israeli society. Far from passive, these places and the experiences they create for the characters actually instigate paralysis by disrupting their movement both within and among places, thus confirming the ambiguous in-betweenness of their identity. The most familiar places become a foreboding no-man's-land, disrupting Israeli Palestinians' autonomy as free citizens at the same time that they deny them the terrible clarity of outright expulsion.

The anxiety so prevalent in the interactions between people and place in the novels of Castel-Bloom and Kashua threatens Yoel Hoffmann's characters as well. In his novels, vernacular places are at the center of the experience of another group marginalized by nationalist ideology in Israel: diasporic European Jews. Yet his characters find ways to sidestep the demands of this ideology, either recasting Zionist places as benign versions of the horrific Europe they left behind or pressing beyond their boundaries to find acceptance with other ideological misfits. Whether wandering the ambiguous space beyond the kibbutz, dressing up to sit at bourgeois cafés, inhabiting multiple landscapes of the imagination, or celebrating the sanctity of eroticized feminine space, Hoffmann's characters experience a spatiality that defies the centrality of nationalist ideology. The Zionist space thus stripped of its omnipotence poses not an obstacle but a counterpoint to the identity inhabited by Hoffmann's characters, an autonomous identity that, like the places that enable it, is Israeli but not Zionist.

The alternative spatiality presented in Hoffmann's novels is ideological only insofar as it resists Zionist ideology. Ronit Matalon's characters' interactions with vernacular place go so far as to subvert the spatial relations espoused by Zionism. Setting her first and arguably most important novel almost entirely outside Israel, in a space irrelevant to Zionism but at the center of the much broader ideological discourses of colonialism, postcolonialism, and neocolonialism, Matalon from the outset announces her refusal to be bound to conventional Israeli hierarchies of place. Broadening the borders of her characters' multilayered spatial experience, she demonstrates that Israeli identity can be shaped and informed by places far beyond Israel. More significantly, the vernacular places she represents, such as the airport, the house, the terrace and the African shantytown, enable new modes of seeing and encourage the movement so severely constricted in the places Oz represents.

In Israel, Zionism, though continually subject to criticism and revision, continues to reign as the predominant ideological force and is integrated into various facets of Israeli institutions such as education, citizenship and immigration, and land planning. Despite the ever-dwindling influence of overtly Zionist places, such as the kibbutz, elements of Zionist ideology are so deeply ingrained in the Jewish Israeli consciousness as to have become understood as simply Israeli, which in turn has driven the notion that Israeli identity and adherence to Zionist ideology are one and the same phenomenon. In such a climate, criticism of Zionist ideals or the manner of their realization is reflexively understood by some as signaling a vague and unproductive "post-Zionism," anti-Israel sentiments, or, even more problematically, as anti-Semitism. These facile and unfortunate equations demonstrate the pervasiveness of nationalist ideology and the difficulty of articulating an Israeli identity not primarily defined by it—despite the fact that ideals associated with Zionism de facto exclude or marginalize a significant proportion of the Israeli population. Resisting the singularity of the Zionist conception of place and acknowledging the diverse spatial experiences that defy it, far from threatening the notion of Israeli identity, immeasurably enrich it.

Literature continues to contribute prolifically to the discourse of identity by depicting the places of Israelis' lives and demonstrating the breadth of their spatial experience. The interplay of these diverse places with the nation, an interaction imagined sometimes harmoniously and sometimes destructively, demonstrates that from the intimate recesses of the most private spaces to the ordinary sites of mundane domestic routines to lands far beyond Israel's contested borders, the poetics of vernacular place emerge as transformative and potentially empowering agents of identity.

References

Index

References

Abramovitch, Dvir. 2001. "Ronit Matalon's Ethnic Masterpiece." *Australian Journal of Jewish Studies* 15:89–103.

Aciman, André, ed. 1990. *Letters of Transit: Reflections on Exile, Identity, Language, and Loss.* New York: New Press.

———. 2000. *False Papers: Essays on Exile and Memory.* New York: Farrar Straus Giroux.

Ahmed, Sara. 1999. "Home and Away: Narratives of Migration and Estrangement." *International Journal of Cultural Studies* 2, no. 3:329–47.

Almog, Oz. 1997. *Ha-tsabar: dyokan* [The sabra: a portrait]. Tel Aviv: Am Oved.

———. 2000. *The Sabra: The Creation of the New Jew.* Trans. Haim Watzman. Berkeley and Los Angeles: Univ. of California Press.

Alter, Robert. 2005. *Imagined Cities: Urban Experience and the Language of the Novel.* New Haven and London: Yale Univ. Press.

Amir, Eli. 1983. *Tarnegol kaparot* [Scapegoat]. Tel Aviv: Am Oved.

Anderson, Benedict. 1983. *Imagined Communities: Reflections on the Origin and Spread of Nationalism.* London and New York: Verso.

Aran, Gideon, and Zali Gurevitch. 1991. "Al ha-makom: Anthropologiya israelit" [On place: Israeli anthropology]. *Alpayim* 4:9–44.

Aronis, Carolin. 2009. "The Balconies of Tel Aviv: Cultural History and Urban Politics." *Israel Studies* 14, no. 3:157–80.

Ashcroft, Bill. 2001. *Post-Colonial Transformation.* London and New York: Routledge.

Augé, Marc. 1995 [1992]. *Non-Places: Introduction to an Anthropology of Supermodernity.* Trans. John Howe. London and New York: Verso.

Azaryahu, Maoz. 2006. *Tel Aviv: Mythography of a City.* Syracuse: Syracuse Univ. Press.

Azaryahu, Maoz, and Yoram Bar-Gal. 1997. "Israeli Cemeteries and Jewish Tradition: Two Cases." In *Land and Community: Geography and Jewish Studies,* ed. Harold Brodsky, 105–28. Bethesda, MD: Univ. Press of Maryland.

Bachelard, Gaston. 1969 [1958]. *The Poetics of Space*. Trans. Maria Jolas. Boston: Beacon Press.

Bakhtin, Mikhail. 1981. *The Dialogic Imagination*. Trans. Caryl Emerson and Michael Holquist. Austin: Univ. of Texas Press.

Balaban, Avraham. 1995. *Gal aher ba-siporet ha-'ivrit: siporet 'ivrit postmodernistit* [A different wave in Hebrew fiction: postmodernist Hebrew fiction]. Jerusalem: Keter.

Barthes, Roland. 1981. *Camera Lucida: Reflections on Photography*. Trans. Richard Howard. New York: Farrar, Straus and Giroux.

Bartov, Hanoch. 1970. *Shel mi ata yeled* [Whose little boy are you]. Tel Aviv: Am Oved.

———. 1978. *Whose Little Boy Are You?* Philadelphia: Jewish Publication Society of America.

Bashford, Alison, and Carolyn Strange. 2003. "Isolation and Exclusion in the Modern World." In *Isolation: Places and Practices of Exclusion,* ed. Carolyn Strange and Alison Bashford, 1–19. London and New York: Routledge.

Baudrillard, Jean. 1994 [1981]. *Simulacra and Simulation*. Trans. Sheila Faria Glaser. Ann Arbor: Univ. of Michigan Press.

Ben-Ezer, Ehud. 1989. "Early Tel Aviv as Mirrored in Literature." *Modern Hebrew Literature* 2:43–47.

Ben-Gurion, David. 1955. Mashma'ut ha-negev [The significance of the Negev]. Ha-makhon le-moreshet ben-guryon [The institute for the heritage of Ben-Gurion]. Ben-Gurion Archives, Speeches and Articles Division. http://bg archives.bgu.ac.il/moreshet/ben_gurion/mash.html (accessed October 31, 2008).

Ben-Porat, Ziva. 1987. "History in Representations of Jerusalem in Modern Hebrew Poetry." *Neohelicon* 14, no. 2:353–58.

Ben-Zadok, Efraim. 1993. "Oriental Jews in the Development Towns: Ethnicity, Economic Development, Budgets, and Politics." In *Local Communities and the Israeli Polity: Conflict of Values and Interest,* ed. Efraim Ben-Zadok, 91–122. Albany: State Univ. of New York Press.

Benjamin, Walter. 1977. *The Origin of German Tragic Drama*. Trans. John Osborne. London: NLB.

———. 1986 [1955]. *Illuminations*. Trans. Harry Zohn. New York: Schocken.

Bhabha, Homi. 1992. The World and the Home. *Social Text* 31/32: 141–53.

Bloom, Allan, trans. 1991. *The Republic of Plato*. New York: Basic Books.

———. 1994. *The Location of Culture*. London and New York: Routledge.

Blunt, Allison, and Robyn Dowling. 2006. *Home*. New York: Routledge.

Boyarin, Daniel, and Jonathan Boyarin. 1993. "Diaspora: Generation and the Ground of Jewish Identity." *Critical Inquiry* 19:693–725.

———. 2002. *Powers of Diaspora: Two Essays on the Relevance of Jewish Culture*. Minneapolis: Univ. of Minnesota Press.

Brenner, Rachel Feldhay. 2003. *Inextricably Bonded: Israeli, Arab, and Jewish Writers Re-visioning Culture*. Madison: Univ. of Wisconsin Press.

Brenner, Yosef Hayim. 1978–85. *Kol kitvey y. h. brener* [Complete Works of Y. H. Brenner]. Tel Aviv: Hakibbutz Hameuchad.

Casey, Edward S. 1993. *Getting Back into Place: Toward a Renewed Understanding of the Place-World*. Bloomington and Indianapolis: Indiana Univ. Press.

Castel-Bloom, Orly. 1987. *Lo rahok mi-merkaz ha-'ir* [Not far from the center of town]. Tel Aviv: Am Oved.

———. 1989. *Sviva 'oyenet* [Hostile surroundings]. Tel Aviv: Zmora-Bitan.

———. 1990. *Heykhan ani nimtset* [Where am I]. Tel Aviv: Zmora-Bitan.

———. 1992. *Doli siti* [Dolly city]. Tel Aviv: Zmora Bitan.

———. 1993. *Ha-ma'amar ha-avud* [The lost article]. *Yediot aharonot*, June 11, Sifrut [Literature]: 30.

———. 1998. *Ha-sefer he-hadash shel orli kastel-bloom* [Taking the trend; lit., The new book by Orly Castel-Bloom]. Jerusalem: Keter.

———. 2002. *Halakim enoshiyim* [Human parts]. Tel Aviv: Kinneret.

———. 2003. *Human Parts*. Boston: David R. Godine.

———. 2006. *Tekstil* [Textile]. Tel Aviv: Hakibbutz Hameuchad.

———. 2010. *Dolly City*. Champaign and London: Dalkey Archive Press.

Certeau, Michel de. 1984. *The Practice of Everyday Life*. Trans. Steven Rendall. Berkeley and Los Angeles: Univ. of California Press.

Chetrit, Sami Shalom. 2004. *Ha-ma'avak ha-mizrahi be-yisrael: Beyn dikuy le-shihrur, beyn hizdahut le-alternativa* [The Mizrahi struggle in Israel: Between oppression and liberation, between identification and alternative 1948–2003]. Tel Aviv: Am Oved.

Cixous, Hélène. 1998. *Stigmata: Escaping Texts*. London and New York: Routledge.

Cleary, Joe. 2002. *Literature, Partition and the Nation State: Culture and Conflict in Ireland, Israel and Palestine*. Cambridge: Cambridge Univ. Press.

Cohen, Joseph. 1990. *Voices of Israel*. Albany: State Univ. of New York Press.

Dainotto, Roberto M. 2000. *Place in Literature: Regions, Cultures, Communities*. Ithaca and London: Cornell Univ. Press.

Deleuze, Gilles, and Félix Guattari. 1987. *Thousand Plateaus: Capitalism and Schizophrenia*. Trans. Brian Massumi. Minneapolis: Univ. of Minnesota Press.

Di Stefano, John. 2002. "Moving Images of Home." *Art Journal* 61, no. 4 (Winter): 38–53.

Docker, John. 1994. *Postmodernism and Popular Culture: A Cultural History*. Cambridge, MA: Cambridge Univ. Press.

Douglas, Mary. 1991. "The Idea of a Home: A Kind of Space." *Social Research* 58, no. 1 (Spring): 287–307.

Eileraas, Karina. 2003. "Reframing the Colonial Gaze: Photography, Ownership, and Feminist Resistance." *MLN* 118, no. 4:807–40.

Elad-Bouskila, Ami. 1999. *Modern Palestinian Literature and Culture*. London and Portland, OR: Frank Cass.

———. 2001. "Symbol of Confrontation: Jerusalem in Israeli-Arab Literature During the Intifada." In *Linguistic and Cultural Studies on Arabic and Hebrew*, ed. Judith Rosenhouse and Ami Elad-Bouskila, 255–75. Wiesbaden: Harrassowitz Verlag.

Ezrahi, Sidra DeKoven. 2000. *Booking Passage: Exile and Homecoming in the Modern Jewish Imagination*. Berkeley and Los Angeles: Univ. of California Press.

———. 2007. "'To What Shall I Compare You?': Jerusalem as Ground Zero of the Hebrew Imagination." *PMLA–Publications of the Modern Language Association of America* 122, no. 1:220–34.

Feder, Lillian. 1980. *Madness in Literature*. Princeton: Princeton Univ. Press.

Finnane, Mark. 2003. "The Ruly and the Unruly: Isolation and Inclusion in the Management of the Insane." In *Isolation: Places and Practices of Exclusion*, ed. Carolyn Strange and Alison Bashford, 89–103. London and New York: Routledge.

Foucault, Michel. 1986. "Of Other Spaces." *Diacritics* 16, no. 1 (Spring): 22–27.

———. 1994 [1973]. *The Birth of the Clinic*. Trans. A. M. Sheridan Smith. New York: Vintage Books.

———. 1995 [1977]. *Discipline and Punish: the Birth of the Prison*. Trans. Alan Sheridan. New York: Vintage Books.

———. 2000. *Power*. Ed. James D. Faubion; trans. Robert Hurley. New York: New Press.

Gertz, Nurith. 1980. *'Amos 'oz: monografiya* [Amos Oz: monograph]. Tel Aviv: Sifriyat Poalim.

Gertz, Nurith, and George Khleifi. 2005. "Palestinian 'Roadblock Movies.'" *Geopolitics* 10:316–34.

Goldberg, Leah. 1964. *'Im ha-layla ha-ze* [With this night]. Tel-Aviv: Sifriyat Poalim.

Govrin, Nurit. 1989. "Jerusalem and Tel Aviv as Metaphors in Hebrew Literature." *Modern Hebrew Literature* 2:23–27.

Gregory, Derek. 2005. "Splintering Palestine." In *B/ordering Space*, ed. Henk Van Houtum, Olivier Thomas Kramsch, Oliver Kramsch, and Wolfgang Zierhofer, 123–37. Burlington, VT: Ashgate.

Grossman, David. 2002. *The Yellow Wind*. New York: Picador USA.

Gur, Batya. 2005. *Lama she-aravim kaeylu yirkedu disko?* [Why should Arabs like these dance disco?]. In *Mi-bli daleg 'al af daf* [Without missing a page], ed. F. Bezhizinski and Ariel Hirschfeld, 391–95. Jerusalem: Keter.

Gurevitch, Zali. 1997. "The Double Site of Israel." In *Grasping Land: Space and Place in Contemporary Israeli Discourse and Experience*, ed. Eyal Ben-Ari and Yoram Bilu, 203–16. Albany: State Univ. of New York Press.

———. 2007. *Al ha-makom* [On place]. Tel Aviv: Am Oved.

Guyer, Jane. 2002. Preface to *Architecture and Power in Africa*, by Nnamdi Elleh, xiii–xvi. Westport, CT: Praeger.

Hamilton, Edith, and Huntington Cairns, ed. 1961. *The Collected Dialogues of Plato*. New York: Bollingen Foundation.

Handelman, Susan A. 1991. *Fragments of Redemption: Jewish Thought and Literary Theory in Benjamin, Scholem, and Levinas*. Bloomington and Indianapolis: Indiana Univ. Press.

Hareven, Shulamith. 1972. *Ir yamim rabim* [City of many days]. Tel Aviv: Am Oved.

———. 1977. *City of Many Days*. Garden City, NY: Doubleday.

Harvey, David. 1990. *The Condition of Postmodernity: An Enquiry into the Origins of Cultural Change*. Cambridge, MA, and Oxford: Blackwell.

Hasak-Lowy, Todd. 2008. *Here and Now: History, Nationalism, and Realism in Modern Hebrew Fiction*. Syracuse: Syracuse Univ. Press.

Helphand, Kenneth. 2002. *Dreaming Gardens: Landscape Architecture and the Making of Modern Israel*. Santa Fe, NM, and Harrisonburg, VA: Center for American Places.

Hertzberg, Arthur. 1972 [c1959]. *The Zionist Idea*. New York: Atheneum.

———. 2003. *The Fate of Zionism: A Secular Future for Israel and Palestine*. New York: HarperCollins.

Herzl, Theodor. 1896. *Der Judenstaat*. Leipzig and Vienna: Verlags-Buchhandlung.

———. 1917. *A Jewish State: An Attempt at a Modern Solution of the Jewish Question*. Trans. Sylvia D'Avigdor. New York: Federation of American Zionists.

Hever, Hanan. 2000. *Kol ehad tsarikh lada'at et ha-makom shelo* [Everyone must know his place]. *Haaretz*, Feb. 2, Sfarim [Books]: 1+.

————. 2006. *El ha-hof ha-mekuve: ha-yam ba-tarbut ha-'ivrit u-va-sifrut ha-'ivrit ha-modernit* [Toward the longed-for shore: the sea in Hebrew culture and modern Hebrew literature]. Jerusalem and Tel Aviv: The Van Leer Institute and Hakibbutz Hameuchad.

————. 2007. *Ha-sipur ve-ha-le'om* [The narrative and the nation]. Tel Aviv: Resling.

Hochberg, Gil. 2004. "'Permanent Immigration': Jacqueline Kahanoff, Ronit Matalon, and the Impetus of Levantinism." *Boundary 2* 31, no. 2 (Summer): 219–43.

————. 2007. *In Spite of Partition: Jews, Arabs, and the Limits of Separatist Imagination.* Princeton: Princeton Univ. Press.

Hoffmann, Yoel. 1988. *Sefer yosef* [Book of Joseph]. Jerusalem: Keter.

————. 1989. *Bernhard.* Jerusalem: Keter.

————. 1991. *Kristus shel dagim* [Christ of fish]. Jerusalem: Keter.

————. 1995. *Ma shlomekh dolores* [How do you do, Dolores?]. Jerusalem: Keter.

————. 1998a. *Bernhard.* New York: New Directions.

————. 1998b. *Katschen & the Book of Joseph.* New York: New Directions.

————. 1999. *Christ of Fish.* New York: New Directions.

————. 2003. *Efrayim.* Jerusalem: Keter.

Jabès, Edmond. 1991. "This Is the Desert, Nothing Strikes Root Here." Interview. In *Routes Of Wandering*, ed. Sarit Shapira, 246–56. Jerusalem: The Israel Museum.

Jackson, John Brinckerhoff. 1984. *Discovering the Vernacular Landscape.* New Haven and London: Yale Univ. Press.

Jameson, Frederic. 1991. *Postmodernism, or, the Cultural Logic of Late Capitalism.* Durham, NC: Duke Univ. Press.

Kalderon, Nissim. 1995. *Lo hakol sipur ehad* [Not everything is one story]. *Rehov* 2: 48–58.

Kashua, Sayed. 2002. *Aravim rokdim* [Dancing Arabs]. Ben Shemen Moshav: Modan.

————. 2004a. *Dancing Arabs.* New York: Grove Press.

————. 2004b. *Va-yehi boker* [Let it be morning]. Jerusalem: Keter.

————. 2006. *Let It Be Morning.* New York: Grove/Atlantic Inc.

Kayyal, Mahmoud. 2008. "Arabs Dancing in a New Light of Arabesques": Minor Hebrew Works of Palestinian Authors in the Eyes of Critics. *Middle Eastern Literatures* 11, no. 1:31–51.

Kenaz, Yehoshua. 1986. *Hitganvut yehidim* [Infiltration]. Tel Aviv: Am Oved.

Keret, Etgar. 1998. *Ha-keytana shel kneler* [Kneller's happy campers]. Jerusalem: Keter and Zmora Bitan.

———. 2004. *The Bus Driver Who Wanted to Be God and Other Stories*. New Milford, CT, and London: The Toby Press.

Kolirin, Eran, dir. 2007. *Bikur ha-tizmoret* [The band's visit].

Kort, Wesley A. 2004. *Place and Space in Modern Fiction*. Gainesville: Univ. Press of Florida.

Kotef, Hagar, and Merav Amir. 2007. (En)Gendering Checkpoints: Checkpoint Watch and the Repercussions of Intervention. *Signs: Journal of Women in Culture and Society* 32, no. 4:973–96.

Lacan, Jacques. 1977 [1966]. *Écrits: A Selection*. Trans. Alan Sheridan. New York and London: W. W. Norton.

———. 1981 [1973]. *The Four Fundamental Concepts of Psychoanalysis: The Seminar of Jacques Lacan, Book XI*. Ed. Jacques-Alain Miller; trans. Alan Sheridan. New York: W. W. Norton.

Laor, Yitzhak. 1995. *Anu kotvim otakh moledet* [Narratives with no natives: essays on Israeli literature]. Tel Aviv: Hakibbutz Hameuchad.

Leeds, Anthony, and Elizabeth Leeds and Peter Lloyd. 1979. "On the 'Shantytown' Conference Report." *Current Anthropology* 20, no. 2:460–62.

Lefebvre, Henri. 1991 [1974]. *The Production of Space*. Trans. Donald Nicholson-Smith. Malden, MA: Blackwell.

Levinas, Emmanuel. 1979. *Totality and Infinity*. The Hague and Boston: M. Nijhoff.

Levy, Lital. 2008. "Self-Portraits of the Other: Toward a Palestinian Poetics of Hebrew Verse." In *Transforming Loss into Beauty: Essays on Arabic Literature and Culture in Honor of Magda al-Nowaihi*, ed. Marlé Hammond and Dana Sajdi, 343–402. Cairo and New York: American Univ. in Cairo Press.

Lie, Rico. 2003. *Spaces of Intercultural Communication: An Interdisciplinary Introduction to Communication, Culture, and Globalizing/Localizing Identities*. Cresskill, NJ: Hampton Press.

Lloyd, Peter C. 1979. "Shantytowns in Developing Nations." *Current Anthropology* 20, no. 1:114–17.

Lupack, Barbara Tepa. 1995. *Insanity as Redemption in Contemporary American Fiction: Inmates Running the Asylum*. Gainesville: Univ. Press of Florida.

Lutwack, Leonard. 1984. *The Role of Place in Literature*. Syracuse: Syracuse Univ. Press.

Mabogunje, Akin L. 1990. "Urban Planning and the Post-Colonial State in Africa: A Research Overview." *African Studies Review* 33, no. 2:114–17.

Mallett, Shelley. 2004. "Understanding Home: A Critical Review of the Literature." *The Sociological Review* 52, no. 1:62–89.

Mann, Barbara. 2001. "The Vicarious Landscape of Memory in Tel Aviv Poetry." *Prooftexts* 21, no. 3:350–78.

———. 2006. *A Place in History: Modernism, Tel Aviv, and the Creation of Jewish Urban Space*. Stanford: Stanford Univ. Press.

Massey, Doreen. 1993. "Politics and Space/Time." In *Place and the Politics of Identity*, ed. Michael Keith and Steve Pile, 141–61. London and New York: Routledge.

———. 1994. *Space, Place, and Gender*. Minneapolis: Univ. of Minnesota Press.

Matalon, Ronit. 1992. *Zarim ba-bayit* [Strangers at home]. Tel Aviv: Hakibbutz Hameuchad.

———. 1995. *Ze im ha-panim eleynu* [The one facing us]. Tel Aviv: Am Oved.

———. 1998a. Ha-lashon ve-ha-bayit [Language and home]. *Mikarov: A Journal for Literature and Culture* 2:169–71.

———. 1998b. *The One Facing Us*. New York: Metropolitan Books.

———. 2000. *Sara, Sara* [Bliss]. Tel Aviv: Am Oved.

———. 2001. *Kroh u-khtov* [Reading and writing]. Tel Aviv: Hakibbutz Hameuhad.

———. 2003. *Bliss*. New York: Metropolitan Books.

———. 2008. *Kol tsa'adeynu* [The sound of our steps]. Tel Aviv: Am Oved.

Mazor, Yair. 1998. *Lituf ba-afela: al siporet 'amos 'oz* [Somber lust: the art of Amos Oz]. Jerusalem: Keter.

———. 2002. *Somber Lust: The Art of Amos Oz*. Trans. Marganit Weinberger-Rotman. Albany: State Univ. of New York Press.

Mendelson-Maoz, Adia. 1996. "Olamot efshariyim bitsiratam shel orli kastel-bloom ve-etgar keret" [Possible worlds in the works of Orly Castel-Bloom and Etgar Keret]. *'Aley siyah* 38 (Winter): 39–64.

Mills, Sara. 2006. *Gender and Colonial Space*. Manchester: Manchester Univ. Press.

Myers, David N. 2008. *Between Jew and Arab: The Lost Voice of Simon Rawidowicz*. Lebanon, NH: Univ. Press of New England.

Naveh, Hannah. 1993. *Bi-shvi ha-evel: ha-evel bi-r'i ha-sifrut ha-'ivrit ha-hadasha* [Captives of mourning: perspectives of mourning in Hebrew literature]. Tel Aviv: Hakibbutz Hameuchad.

———. 2002. *Nos'im ve-nos'ot: sipurey mas'a ba-sifrut ha-'ivrit ha-hadasha* [Men and women travelers: travel narratives in modern Hebrew literature]. Tel Aviv: Misrad Ha-bitahon.

Nesher, Avi, dir. 2004. *Sof ha-'olam smola* [Turn left at the end of the world].

Newton, Adam. 2005. *The Elsewhere: On Belonging at a Near Distance.* Madison: Univ. of Wisconsin Press.

Nimni, Ephraim. 2003. "Introduction." In *The Challenge of Post-Zionism: Alternatives to Israeli Fundamentalist Politics,* ed. Ephraim Nimni, 1–19. London and New York: Zed Books.

Njoh, Ambe J. 2000. "Continuity and Change in Cameroonian Land Policy." *Planning Perspectives* 15, no. 3:241–65.

Omer-Sherman, Ranen. 2006a. *Israel in Exile: Jewish Writing and the Desert.* Urbana and Chicago: Univ. of Illinois Press.

———. 2006b. "Yehuda Amicha's Exilic Jerusalem." *Prooftexts* 26, no. 1–2:212–39.

Ophir, Adi. 2000. "The Identity of the Victims and the Victims of Identity: A Critique of Zionist Ideology for a Post-Zionist Age." In *Mapping Jewish Identities,* ed. Laurence J. Silberstein, 174–200. New York and London: New York Univ. Press.

Oz, Amos. 1965. *Artsot ha-tan* [Where the jackals howl]. Tel Aviv: Massada.

———. 1966. *Makom aher* [Elsewhere, perhaps]. Merhaviya: Sifriyat Poalim.

———. 1976. *Har ha-'etsa ha-ra'a* [The hill of evil counsel]. Tel Aviv: Am Oved.

———. 1978. *The Hill of Evil Counsel.* New York and London: Harcourt Brace Jovanovich.

———. 1981. *Where the Jackals Howl and Other Stories.* New York and London: Harcourt Brace Jovanovich.

———. 1982. *Menuha nekhona* [A perfect peace]. Tel Aviv: Am Oved.

———. 1985. *A Perfect Peace.* New York: Harcourt Brace Jovanovich.

———. 1989. *Lada'at isha* [To know a woman]. Jerusalem: Keter.

———. 1991. *To Know a Woman.* San Diego: Harcourt Brace Jovanovich.

———. 1994. *Al tagidi layla* [Don't call it night]. Jerusalem: Keter.

———. 1995. *Under This Blazing Light.* Cambridge: Cambridge Univ. Press.

———. 1996. *Don't Call It Night.* San Diego: Harcourt Brace.

———. 2002. *Sipur al ahava ve-hoshekh* [A tale of love and darkness]. Jerusalem: Keter.

———. 2004. *A Tale of Love and Darkness.* New York: Harvest Books.

———. 2006. *How to Cure a Fanatic.* Princeton: Princeton Univ. Press.

Pappé, Ilan. 1997. "Post-Zionist Critique on Israel and the Palestinians Part I: The Academic Debate." *Journal of Palestine Studies* 26, no. 2:29–41.

Pardes, Ilana. 2000. *The Biography of Ancient Israel: National Narratives in the Desert.* Berkeley and Los Angeles: Univ. of California Press.

Parmenter, Barbara M. 1994. *Giving Voice to Stones: Place and Identity in Palestinian Literature*. Austin: Univ. of Texas Press.

Peleg, Yaron. 2005. *Orientalism and the Hebrew Imagination*. Ithaca and London: Cornell Univ. Press.

Pianko, Noam. 2010. *Zionism and the Roads Not Taken: Rawidowicz, Kaplan, and Kohn*. Bloomington: Indiana Univ. Press.

Prineas, James. 2006. The Spirit of Sumud. Photography exhibit. http://www.sumud.net (accessed August 30, 2008).

Raab, Esther. 1964. *Shirey esther raab* [The poems of Esther Raab]. Tel Aviv: Masada.

Ram, Uri. 1999. "The State of the Nation: Contemporary Challenges to Zionism in Israel." *Constellations* 6, no. 3:325–38.

Rattok, Lily. 1997. "My Gaze Was All I Had: The Problem of Representation in the Works of Ronit Matalon." *Israel Social Science Research* 12, no. 1:44–55.

———. 2000. "Stranger at Home: The Discourse of Identity in Ronit Matalon's *The One Facing Us*." In *Discourse on Gender/Gendered Discourse in the Middle East*, ed. Boaz Shoshan, 95–115. Westport, CT: Praeger.

Raz-Krakotzkin, Amnon. 1997. "Historical Consciousness and Historical Responsibility." In *From Vision to Revision: A Hundred Years of Historiography of Zionism*, ed. Yechiam Weitz, 97–134 [Hebrew]. Jerusalem: Zalman Shazar Center.

Relph, E. 1976. *Place and Placelessness*. London: Pion Limited.

Riklis, Eran, dir. 2008. *Ets limon* [Lemon tree].

Said, Edward. 1999. *After the Last Sky: Palestinian Lives*. New York: Columbia Univ. Press.

Sartre, Jean-Paul. 1956. *Being and Nothingness: An Essay on Phenomenological Ontology*. Trans. Hazel E. Barnes. New York: Philosophical Library.

Schwartz, Yigal. 1995. "Mi-makom aher le-doli siti" [From *Elsewhere, Perhaps*, to *Dolly City*]. *Haaretz*, June 16, Tarbut ve-sifrut [Culture and literature], 8b–9b.

———. 2007. *Ha-yada'ata et ha-arets sham ha-limon pore'ah: handasat ha-adam u-mahshavat ha-merhav ba-sifrut ha-'ivrit ha-hadasha* [Do you know the land where the lemon tree blooms: the design of man and the conceptualization of landscape in Hebrew literature]. Or Yehuda, Israel: Kinneret, Zmora-Bitan, Dvir.

Shalev, Meir. 1988. *Roman rusi*. Tel Aviv: Am Oved.

———. 1994. *Ke-yamim ahadim* [As a few days; available in English as *The Loves of Judith* and *Four Meals*]. Tel Aviv: Am Oved.

Shamir, Moshe. 1951. *Be-mo yadav: pirkey elik* [With his own hands]. Tel Aviv: Sifriyat Poalim.

——. 1970. *With His Own Hands*. Jerusalem: Israel Universities Press.

Shammas, Anton. 1979. *Shetah hefker: shirim* [No man's land: poems]. Tel Aviv: Hakibbutz Hameuhad.

——. 1987. "Kitsch 22, o: gvul ha-tarbut" [Kitsch 22, or: the boundary of culture]. *Iton 77* 84–85 (Jan.–Feb.): 24–26.

Shapira, Anita. 1992. *Land and Power: The Zionist Resort to Force, 1881–1948*. New York: Oxford Univ. Press.

——. 1995. "Politics and Collective Memory: The Debate over the 'New Historians' in Israel." *History and Memory* 7, no. 1:9–40.

Shaul, Dror, dir. 2006. *Adama meshuga'at* [Sweet mud].

Shemtov, Vered. 2005. "Between Perspectives of Space: A Reading in Yehuda Amichai's 'Jewish Travel' and 'Israeli Travel.'" *Jewish Social Studies* 11, no. 3:141–61.

Shohat, Ella. 1999. "The Invention of the Mizrahim." *Journal of Palestine Studies* 29, no. 1:5–20.

——. 2003. "Rupture and Return: Zionist Discourse and the Study of Arab Jews." *Social Text 75* 21, no. 2 (Summer): 49–74.

Siegel, Dina. 1998. *The Great Immigration: Russian Jews in Israel*. New York and Oxford: Berghahn, 1998.

Slyomovics, Susan. 1998. *The Object of Memory: Arab and Jew Narrate the Palestinian Village*. Philadelphia: Univ. of Pennsylvania Press.

Soja, Edward W. 1989. *Postmodern Geographies: The Reassertion of Space in Critical Social Theory*. London and New York: Verso.

Sokoloff, Naomi B. 1983. "Longing and Belonging: Jerusalem in Fiction as Setting and Mindset." *Hebrew Studies* 24:137–49.

Stahl, Neta. 2008. *Tselem yehudi: Representations of Jesus in Twentieth-Century Hebrew Literature* [Hebrew]. Tel Aviv: Resling Academic Press.

Starr, Deborah A. 2000. "Reterritorializing the Dream: Orly Castel-Bloom's Remapping of Israeli Identity." In *Mapping Jewish Identities*, ed. Laurence J. Silberstein, 220–49. New York and London: New York Univ. Press.

Steiner, George. 1985. "Our Homeland, The Text." *Salamagundi* 66:4–25.

Tchernichovsky, Saul. 1990–2003 [1929–1932]. *Kol kitvey shaul chernihovski* [Complete works of Saul Tchernichovsky]. Tel-Aviv: Am Oved.

Troen, S. Ilan. 1995. "New Departures in Zionist Planning: The Development Town." In *Israel: the First Decade of Independence*, ed. S. Ilan Troen and Noah Lucas, 441–60. Albany: State Univ. of New York Press.

Tuan, Yi-Fu. 1977. *Space and Place: The Perspective of Experience*. Minneapolis: Univ. of Minnesota Press.

Turner, Mark. 1996. *The Literary Mind*. New York: Oxford Univ. Press.

Upton, Dell. 1997. "Seen, Unseen, and Scene." In *Understanding Ordinary Landscapes*, ed. Paul Groth and Todd W. Bressi, 174–79. New Haven and London: Yale Univ. Press.

Van Schepen, Randall K. 2007. "Benjamin's Aura, Levine's Homage and Richter's Effect." *InterCulture* 4, no. 2 (Summer). http://iph.fsu.edu/interculture/pdfs/van%20schepen%20randall.pdf (accessed September 22, 2008).

Waterman, Stanley. 2004. "Land, House, and Garden: Evolving Landscapes in Israel." *Social & Cultural Geography* 5:663–69.

Waters, Michael. 1988. *The Garden in Victorian Literature*. Aldershot, England: Scolar Press.

Wirth-Nesher, Hana. 1996. *City Codes: Reading the Modern Urban Novel*. Cambridge and New York: Cambridge Univ. Press.

Wolin, Richard. 1982. *Walter Benjamin: An Aesthetic of Redemption*. New York: Columbia Univ. Press.

Yehoshua, A. B. 1968. *Mul ha-ye'arot, sipurim*. [Facing the forests: stories]. Tel Aviv: Hakibbutz Hameuhad.

Yeshurun, Yitzhak, dir. 1982. *No'a bat 17* [Noa at 17].

Yizhar, S. 1949. *Sipur hirbet hiz'eh ve-ha-shavuy* [The story of Hirbet Hizeh and the prisoner]. Tel Aviv: Sifriyat Poalim.

———. 2008. *Khirbet Khizeh*. Jerusalem: Ibis Editions, 2008.

Zanger, Anat. 2005. "Blind Space: Roadblock Movies in the Contemporary Israeli Film." *Shofar: An Interdisciplinary Journal of Jewish Studies* 24, no. 1:37–48.

Zeedani, Said. 2005. "A Palestinian Perspective on the Checkpoints." *Occupation Magazine: Life Under Occupation*. Sept. 29. http://kibush.co.il/show_file.asp?num=9277 (accessed July 29, 2008).

Zerubavel, Yael. 2008. "Desert and Settlement: Space Metaphors and Symbolic Landscapes in the Yishuv and Early Israeli Culture." In *Jewish Topographies: Visions of Space, Traditions of Place*, ed. Julia Brauch, Anna Lipphardt, and Alexandra Nocke, 201–22. Burlington, VT: Ashgate.

———. Forthcoming. *Desert in the Promised Land: Nationalism, Politics, and Symbolic Landscapes*. Chicago: Univ. of Chicago Press.

Index

77, 80–86, 109–10, 111; and exile, 12, 15, 53, 157; genealogy as, 214; in Hoffmann's works, 159, 164, 172, 173, 177, 182–87, 194, 197–99; house vs., 229–30; of Jews, 15; of Israeli Palestinians, 6–7, 129, 141–48; in Kashua's novels, 141–48; in Matalon's novels, 204–20, 230–35; movement as, 204–20; objects/fragments creating sense of, 182–87; as "original soil" (Foucault), 99; as prison, 207, 230–35; as process, 205–6; rejection of Israel as, 220; without roots, 204, 205–7; in state of supermodernity, 23; and street, 78–86, 109–10, 111; symbolism of, 48; transcendence of place/ethnicity/language, 172; transnational paradigm of, 208–9; and "unhomeliness" (Bhabha) 20; womb as, 197–98

hospital: effect on patients, 98, 250; erasure of social/economic boundaries, 97–98, 100; as heterotopia of deviation, 77, 98–99; isolation of, 77, 89, 98–99, 100, 121, 122; as place of community, 97–98; as place of reflection on social order, 89, 97, 100; power structure in, 87; as space of confinement/exclusion, 88, 97–101; structure of in *Human Parts*, 98

Hostile Surroundings (Castel-Bloom), 78

house-key, 137, 138, 141

houses: homes vs., 229–30; as intimate/private space, 229, 230; Israeli Palestinians' decoration of, 139–41; metaphor of for Israeli Palestinians, 138–39; neocolonial, 231–40; as potential ruin, 137–38; as prison, 207, 231, 233, 234–35; protection expected from/vulnerability of, 139, 142–44, 146, 232, 233; representation

of Palestine, 141, 250; in shantytown, 241–43; symbolism of in Palestinian literature, 137–39; tyranny of postcolonial, 7–8, 229–40; "unhomeliness" of, 20, 141n11, 230–31

How Do You Do, Dolores? (Hoffmann), 166

Human Parts (Castel-Bloom): depiction of urban spaces, 107, 115–21; emphasis on street names, 116–17; experiences of death/burial in, 105–7; loneliness in hospitals, 97–101; reflection on alienating social order in, 89, 120–21; setting of, 87, 115–16

Hyman, Sy, 49n13

hypersight: "ability to see more" (Matalon), 221–23; in *Dolly City*, 87–97, 160, 222; in Hoffmann, 161, 187–89, 191, 195, 198–99, 222. *See also* Cyclops; eye; prophecy; sight/seeing

identity (GENERAL): Israeli, 4–6, 8–10, 12–13, 25–27, 32, 38–39, 47–52, 57–58, 60–61, 62–63, 78, 83, 122, 160, 162–67, 201–2, 205, 248–49, 251–52; Israeli Palestinian, 7, 123–37, 140–41, 148–57, 250; Jewish, 14–17, 191, 194–95; Levantine, 221, 223–24; link to sight/gaze, 167–72, 201, 221, 223–24, 228–29, 234, 236–40, 244–45; name as signifier of, 165–68, 170, 172, 194–95; national, 6, 10, 26–27, 38–39, 122, 162–65, 181, 198, 212, 246. *See also* identity (RELATION TO PLACE)

identity (RELATION TO PLACE): balconies and, 78, 250; on complexity of notion of home for Palestinian Israelis, 6–7; effect of heterotopia of deviation, 6; for European Israelis, 165;